POLITICAL SCIENCE

A Bibliographical Guide to the Literature

by

Robert B. Harmon

San Jose State College

The Scarecrow Press, Inc.

New York and London   1965

To Merlynn, Marriner John
and Jane Anne

"I teach my people correct principles
and they govern themselves."

Joseph Smith

Preface

Structurally political science is similar to a large
building that is composed of many bricks held together by
the mortar of tradition and new approaches. Interest in the
primary correlates or determinants of the political process
indicates that the study of political science is of prime importance to scholars, students and citizens alike. This work
offers a taxonomy of the entire field drawing upon both traditional and contemporary sources.

The purpose for this taxonomy is to provide the student with a useful framework for ordering the components of
the literature. As a guide for such a broad area of knowledge the number of materials included in this work cannot
pretend to be comprehensive or the categories all inclusive.
Consequently the areas and works innumerated are merely
suggestive. There will undoubtedly be a questioning by many
as to the placement of works in certain categories or in the
inclusion or exclusion of various materials. I have at-
tempted to provide a representative selection of the major
subjects and works having some measure of significance to
political science. For any errors either of comission or
omission I assume full responsibility.

No work of this size could possibly be the product of
one person. The debts of gratitude I owe are many, particularly to those who played a part in guiding my educational
development. To the professors and instructors in the Political Science and History Departments of Brigham Young University and the Graduate School of Library Service at Rutgers-
The State University I give special recognition for their vali-
ant efforts to teach this student the value of sound and systematic scholarship. My colleagues at San Jose State College
deserve much credit for their help in reading the manuscript
and pointing out the many errors and inconsistencies contained therein. Lastly I am deeply indebted to my wife whose
patience and help in typing, criticizing and correcting the
manuscript proved invaluable to the completion of this work.

Robert Bartlett Harmon

Contents

CHAPTER I

The Literature of Political Science

Introduction

The literature of any field of scholarly inquiry is delimited by the nature of its content as well as the trends and tangents promulgated by its practitioners. Political science is one of the most diverse of the social sciences and has been marked by an increasing fragmentation of subject matter. The resultant problems are numerous and highly complex, especially in those approaches based on interdisciplinary relationships in the conduct of political behavior.

Many definitions of political science have been set forth in the past, and an attempt to do so here would serve no useful purpose. There are, however, a number of important elements that can be culled from many of these definitions that would be essential to a proper understanding of the literature. Political science, first of all, is considered to be an important branch of the social sciences. As such it broadly deals with the theory, organization, government and practice of the state.[1] Even more generally, political science encompasses social processes and patterns of behavior exhibited by individuals, groups, communities and societies as they attempt to resolve problems collectively.[2]

Development of Political Science

It has been said that politics is as old as man himself. If this is true then certainly it is worthy of man's best efforts to understand and use for his benefit. The ancient Greeks were the first to speculate upon political activity and to formulate their thinking into prescriptive utopian theories. Since the Renaissance, political science has discarded the traditional bonds of ethics, law and history in an attempt to become a truly empirical science. In this process it has discovered a particular affinity for other areas of the social sciences, most prominent of which are sociology and psychology.

9

In its development, political science, as a separate discipline, is largely an American phenomenon. The influence of its European legalistic and formalistic orientation was not broken until after the first World War. The efforts of such prolific thinkers as Arthur F. Bentley and Charles E. Merriam to stress the importance of the process and inter-disciplinary concepts did not bear fruit until recently. Much of the raw data for research as well as methodology is being drawn from other disciplines as illustrated in the works of Harold D. Lasswell, Richard C. Snyder, Gabriel Almond and others.

The viability of political science rests in the many fresh approaches that are helping to clarify meaningful relationships among political phenomena. New attempts to apply mathematical and purely abstract models to analyze the functions of political systems have broadened the horizons for political research. Comparative politics and political theory have received rejuvenation through the formulation of new categories of analysis. A concentrated effort is being made to study the many complex relationships between fact and value by means of establishing political science as a "policy science."[3] The institutional-descriptive approach is being discarded for the study of human behavior in individuals and groups. New methods of research such as content analysis and survey research also enhance prospects for the field. It must be reiterated, however, that a dynamic and ever changing academic discipline such as political science is not without its many problems.

Structure of Political Science

The paramount problem is the fragmentation mentioned above. It is clearly evident that the field as a whole encompasses an extremely broad spectrum of information, methodology and theory. Prior to World War I, politics was largely considered within the framework of governmental institutions or legal procedures. These two categories made the study of political action rather myopic. The modern political scientist now finds himself confronted with a field of study that is split into many parts and some of the parts fractionalized still further. It is becoming increasingly difficult, as one professor put it, "to teach another colleague's classes."

Attempting to assign useful designations to the many sub-disciplines is somewhat hazardous, but I do not know how

to avoid it sensibly.   Below is a brief table of what can be
considered the present structural orientation of political science.

Sub-discipline	Specialized Areas (examples)
Politics	Political Psychology Political Sociology Political Economy
Comparative Government	American African Asian European Middle Eastern
State and Local Government	Community Power Structures Interstate and Intrastate rela- tions Local Governmental Functions
Law	Public Law Administrative Law Jurisprudence
Political Theory	Greek Renaissance Modern American
Public Administration	Bureaucracy Personnel Administration Supervision Urban Renewal
Parties, Public Opinion and Electoral Processes	Role and Functions of Political Parties Influence of Public Opinion on Public Policy Electoral Functions on all Levels of Government
International Relations	International Politics International Organization International Law

Several of these categories are traditional; others are

rather arbitrarily designated. Courses of instruction in political science, as given in the institutions of higher education in the United States are moulded from these sub-divi-
sions as are the text books for instructional purposes. The
ever changing foci of political science are reflected by the
large textural material for college courses as new fields of
interest and divergent approaches are emphasized by their
exponents.

Approaches in Political Science

Political science, within its organizational and procedural structure, is being studied by means of new and
complex approaches. An approach, as used within the context of the discipline, includes not only methodology but abstract models by which political data may be analyzed and
interpreted.[4] There are many places where these approaches
overlap, and they are often beset with theoretical and methodological difficulties. The difficulties most frequently encountered include the interpretation of empirically gathered
data as well as testing and measuring the validity of concepts
formulated from this information. Below is a selective list
of approaches that have been and some that are most currently in vogue, along with a listing of a few of their leading
proponents.

Approach	Proponents
Historical-Descriptive	V. O. Key, Jr. Leonard White
Behavioral	Heinz Eulau Sidney Verba John Wahlke
Case Study	Ernest Griffith Herbert Simon
Decision-Making	Richard C. Snyder Burton W. Sapin Duane Marvick Harold D. Lasswell
Power	Hans J. Morgenthau, Jr. Machiavelli Thomas Hobbes

Approach	Proponents
Structional-Functional	Gabriel Almond David Apter Edward Banfield
Conflict Analysis	Kenneth Boulding Robert C. North
System-Models	Morton Kaplan George Liska David Easton

All of the approaches listed above, as well as many others, cannot be considered as mutually exclusive. Often they are combined as separate elements for analytical purposes. The historical-descriptive approach is employed in most of the other approaches. Power is also almost universally used, although its meaning is vague, and its use is largely associated with the study of international politics.

The application of these approaches is being made to the behavior of judicial and legislative bodies, individuals and groups. Data from supporting disciplines such as anthropology and economics gives new dimensions to the analysis of the decision process and the structural-functional approach. Comparative politics has been buttressed by the combination of structural-functional formulations and equilibrium theories. Such groups as legislative bodies, elites and military planners are also being analyzed by means of role analysis in terms of systematic orientations.

Intellectual ferment within political science is suggestive of the state of flux which permeates the field generally. It is not improbable that the discipline is changing in character with the advent of new techniques and approaches.

Types of Sources

Most of the sources for political science fall within the two broad categories of expository matter and reference materials. The content of this vast body of literature is dependent upon the demands of its selective clientele. These sources serve as the tools for obtaining knowledge and as guides to the applications of that knowledge in a creative manner.

The former class consists mainly of monographic
works, pamphlets, and articles in periodicals and journals.
The material in this class of sources differs in nature ac-
cording to the specialized or general problem being treated.
It also varies with the method of approach, or the degree of
systematization utilized in presenting and analyzing a politically relevant problem. The wide distribution of scholarly
journals, as well as the broad range of topics treated, has
increased the currency of information on specialized problems
and research.

Reference materials in political science have become
more numerous in the last two decades. As in most fields,
the types of reference tools, particularly for specialized
areas within the field, have been extensive for some and almost non-existent for others.

Since Burchfield's masterful Student's guide to materials in political science (B91) no extensive guide to the literature has been produced for political science. It is this de-
ficiency which the present work is designed to ameliorate. A
good, brief guide was given in Hitchner's Modern government
(B150) although its usefulness is limited.

There is a genuine demand, especially by undergradu-
ate students, for more effective means of evaluating the literature. Reviews have been confined to the scholarly journals, but it would be useful if this function were to be cen-
tralized, either by means of a book reviewing organ or an
extensive inventory of research progress issued quarterly or
annually.

International political science abstracts (B46), although
not an evaluation tool, is an aid for finding materials. In
describing the essential elements of an article or book,
search for materials is quickened immeasurably. Abstracts
and digests for any or all of the specialized sub-disciplines
of political science would certainly facilitate the research
process.

As finding devices for information, bibliographies and
indexes for political science have been adequate for retrospective purposes; however, a problem arises from the need to
have adequate bibliographic coverage of current information.
At present, for most areas of the discipline, current bibliographic information is sometimes sporadic as well as slow in
becoming available for use.

Political science has always placed particular emphasis upon the definition of terms and concepts. The last ten years has seen a flood of dictionaries which provide a wide range of treatment for political terminology.

Since Lalor's monumental Cyclopedia of political science (B82) there has not been published any encyclopedic work of comparable scope. There is need for a current work which places the field in historical perspective, identifies those who have furthered its progression and considers the most pertinent literature.

Directories and biographical dictionaries about political scientists, organizations within the field and places and things of a relevant nature have been scattered and incomplete. The biographical directory of the American Political Science Association could be more helpful if it were produced annually.

Only in the field of international relations has there been published a number of useful atlases or pictorial works that depict world events. To a limited extent structural organization of branches of government has been utilized by other sub-disciplines within the field.

The use of handbooks and manuals has largely been confined to applications of parliamentary and legislative procedures. Manuals for research techniques have been a recent innovation and have encouraged wider and more extensive use of this type of tool.

International relations and public administration have benefited from the use of yearbooks that report systematic accounts of current developments and new techniques. In the area of comparative government, organizations such as the United Nations provide a variety of yearbooks that list useful data on their activities. Yearbooks could also be used to review current research in other sub-disciplines of political science.

Utilization of statistical sources for the entire field has not been extensive. The areas that are more amenable to statistical study (e.g. voting patterns and behavior) are receiving exhaustive treatment, and it is not improbable that as technology advances the applications to other sub-disciplines within the field will do the same.

The discussion above by no means exhausts the types of sources available to the student of political science. It is merely suggestive of the diversity of these sources and possible areas in which they could be made more useful.

Characteristics of the Literature

It is exceedingly difficult to assess the leading characteristics of any body of literature. The task for political science is not made easier by the lack of consensus inherent in the discipline as a whole. What follows, therefore, is a brief summation of what can be considered the most prominent characteristics which pervade the pages of the literature of political science.

Voltaire was once credited with saying, "If you wish to converse with me define your terms." Political science is a field of study with a highly developed and complex terminology. Many of these terms that are employed for the more precise understanding of political phenomena are being borrowed from other disciplines such as mathematics and economics. Since it is impossible to strictly control the meaning of these terms, an abstruse or involved jargon has resulted which has made the communicative process within the field difficult at times.

Over the years the writings on politics follow fashion. Similar to the changes that occur in women's fashions from time to time, the literature of political science adopts new styles, themes and goals. These fashions are the product of historical events and the impact of traditional notions and concepts.[5]

At the beginning of this brief essay the fragmentation of political science into specialized sub-disciplines was emphasized. The literature naturally reflects this trend and thereby imposes a myopic understanding of the relationships among the parts that comprise the field as a whole. It appears from a cursory survey of this specialized literature that the necessary linking of the parts to the whole is not being done adequately. Concomitant to the fragmentation of the field is the development of a rapidly changing methodology. General systems theory, mathematical models, simulation, game theory and systematic constructs are only a few of the relatively new methods now being employed to gain a more meaningful understanding of political phenomena.

Perhaps the chief characteristic of the literature in general, however, is its disposition toward obsolescence. This is due largely to the rapid change that politics and government are undergoing, the absence of a stable and agreed upon theoretical structure and the advent of the methodological innovations mentioned earlier. [6]

Trends in the Literature

There have been, in the course of time, many important trends developing within the multifarious branches of political science. A large scale consensus is not evident among political scientists as to the nature of these trends or their impact upon the study of their discipline. The brief summarizing of a few of these trends in the main branches of political science will aid in the understanding of some important factors that are reflected in the literature.

Political Theory

Western political thought has been largely shaped by three major trends or movements. First was the philosophical idealism of the ancient Greeks as expressed in the writings of Plato and Aristotle. Second was the development of materialism as an off-shoot of Renaissance humanism. Third and most recent is the empiricism illustrated in the writings of Laski, Cole, Lasswell and others. [7]

Traditionally, political thought is concerned with the ordering of political phenomena in an attempt to understand them and their complex interrelationships. The basic elements of political thought are concepts or generalized abstractions. Therefore, it is much more than merely the history of ideas.

The historical-descriptive approach as exemplified by George H. Sabine and Charles H. McIlwain has been the most instrumental in the study of political thought. Only in the last two decades has there been a real attempt to systematize the basic concepts expressed by the many thinkers in politics into meaningful and coherent patterns. There are two basic types of political concepts that have been explored in the literature, viz. prescriptive and descriptive. The former refers to the establishment of prescriptive formulas to political action or the "what ought to be." The latter is termed "empirical political theory" and attempts to avoid value statements. Its goal is to elucidate empirically relevant propositions that are causal, functional or correlational in nature. [8] This type of political thought primarily deals with "what is" in terms of political behavior.

The prime focus of political thought is the search for understanding, and scholarly writing of this genre is dedicated to this aim. The literature of political theory is expressed in terms of probability not certainty. It cannot prove but can only suggest. [9] Indeed, one of the basic problems of political thought lies in the difficulty of determining the validity of concepts. It is possible that the viability of political thought in the current century is dependent upon the application of new methods of measurement to test the reliability of concepts both old and new.

Comparative Government and Politics

Comparative government as a separate specialty within political science has been inexorably fastened to the study of structure and formal institutionalism. Since Aristotle's study of Athenian constitutions, no empirical study of governmental institutions was formulated until Giovanni Batista Vico in the first part of the 18th century made a thorough comparison of various political institutions. Up to the current period the study of comparative government has been mainly concerned with the description of individual state systems or specific institutional structures within them.

Modern writing on comparative government is expanding into new and more fruitful areas. Comparative analyses of political systems are now exploring the relationships of cultural traditions, economic conditions, class structure and geographical situations to the development of governmental structures. In short, more attention is being given to the broader cultural and social milieus in the development of political systems.

Local Government, Political Parties and Public Opinion

The study of local governmental structures and problems has been a relatively recent development. Most of the literature in this area represents a departure from the mere study of governmental institutions and has focused on the development and function of community power structures as exemplified in the writings of Robert A. Dahl and Nelson W. Polsby. In local government the number of problems stemming from executive, legislative, judicial and electoral func-

tions is almost endless as are the multiple methods of dealing with them.

Political parties in political systems are receiving
more attention in recent years. The study of their development and role in the political process has been treated in
terms of historical evolution devoid of any theoretical orientations.

In this strictest sense, public opinion is not considered as a branch of political science; however, its function in the political process contains many relevant implications. Current works on public opinion concentrate on the
methods of collecting and analyzing pertinent data as well as
finding valid measuring devices.

Law and Jurisprudence

From the development of Hammurabi's Code, the jus
civile and jus gentium of Rome to the present, the literature
of the law has its roots in legislative enactments or decisions of judicial tribunals. Because of this it is understand-
able that this large body of literature is in the form of com-
pends and collections. Jurisprudence has been characterized
by schools of thought such as the sociological school under the
leadership of Roscoe Pound. Recent innovations in the study
of judicial behavior have been instituted to broaden understanding of the judicial process within the framework of politics.

Public Administration

The literature concerning public administration is le-
gion with emphasis on bureaucratic structures and the formulation of public policy. Primary attention is given to administrative functions summed up in the word POSDCORB
first enunciated by Luther Gulick and Lyndall Urwick. The
word stands for the functions of planning, organizing, staffing,
directing, coordinating, reporting, and budgeting.

Through the efforts of such men as Herbert A. Simon
and Dwight Waldo a more conceptual approach has developed
toward more generalized theories of organization. Related
concepts from sociology and psychology are also being used
to study administrative organization, function and behavior.
Perhaps the most current development in the field has been
the use of applied techniques through case studies. This al-

lows the student a maximum of actual experience in the
study of the administrative process.

International Relations

Currently composed of three broad sub-disciplines, the
study of international relations is an amalgam of many diverse elements. Since the beginning of the nation-state system in the sixteenth century, relations between states have
been of keen interest to students and statesmen alike.

International politics has dealt with such factors as
economic and human geography and their effect on the power
of a state, political history, national psychology, and economic, military, and foreign policies. The formulation and
control of foreign policy has been of particular interest in the
literature with a great amount of space being dedicated to the
effects of the idealism versus realism approaches. Scholarly
writing in this area is leaning toward conceptual frames of
reference to provide a better understanding of interaction on
the international level.

The development of international organization since the
early 1920's has given rise to an increasingly important body
of literature. Most of the writing in this area has concentrated on formal institutions and their role in peacefully re-
solving international conflict.

International law has had a specialized literature of
its own, although it maintains a close theoretical tie with international organizations. Largely customary in nature, international law has developed through the adjudication of cases
by various international tribunals although it is unable to im-
pose sanctions for disobedience.

Summary

From this cursory overview it can be readily seen that
political science is a composite of large collectives, governmental structures, theoretical concepts and constructs, factor
specialization and human behavior. Exponents of the "policy
science" approach such as Harold D. Lasswell and James K.
Pollock advocate the sharing of political problems with the
other social sciences. [10] The future of political science may
rest in the relationship it shares with its sister disciplines
in the development of new and imaginative approaches, theoretical frameworks and techniques that lead to a greater un-

derstanding of the world in which we live.

Footnotes

1. Edward C. Smith, ed., Dictionary of American politics (New York: Barnes & Noble, 1955), p. 293.

2. Heinz Eulau, "Political science." In Carl M. White, Sources of information in the social sciences (Totowa, N. J.: Bedminster Press, 1964), p. 359.

3. Ibid. p. 389.

4. Ibid. p. 364. Dr. Eulau states that an approach means "not the particular methods of inquiry and research, but the models in terms of which the data government and politics are analyzed and interpreted." Not doubting the plausibility of this view, this writer cannot divorce methodology from approach so easily. Simulation models become unmanageable, for instance, unless handled by means of computer methods or applications.

5. Heinz Eulau, "Political science." In Bert F. Hoselitz, ed. A reader's guide to the social sciences. (Glencoe, Ill.: Free Press, 1959), p. 89.

6. Eulau, op. cit., p. 358.

7. William Ebenstein, Political thought in perspective. (New York: McGraw-Hill, 1957), p. 1.

8. Heinz Eulau, "Political science." In Carl M. White, Sources of information in the social sciences (Totowa, N. J.: Bedminster Press, 1964), p. 369.

9. Michael Curtis, The great political theories (New York: Avon Books, 1962), p. 17.

10. Alfred de Grazia, Politics and government. vol. I. (New York: Collier Books, 1962), p. 64.

CHAPTER II

General Research Materials

The foci of the social sciences are men and the many complex relationships that result from interaction among men. Political relationships form only a part of the larger social matrix which contains many diverse elements. Illustrated in this chapter are a number of works dealing with the social sciences in general. All of these are partially relevant to political science and a large number are valuable source materials for research purposes.

A Bibliography of
Social Science Research and Methodology

American Council of Learned Societies Devoted to Humanistic Studies. Research in the humanistic and social sciences; report of a survey conducted for the American Council of Learned Societies, by Frederick Austin Ogg... New York, Century, 1928. 454p. (A1)

---- ----. The social studies and the social sciences, Bernard Berelson and others. New York, Harcourt, Brace & World, 1962. 303p. (A2)

Barnes, Harry Elmer, ed. The history and prospects of the social sciences. New York, Knopf, 1925. 534p. (A3)

Berelson, Bernard, ed. The behavioral sciences today. New York, Basic Books, 1963. 278p. (A4)

Brookings Institution, Washington, D.C. Committee on Training. Essays in research in the social sciences. Washington, Brookings Institution, 1931. 194p. (A5)

Charlesworth, James Clyde, ed. Mathematics and the social sciences; the utility and inutility of mathematics in the study of economics, political science, and sociology. Philadelphia, American Academy of Political and Social Science, 1963. 121p. (A6)

Gee, Wilson, ed.   Research in the social sciences; its fundamental methods and objectives.   New York, Macmillan,
1929.   305p.   (A7)

---- ----.   Social science research methods.   New York,
Appleton-Century-Crofts, 1950.   390p.   (A8)

---- ----.   Social science research organization in American universities and colleges.   New York, D. Appleton,
1934.   275p.   (A9)

Green, Bert F.   Digital computers in research, an introduction for behavioral and social scientists.   New York, Mc-
Graw-Hill, 1963.   333p.   (A10)

Holbrook, Franklin Fisk.   Survey of activities of American
agencies in relation to materials for research in the social
sciences and the humanities.   Washington & New York,
Published for the Council of Learned Societies and the Social Science Research Council, 1932.   184p.   (A11)

Hoselitz, Berthold Frank, ed.   A reader's guide to the social sciences.   Glencoe, Ill., Free Press, 1960, c1959.
256p.   (A12)

House, Floyd Nelson.   The range of social theory; a survey
of the development, literature, tendencies and fundamental
problems of the social sciences.   New York, Holt, c1929.
587p.   (A13)

Kaufmann, Felix.   Methodology of the social sciences.   New
York, Humanities Press, 1958.   272p.   (A14)

Lazarsfeld, Paul Felix.   The academic mind; social scientists in a time of crisis.   With Wagner Thielens, Jr.
Glencoe, Ill., Free Press, 1958.   460p.   (A15)

---- ----, ed.   The language of social research; a reader in
the methodology of social research.   Edited with Morris
Rosenberg.   Glencoe, Ill., Free Press, 1955. 590p.
                                                          (A16)
Lerner, Daniel, ed.   The policy sciences; recent developments in scope and method.   Edited with Harold D. Lasswell.   Stanford, Calif., Stanford University Press, 1951.
344p.   (A17)

Lundberg, George Andrew.   Social research, a study in

methods of gathering data. New York, Longmans, Green, 1942. 426p. (A18)

McCormick, Thomas Carson. Methods of research in the behavioral sciences. With Roy G. Francis. New York, Harper, 1958. 244p. (A19)

Michigan State University of Agriculture and Applied Science, East Lansing. Dept. of Social Science. Introduction to social science: the scientific method and social problems. East Lansing, Michigan, State University Press, 1962. 117p. (Its Social science series, 1) (A20)

Odum, Howard Washington. An introduction to social research. New York, Holt, c1929. 488p. (A21)

Ogburn, William Fielding, ed. The social sciences and their interrelations. Boston, Houghton Mifflin, c1927. 506p. (A22)

Passfield, Sidney James Webb. Methods of social study. New York, Longmans, Green, 1932. 263p. (A23)

Ray, Donald P., ed. Trends in social science. New York, Philosophical Library, 1961. 169p. (A24)

Recent developments in the social sciences, by Charles A. Ellwood and others. Philadelphia, Lippincott, c1927. 427p. (A25)

Rueff, Jacques. From the physical to the social sciences: introduction to a study of economic and ethical theory. Baltimore, the Johns Hopkins Press, 1929. 159p. (A26)

Social Science Research Council. Committee on Scientific Method in the Social Sciences. Methods in social science, a case book. Chicago, University of Chicago Press, 1937. 822p. (A27)

Spahr, Walter Earl. Methods and status of scientific research with particular application to the social sciences. New York, Harper, 1930. 533p. (A28)

White, Leonard Dupee, ed. The new social science. Chicago, University of Chicago Press, c1930. 132p. (A29)

Reference Works and Bibliographies
in the Social Sciences

Research Methods, Style Manuals and Guides

Appel, Livia. Bibliographical citation in the social sciences
and the humanities; a handbook for authors, editors and
students. 3d ed. Madison, University of Wisconsin Press,
c1949. 32p.   (A30)

Barzun, Jacques. The modern researcher. With Henry F.
Graff. New York, Harcourt, Brace and World, 1963,
c1957. 386p.

Although basically concerned with research problems in
history and its auxiliary sciences it is useful to any student engaged in research and report writing. Includes
sections on methods of research, evaluation and interpretation of facts, and the verification of citations. (A31)

Clarke, Jack Alden. Research materials in the social sciences. Madison, University of Wisconsin Press, 1959.
42p.

An annotated listing of the more important research aids
in the social sciences including bibliographies, reference
works and periodicals.   (A32)

Hurt, Peyton. Bibliography and footnotes; a style manual for
college and university students. Rev. and enl. by Mary L.
Hurt Richmond. Berkeley, University of California Press,
1957, c1949. 167p.

Perhaps the most useful guide to proper citation for the
political scientist because of its emphasis on political and
governmental materials.   (A33)

Lewis, Peter R. The literature of the social sciences; an
introductory survey and guide. London, Library Association, 1960. 222p.

A general guide to the social sciences. It is slanted toward British usage and tools but is useful because it includes excellent coverage of political science.   (A34)

White, Carl Milton. Sources of information in the social
sciences; a guide to the literature. With associates.

Totowa, N. J. , Bedminster Press, 1964. 498p.

A general work on the social sciences. Section on political science written by Heinz Eulau gives a good capsule view of the field. Many reference works are annotated for evaluation.   (A35)

Bibliographies and Encyclopedias

Encyclopedia of the social sciences; editor-in-chief, Edwin R. A. Seligman; associate editor, Alvin Johnson... New York, Macmillan, 1930-35.   15 v.

A comprehensive encyclopedia of the entire field of the social sciences prepared under the auspices of ten learned societies. Articles are by specialists and signed. They are accompanied by bibliographies and many biographies of deceased persons. A revision is now in preparation.
(A36)

Hoffman, Bernard G. Tentative check list of social science periodicals and monograph series published in the United States and Canada. Washington? 1961. 21p.

A brief but useful bibliography.   (A37)

A London bibliography of the social sciences, being the subject catalogue of the British Library of Political and Economic science... London, London School of Economics and Political Science, 1931+   v. 1+

In its field the most extensive subject bibliography. It is arranged alphabetically by subjects, with brief but adequate information-author, title (often abbreviated) paging, date, location and other information as to whether the work contains a bibliography - with a large number of cross references.   (A38)

New York. State Library, Albany. Checklist of books and pamphlets in the social sciences; including anthropology, economics, philosophy, political science, psychology, welfare but not including education, history and law. Albany, 1956.   142p.   (A39)

Samford, Clarence D. Social studies bibliography: curriculum and methodology. Carbondale, Southern Illinois University Press, 1959. 101p.   (A40)

Indexes and Abstracts

International index, a quarterly guide to periodical literature
in the social sciences and humanities. New York, Wilson,
1916+ v. 1+

> This valuable cumulation indexes selected English language
> journals published in the United States and abroad. It al-
> so includes society publications. It is arranged by author,
> subject and title, is issued quarterly and cumulated peri-
> odically.   (A41)

Public affairs information service. Bulletin in annual cumulation. New York, Wilson, 1915+ v. 1+

> Issued in three forms: (1) weekly bulletins; (2) cumula-
> tions published five times a year, the fifth cumulated issue
> forming (3) the annual cumulation. It is a subject index
> to the current literature in political science, government,
> economics and the rest of the social sciences. Indexes
> periodicals as well as books, documents, pamphlets, articles
> and multigraphed materials.   (A42)

Social science abstracts: a comprehensive abstracting and
indexing journal of the world's periodical literature in the
social sciences. New York, Social Science Abstracts, Inc.,
Columbia University, 1929-33. 5v.

> This is an extensive bibliography with the abstracts having
> been written by specialists. Each annual volume includes
> an index of authors as well as detailed index of subjects.
> It was discontinued for lack of funds but is excellent for
> its period of coverage.   (A43)

Miscellaneous Reference Works

American men of science, a biographical directory. Edited
by Jacques Cattell, 10th ed. Tempe, Ariz., Jacques Cattell Press, 1962. v. 5. The social and behavioral sciences.
1220p.

> Volume 5 of the current 10th ed. contains the biographical
> data including full name, position, address, field of spe-
> cialization, birth place, degrees, etc., of persons in the be-
> havioral and social sciences.   (A44)

Chamberlin, Jo Hubbard. Careers for social scientists:

anthropology, economics, history, political science, sociology. New York, H.A. Walack, 1961. 108p.

Although written on the adolescent level, this work is still
useful in indicating the opportunities open to political scientists.   (A45)

Gale Research Company. Acronyms dictionary; a guide to
alphabetic designations, contractions, and initialisms; associations, aero space, business, electronic, governmental,
international, labor, military, public affairs, scientific,
societies, technical, transportation, United Nations. Detroit, 1960.   211p.   (A46)

United Nations Educational, Scientific and Cultural Organization.   Theses in the social sciences; an international analytical catalogue of unpublished doctorate theses, 1940-1950.
Paris, 1952. 236p.

A useful but somewhat limited work covering only a ten
year period.   (A47)

Who's who in Soviet social sciences, humanities, art and
government.   Compiled by Ina Telberg. New York, Telberg Book Co., 1961.   (A48)

Zadrozny, John Thomas. Dictionary of social science.
Washington, Public Affairs Press, 1959. 367p.

For political as well as social scientists this work gives
actual usages of the more important terms in the major
social sciences.   (A49)

Generally Useful Reference Works
and Bibliographies

Materials covering an even wider scope than those
lised in the previous section cannot be ignored because of
their great value to the researcher. Reference tools of a
wide general nature ranging from bibliographies to atlases
will be of interest to the political scientist and student who
will need a breadth of coverage to select the most useful materials for their various purposes.

Guides to Reference Works

Enoch Pratt Free Library, Baltimore.   Reference books: a

brief guide for students and other users of the library,
compiled by Mary Neill Burton.   5th ed.   Baltimore, 1962.
135p.

Although brief, it is an extremely useful guide which includes a section on political science.   (A50)

Winchell, Constance Mabel.   Guide to reference books. 7th
    ed.   Chicago, American Library Association, 1951. 645p.

An extensive and useful guide to many types of reference
works with a large number of helpful annotations.   Supplements have been issued for the years 1950/52; 1953/55;
1956/58; and 1959/62.   (A51)

Bibliographies of Bibliographies

Besterman, Theodore.   A world bibliography of bibliographies
    and of bibliographical catalogues, calendars, abstracts,
    digests, indexes, and the like.   3d ed.   New York, Scare-
    crow Press, 1955. 4 v.

This monumental work lists 80, 000 separately published
bibliographies.   Arrangement is alphabetical and classified.
Volume four is an index of authors, editors, translators,
libraries, etc.   (A52)

Bibliographic index; a cumulative bibliography.   New York,
    H.W. Wilson, 1937+   v.1+

An alphabetical subject arrangement of recent bibliographies appearing in books, pamphlets, and articles.   Includes over one thousand periodicals, many in foreign languages, which are examined regularly.   (A53)

Collison, Robert Lewis.   Bibliographies, subject and national;
    a guide to their contents, arrangement and use.   2d ed.
    New York, Hafner, 1962.   185p.

Basically a handbook that includes three to four hundred
carefully selected references to bibliographies.   (A54)

Index bibliographicus, directory of current periodical ab-
    stracts and bibliographies. 3d ed. Paris, UNESCO, 1951-52.
    2v.

A guide to bibliographies appearing in current periodicals

and society publications. Arrangement of bibliographies and
abstracting journals is by the Universal Decimal Classification scheme. Indication is given of the language of the abstracts, the coverage, frequency of issue and address of
the publisher. Volume 2 handles the social sciences.
                                                        (A55)

U.S. Library of Congress. General Reference and Bibliography Division. Current national bibliographies, compiled by
Helen F. Conover. Washington, 1955. 132p.

An annotated list of national bibliographies. Its extensive
coverage makes it extremely useful.   (A56)

National Bibliographies

American

American catalogue of books, 1876-1910. New York, Publishers Weekly, 1876-1910. 9v. in 13.

Volume one lists books in print in 1876 and is therefore a
guide to books published prior to that date. Included are
society proceedings and a section on government documents.
Up to 1905 the subjects and authors are entered in one
alphabet.   (A57)

The Cumulative book index. Minneapolis, New York, H.W.
Wilson, 1898+ v.1+

Issued monthly, cumulated twice yearly, yearly, bi-yearly
and every four or five years. Like the U.S. Catalog which
it supplements, the Cumulative Book Index contains society
publications along with the works of personal authors. A
selection of important government documents is also included in both works. Since 1925 the Cumulative Book Index has included books in the English language published
outside the United States.   (A58)

The United States Catalog; books in print January 1, 1928.
New York, H.W. Wilson, 1900-1928. v.1+

Lists books in print under author and subject, in 1899,
1902, 1920, and 1928. Though many books went out of
print between those dates, these volumes are valuable because of their detailed subject entries.   (A59)

U.S. Library of Congress. A Catalog of books represented

by the Library of Congress printed cards issued to July 31, 1942. Ann Arbor, Mich., Edwards Bros., 1942-46. 167v.
(A60)

---- ----. Supplement: Cards issued August 1, 1942-December 31, 1947. Ann Arbor, Mich., Edwards Bros., 1948. 42v. (A61)

---- ----. The Library of Congress author catalog; a cumulative list of works represented by the Library of Congress printed cards, 1948-1955. Washington, Library of Congress, 1948-55. 46v. (A62)

---- ----. The National union catalog: a cumulative author list representing Library of Congress printed cards and titles reported by other American libraries, 1956+ Washington, Library of Congress, 1956+ v.1+

The Library of Congress has held the copyright depository privilege for books published in the United States since 1846. It includes, in addition to personal authors, society publications and titles of periodicals. This entire set of books consists chronologically of the basic set of 167 volumes, the 1948 supplement, another set covering the years 1948-1952, yet another covering the years 1953-1957, and a new set covering 1958-1962. A cumulative set of the National Union Catalog is issued annually and cumulated about every five years. (A63)

Vertical file index, an annotated subject catalog of pamphlets. New York, H.W. Wilson, 1932+ v.1+

Issued monthly with annual cumulations. (Formerly known as the Vertical file service catalog.) It is a guide, arranged under broad subject entries with author indexes. Includes a large number of pamphlets in the English language only, issued by societies, universities and commercial organizations. (A64)

British

British national bibliography. London, Council of the British Bibliography, British Museum, 1950+ v.1+

A weekly bibliography of books published in Great Britain. There is a monthly author and title index and it is cumulated annually with a three volume cumulation every five years. (A65)

Whitaker's Cumulative book list, a classified list of publications, London, Whitaker, 1924+ v. 1+

Issued quarterly, cumulating yearly and every few years.
Each issue consists of a classified list of recent publications and has a detailed author and title index.   (A66)

French

Biblio, catalogue des ouvrages parus en langue française dans
le monde entier. Paris, Service Bibliographique des Mes-
sageries Hachette, 1933+ v.1+

Issued monthly and cumulated annually, it is a dictionary
catalog, entering each book under author, subject and title
with many cross references.   (A67)

Bibliographie de la France; ou, Journal général de l'imprim-
erie et de la librairie. Paris, Cercle de la Librairie,
1811+   v.1+

A weekly list including books, pamphlets, official publications, music, prints, and a monthly record of gifts to the
Bibliothèque Nationale.   (A68)

German

Deutsche Bibliographie. Frankfurt am Main, Buchhandler-
Vereinigung GMBH, 1952+   v. 1+

Compiled by the Deutsche Bibliothek, the official depository
library for Western Germany. Arranged basically in two
parts by author and title which are cumulated from fasci-
cles annually.   (A69)

Deutsche Nationalbibliographie. Leipzig, Deutschen Bucherei
und Borsenverein der deutschen Buchhandler, 1931+ v.1+

This is a weekly classified list of books, pamphlets, seri-
als and documents. It is indexed by author and keyword
of title. East German.   (A70)

Periodical Directories

Ayer, Firm, newspaper advertising agents. N.W. Ayer &
son's directory of newspapers and periodicals; a guide to
publications printed in the United States and possessions...

Philadelphia, N.W. Ayer, 1880+   v. 1+

An annual that includes periodicals arranged by place of
publication, with classified lists serving as a guide to their
subject content. Each volume lists current periodicals.
                                                        (A71)
Ulrich's periodicals directory: a classified guide to a selected list of current periodicals, foreign and domestic.
New York, R.R. Bowker, 1932+   v. 1+   (Current ed. 10th,
1962)

In essence a world list.   Each edition includes a selective
but extensive list of current periodicals.   Titles are arranged under broad subjects.   A new two volume edition
is now in preparation.   (A72)

Periodical Indexes

Nineteenth century readers' guide to periodical literature,
    1890-1899, with supplementary indexing, 1900-1922. New
    York, H.W. Wilson, 1944. 2v.

    This is an author and subject index of 59 English and
    American nineteenth-century periodicals.   (A73)

Poole's index to periodical literature, 1802-81.   Rev. ed.
    Boston, Houghton Mifflin, 1891. 2 v. (Supplements, Janu-
    ary 1882-January 1, 1907.   Boston, Houghton Mifflin,
    c1887-1908,   5v.)

    Only a subject index, except for poems and short stories
    which are entered under title.   It excludes society publica-
    tions and foreign language periodicals.   (A74)

Readers' guide to periodical literature...Author and subject
    index to a selected list of periodicals.   New York, H.W.
    Wilson, 1901+   v.1+

    Contains both author and subject entries.   Periodicals in
    the English language only are included and society publica-
    tions are omitted.   (A75)

Subject index to periodicals, 1915+   London, Library Asso-
    ciation, 1919+   v.1+

    An annual more popularly known as the Athenacum Subject
    Index, 1915-18.   Includes subject entries, with author in-

dexes covering the years 1915-16 and 1917-19.   (A76)

Guides to Dissertations Listed Chronologically

U.S. Library of Congress. Catalog Division. A list of
American doctoral dissertations printed in 1912-1938.
Washington, U.S. Govt. Print. Off., 1913-1939. 27v.

Includes dissertations classified under broad subjects, with
detailed subject index. Indicates dissertations published in
periodicals and society publications or in separate forms.
                                                   (A77)
Doctoral dissertations accepted by American universities.
no. 1-22. New York, H.W. Wilson, 1934-55. 22v.

Dissertations in this publication are classified under broad
subjects. There is also an author index. For a list of
the universities from which doctoral dissertations may be
obtained see the most recent volume. Is no longer published; however, the indexes are continued annually in
Dissertation Abstracts.   (A78)

Dissertation abstracts; abstracts of dissertations and monographs in microfilm. Ann Arbor, Mich., University Microfilms, 1938+ v.1+

Useful for the dissertations it abstracts and its complete
list of all dissertations written in the United States. The
user must be aware that all dissertations are not abstracted
in this publication. A list of the universities submitting
these abstracts is given in the front of each issue. (A79)

Guides and Indexes to Newspapers

Annuaire de la presse française et étrangère et du monde
politique. Paris, Administration et Rédaction, 1880+ v.1+

Arranged by place of publication with each volume containing only currently published newspapers and listing their
political affiliation.   (A80)

The New York Times index for the published news. New
York, New York Times Co., 1913+ v.1+

Due to its wide coverage of news this index may be used to
locate material in other newspapers. Particularly valuable
for its detailed subject entries. Cumulates annually. (A81)

New York Tribune.   New-York daily tribune index.   New
   York, The Tribune Association, 1876-1907.   v. 1+

   An annual now discontinued.   The subject entries are
   somewhat less detailed than those in the N.Y. Times Index.
                                                          (A82)
The Times London.   The official index to the Times, London,
   J. P. Bland at the Times office, 1914+   v. 1+

   Like the New York Times Index this annual publication may
   be used to locate material in other newspapers.   Subject
   entries are greatly detailed.   (A83)

---- ----.   Palmer's index to the Times newspaper... London, S. Palmer, 1868+   v. 1+

   Less detailed than the Official Index, but is valuable because of the long period of time it covers.   (A84)

Willing's Press guide.   London, Willing, 1874+   v. 1+

   Issued annually, the arrangement is by place.   Each volume lists only newspapers published currently and indicates
   political affiliation.   (A85)

Biographical Materials

Biography index; a cumulative index to biographical material
   in books and magazines.   New York, H.W. Wilson, 1946+
   v. 1+

   Indexes biographical material in current books in the English language, with each issue containing an index to pro-
   fessions and occupations.   (A86)

Directory of American scholars; a biographical directory.
   New York, R. R. Bowker, 1942, 1951, 1957, 1963+   v. 1+

   A biographical listing of persons particularly associated
   with institutions of higher education.   Now issued in four
   volumes: v. 1. History, v. 2. English speech and drama,
   v. 3. Foreign languages, linguistics and philology, v.4.
   Philosophy.   (A87)

Miscellaneous Aids

The Book review digest... Annual cumulation.   New York,

H.W Wilson, 1905+   v.1+

A digest of selected books published annually, with an author and title index.   (A88)

Facts on file yearbook... Person's index of world events.
New York, Person's Index, Facts on File, Inc., 1942?+
v. 1+

This is a weekly publication with annual cumulations.   It is
a useful general source in the field of current affairs on
world-wide scope.   (A89)

Shepherd, William Robert.   Historical atlas. 8th ed. New
York, Barnes & Noble, 1956. 248p.

Covering the period from 2000 B.C. to 1955, it is one of
the best historical atlases available.   (A90)

Times, London.   The Times atlas of the world.   Mid-century
ed. London, Times Pub. Co., Boston, Houghton Mifflin,
1955-1959.   5v.

Perhaps the most excellent of world atlases, it gives attention to islands, includes inset maps for many cities and
has great accuracy and beauty in its maps.   (A91)

World almanac and book of facts, 1868+   New York, New
York World Telegram, 1868+

Of the American almanacs now available, this is perhaps
the most comprehensive and useful.   Gives a variety of information on current affairs, contains statistical data and
has a good, detailed index.   (A92)

CHAPTER III

Political Science and the Study of Politics

Generally the field of political science encompasses an extremely broad spectrum including specialized sub-disciplines. The literature contains many works that broadly outline the subject content of the field and seek to clarify the relationship of the various sub-disciplines to each other. The study of politics and the political process (no matter how one defines them) is central to political science, and recent writing trends treat them from divergent perspectives. Frequently political scientists consider the political process as a type of social interaction usually identified by the influence relationships between men, men and the state and between states with control being, more or less, the basic goal or objective.

Although the concentration of this chapter is on the more general treatises, inclusion of pertinent works in a number of peripheral areas such as political economy and geography will provide some additional information.

Research and Methodology in Political Science

Below is a short bibliography of the more important general summarizing works that relate to the trends and status of research and methodology in political science.

American Political Science Association. Committee for the Advancement of Teaching. Goals for political science; report. New York, Sloane, 1951. 319p. (B1)

---- ----. Research Committee. Research in political science: The work of the panel of the committee; ed. by Ernest S. Griffith. Chapel Hill, University of North Carolina Press, 1948. 238p. (B2)

Backstrom Charles Herbert. Survey research, with Gerald D. Hursh. Chicago, Northwestern University Press, 1963. 192p. (B3)

Barker, Ernest.   The study of political science and its relation to cognate studies.   Cambridge, Eng., University
Press, 1928. 50p.   (B4)

Brane, Dennis DeWitt.   A sequential science of government;
a study in systematic political science.   Cleveland, Western Reserve University Press, 1934.   90p.   (B5)

Brookings Institution, Washington, D.C.   Institute for government research, an account of research achievements.
Washington, 1956. 48p.   (B6)

Dahl, Robert Alan.   Modern political analysis.   Englewood
Cliffs, N.J., Prentice-Hall, 1963.   118p.   (B7)

Dauer, Manning Julian.   Political science scope and method:
an introductory manual.   With the collaboration of: Dwynal
Pettingill, Hugh Douglass and Robert J. Frye. Rev.
Gainesville, Fla., 1959. 145p.   (B8)

Deutsch, Karl Wolfgang.   The nerves of government; models
of political communication and control.   London, Free
Press of Glencoe, 1963.   316p.   (B9)

Easton David.   The political system, an inquiry into the
state of political science.   New York, Knopf, 1953. 320p.
                                                          (B10)
Ewing, Russell Howard.   Political science seminar manual;
research methods, problems, bibliography.   Clinton, New
York, Hamilton College, 1949.   15 p.   (B11)

Friedrich, Carl Joachim.   Man and his government; an empirical theory of politics.   New York, McGraw-Hill, 1963.
737p.   (Bibliography: p. 677-715)   (B12)

Hacker, Andrew.   The study of politics: the western tradition and American origins.   New York, McGraw-Hill, 1963.
105p.   (B13)

Hyneman, Charles Shang.   The study of politics; the present
state of American political science.   Urbana, University of
Illinois Press, 1959. 232p.   (B14)

Lasswell, Harold Dwight.   The future of political science.
New York, Atherton Press, 1963.   256p.   (B15)

Leonard, Norman H.   Political science and political goals.

Dubuque, Iowa, W.C. Brown, 1955. 216p.   (B16)

Lewis, George Cornewal.   A treatise on the methods of observation and reasoning in politics.   London, J.W. Parker
and son, 1852.   2v.   (B17)

Macdonald, Austin Faulks.   Elements of political science research: sources and methods.   New York, Prentice-Hall,
1928.   94p.   (Sources: p. 85-94)   (B18)

Macpherson, C.B.   Report on research in political science.
Paris, International Political Science Association, 1953.
20p.   (Mimeo)   (B19)

Merriam, Charles Edward.   New aspects of politics.   Chicago, University of Chicago Press, c1925.   253p. (B20)

Michigan.   University.   Dept. of Political Science.   The status and prospects of political science as a discipline.   Ann
Arbor, 1960.   54p.   (B21)

Michigan.   University.   Survey Research Center.   The proper-
ties of political issues, by Angus Campbell.   Ann Arbor,
1957?   23p.   (B22)

Research frontiers in politics and government, by Stephen K.
Bailey and others.   Washington, Brookings Institution, 1955.
240p.   (B23)

Royal Institute of Public Administration.   Register of research
in political science.   Prepared for the Political Studies Association and the Public Administration Committee of the
Joint University Council for Social and Political Administration.   London, 1960?   16 leaves.   (Includes supplement for
1960/61+)   (B24)

United Nations Educational, Scientific and Cultural Organization.   Contemporary political science; a survey of methods,
research and teaching.   Paris, 1950.   713p.   (B25)

Van Dyke, Vernon.   Political science; a philosophical analysis.   Stanford, Calif., Stanford University Press, 1960.
235p.   (B26)

Verney, Douglas V.   The analysis of political systems.   Glencoe, Ill., Free Press, 1959.   239p.   (B27)

Ward Robert Edward, ed.   Studying politics abroad; field research in the developing areas.   With Frank Bonilla and
others.   Boston, Little, Brown, 1964.   245p. (Bibliography: p. 225-234)   (B28)

Political Science - Study and Teaching
───────────────────────────────────────

A number of monographs are concerned with methods
of teaching political science in institutions of higher education.
Approaches to teaching the subject matter of this field have
undergone a great deal of scrutiny and re-evaluation in the
last two decades.   The works cited below give a general indication of how this has taken place and what areas need further
effort to adjust instructional methods to meet the demands of
a rapidly developing discipline.

Advisory Commission on Graduate Education and Research in
Government in the South.   Graduate education and research
in government in the South, a report.   Atlanta, Southern
Regional Education Board, 1954.   77p.   (B29)

American Political Science Association.   Committee on Instruction.   The teaching of government, report to the
American Political Science Association by the Committee
on Instruction, Charles G. Haines, chm... New York, Macmillan, 1916.   284p. (Bibliography: p. 111-133)   (B30)

Barents, Jan.   Political science in Western Europe, a trend
report.   London, Stevens, 1961. 121p.   (B31)

Brogan, Denis William.   The study of politics.   Cambridge,
Eng. , University Press, 1946.   21p.   (B32)

Field, Oliver Peter.   Political science at Indiana University,
1829-1951.   Bloomington, Bureau of Government Research,
Dept. of Government, Indiana University, 1952. 54p.
                                                     (B33)
Gurland, Arcadius Rudolph Lang.   Political science in Western Germany; thoughts and writings, 1950-1952.   Washington, Library of Congress, Reference Dept. , European Affairs Division, 1952.   118p.   (B34)

Haddow, Anna.   Political science in American colleges and
universities, 1636-1900.   New York, D. Appleton-Century,
c1939.   308p.   (Bibliography: p. 267-296)   (B35)

Hallowell, John Hamilton. Religious perspectives of college teaching in political science. New Haven, Edward W. Hazen Foundation, 1951? 36p. (B36)

Hoxie, Ralph Gordon. A history of the faculty of political science, Columbia University. New York, Columbia University Press, 1955. 326p. (B37)

Knoll, Joachim H. Jugend, Politik und politische Bildung, eine kritische Dokumentation. Heidelberg, Quelle & Meyer, 1962. 79p. (B38)

Kogekar, Sadanand Vasudeo. Political science in India, with A. Appadorai. Delhi, Premier Pub. Co., 1953. 110p. (B39)

Pettersch, Carl Alfred. The teaching of government in the United States, with special reference to secondary schools from 1861-1950. Ann Arbor, University Microfilms, 1954. 256p. (B40)

Rankin, Robert Stanley. Political science in the South. University of Ala., Bureau of Public Administration, University of Alabama, 1946. 61p. (B41)

Reed, Thomas Harrison. Preparing college men and women for politics. With Doris D. Reed. A report to the Citizenship Clearing House, affiliated with the Law Center of New York University. New York, 1952. 180p. (B42)

Robson, William Alexander. The university teaching of social sciences: political science. A report prepared on behalf of the International Political Science Association. Paris, UNESCO, 1954. 249p. (B43)

Schattschneider, Elmer Eric. A guide to the study of public affairs, with Victor Jones, and Stephen K. Bailey. New York, Sloane, 1952. 135p. (B44)

Waldo, Dwight. Political science in the United States of America, a trend report. Paris, UNESCO, 1956. 84p. (B45)

Reference Materials

There is a wide variety of special reference tools and general bibliographies available in political science. Only a few are cited in this section to indicate the types of informa-

tion that can be gleaned from reference materials.   It should
be noted, however, that there are several areas (e.g. directories, bibliographies) where more extensive and current
works would be useful.

Abstracts

International political science abstracts.   (Documentation
    Politique Internationale)   Oxford, Eng. , International Politi-
    cal Science Association, 1951+   v. 1+

    Abstracts are taken from selected articles in an increasing
    number of periodicals published in various countries.   In
    general, abstracts of articles written in English are also
    in French, while those of articles written in any other lan-
    guage are in English.   Arrangement is alphabetical by au-
    thor.   Also included is a detailed subject index.   (B46)

Bibliographies

Adam, Melchior.   Vitae Germanorum, jureconsultorum et
    politicorum: qvi superiori secul o, et quod excurrit, flouer-
    unt.   Haidelbergae, Impensis heredum J. Rosae, 1620.
    488p.   (B47)

Association for Education in Citizenship.   Bibliography of so-
    cial studies; a list of books for schools and adults.   Lon-
    don, Oxford University Press, 1936.   111p.   (B48)

Bibliographie der Sozialwissenschaften.   Berlin, 1905+ v. 1+
                                                       (B49)
Bibliography in politics, for the Honour School of Philosophy,
    Politics and Economics.   Drawn up by Professor Headlam-
    Morley, and others.   Oxford, Blackwell, 1949. 55p. (B50)

Bibliography of the studies on law and politics, Tokyo, High-
    er Education and Science Bureau, 1952.   (Superseded by
    Japan Science Review; law and politics, periodical) (B51)

Bowker, Richard Rogers.   The reader's guide in economic,
    social and political science, being a classified bibliography,
    American, English, French and German, with descriptive
    notes, author, title and subject index, courses of reading,
    college courses etc.   Ed. by R.R. Bowker and George Ikes.
    New York, The Society for Political Education, 1891. 169p.
                                                       (B52)
Bozza, Tommaso.   Scrittori politici italiani dal 1550-al 1650,

saggio de bibliografia.   Roma, Edizioni di "Storia e lettera-
tura," 1949.   218p.   (Bibliography: p. 17-24)   (B53)

Columbia.   University.   Faculty of Political Science.   A bib-
liography of the Faculty of political science of Columbia
University, 1880-1930.   New York, Columbia University
Press, 1931.   365p.   (B54)

Eaton, Andrew Jackson.   Current political science publications in five Chicago libraries; a study of coverage, duplication and omission.   n. p., 1946. 212p.   (B55)

Grandin, A.   Bibliographie générale des sciences juridiques,
politiques, économiques et sociales de 1800 à 1925-1926,
par, A. Grandin.   Publiée par la Société anonyme du Re-
cueil Sirey, 1926.   3v. (Has supplement, 1926/27+) (B56)

Harmon, Robert Bartlett.   Bibliography of bibliographies in
political science.   San Jose, Calif., Dibco Press, 1964.
16p.   (B57)

Holland, Henry M.   A checklist of paperback books and reprints in political science. Washington, American Political
Science Association, 1962.   47p.   (B58)

International bibliography of political science.   Bibliographie
internationale de science politique. Paris, UNESCO, 1953+
v. 1+   (B59)

Maryland.   University.   Bureau of Governmental Research.
Political science; a selected bibliography of books in print,
with annotations.   Compiled by Franklin L. Burdette, direc-
tor, Jerold H. Willmore, and John V. Witherspoon. College Park, 1961.   97p.   (B60)

Mattei, Rodolfo de.   La storia dottrine politiche. Firenze,
G. C.   Sanonsi, 1938.   173p.   (B61)

Meyriat, Jean, ed.   La science politique en France, 1945-
1958.   Bibliographie.   Pref. de Jacques Chapsal. Paris,
Foundation Nationale des Sciences Politiques, 1960. 134p.
                                                        (B62)
Naude, Gebriel.   Bibliographia politica. Venetiis, F. Baba,
1633.   Torino, Bottega d'Erasmo, 1961.   (B63)

Neue politische Literatur; Berichte über das internationale
schrifttum.   Stuttgart, 1956+ v. 1+ (Supersedes Poli-

tische Literatur)   (B64)

Perticone, Giacomo. Filosofia del dritto e dello stato, a
cura. di Giacomo Perticone. Storia delle dottrine politiche,
a cura de Rodolfo de Mattei. Roma, 1943. 190p. (B65)

The Political register and impartial review of new books.
London, Printed for J. Almon, 1767+ v. 1+   (B66)

Politische Literatur; berichte über das internationale schrifttum zur politik. Frankfurt am Main, Institut für Politische
Wissenschaft der Johann-Wolfgang-Goethe Universität, 1952-
1955. v. 1+   (B67)

Puget, Henry. Essai de bibliographie des principaux ouvrages de droit public (droit public général droit constitu-
tionnel, droit administratif de science politique et de science administrative qui ont paru hors de France de 1945
à 1958. Publié sous la direction de Henry Puget. Sous
les auspices du Centre français de droit comparé et avec
le concours du Centre national de la recherche scientifique.
Paris, Editions de l'Epragne, 1961. 369p.   (B68)

Quarterly check-list of economics & political science. Dari-
en, Conn., American Bibliographic Service, 1958+ v. 1+
                                                              (B69)
Television Information Office, New York. Library. Television in government and politics, a bibliography. New
York, Television Information Office, 1964. 62p.   (B70)

Thompson, Olive. A guide to readings in civic education.
(rev. and enl.) Berkeley, University of California Press,
1924. 140p.   (B71)

U. S. Library of Congress. Division of Bibliography. A selected list of recent books on modern political systems,
compiled by Grace Hadley Fuller. Washington, 1936. 26p.
(Typewritten)   (B72)

Virginia. State Library, Richmond. Finding list of the social sciences, political science, law, and education. (In
its Bulletin. Richmond, 1910. v. 3, no. 1, 2 and 3, p. 3-
352; Classed catalog, with author, title and subject index)
                                                              (B73)
World Affairs Book Fair, 3d, 1956. Third world affairs
book fair, political and cultural, 1956. Catalogue of the
combined book exhibit. New York, Carnegie Endowment

International Center, 1956. 31p.   (B74)

Course Outlines and Examination Questions

Beecroft, Eric Armour. Guide for intermediate course in
political science. Los Angeles? 1937. 46p.   (B75)

College Publishing Corporation, Brooklyn. How to pass government; questions and answers. Brooklyn, 1964. 1v.
(B76)

Ewald, Peter Kenneth. Political science, a study of institutions, first semester; a complete review of the semester's
work in the form of examination type questions...New York,
Arco Pub. Co., c 1948. 49 leaves.   (B77)

Dictionaries

Baker, E. Conrad. Political terms and familiar political al-
lusions. London, Falcon Press, 1948. 78p.   (B78)

Bhandari, Sukhsampattirai. The twentieth century political
dictionary. Brahpuri, Ajmer, Dictionary Pub. House, 1949.
174p.   (B79)

Elliott, Florence. A dictionary of politics. With Michael
Summerskill. Hammondsworth, Eng., Penguin Books,
1957. 328p.   (B80)

Haessly, Mathias John. Political and governmental terms.
Milwaukee, Wis., Caspar, 1936. 48p.   (B81)

Lalor, John Joseph, ed. Cyclopedia of political science, po-
litical economy, and of the political history of the United
States, by the best American and European writers. New
York, Maynard, Merrill, & Co., 1904. 3v.

Although out of date this set of volumes gives adequate
coverage for many subjects.   (B82)

Lewis, George Cornwall. Remarks on the use and abuse of
some political terms. Oxford, Clarendon Press, 1898.
194p.   (B83)

Mansoor, Menahem. English-Arabic dictionary of political,
diplomatic, and conference terms. New York, McGraw-
Hill, 1961. 353p.   (B84)

Montgomery, Hugh.   A dictionary of political phrases and al-
lusions, with a short bibliography.   With Philip G. Com-
bray.   New York, E. P. Dutton, 1906.   406p. (Bibliography:
p. 373-400)   (B85)

Political dictionary; forming a work of universal reference,
both constitutional and legal; and embracing the terms of
civil administration, of political economy and social relations, and of all the more important statistical developments of finance and commerce.   London, C. Knight, 1845-
46.   2v.   (B86)

Raghu, Vira.   A comprehensive English-Hindi dictionary of
governmental and educational words and phrases... Nagpur,
Lokesh Chandra, International Academy of Indian Culture,
1955.   1579p.   (B87)

White, Wilbur Wallace.   White's political dictionary.   Cleveland, World Pub. Co., 1947.   378p.

Basically a popular dictionary, international in treatment,
which includes many names and terms of recent origin,
particularly the names of governmental organizations, conferences, treaties, and political events.   There are many
cross references from abbreviations.   The appendices contain constitutions of the League of Nations and the United
Nations.   (B88)

Directories

American Political Science Association.   Directory.   Evanston, Ill., 1945+   (Now published in Washington, D. C. ?)

Serving as a "Who's who in political science," it gives detailed biographical information of members of the association.   (B89)

Guides

Britannica Library Research Service.   Britannica home study
guide.   Political science.   London, Britannica House,
1950?   16p.   (Supplementary reading: p. 15-16)   (B90)

Burchfield, Laverne.   Student's guide to materials in political
science, prepared under the direction of the Sub-committee
on research of the Committee on policy of the American
Political Science Association.   New York, Holt, c1935.

426p.

A general guide for the student interested in political science. Lists important source materials, finding devices, bibliographies, and general reference works to aid in political research. Now out of date, but still very useful.
(B91)

Ward, Robert Edward. A guide to Japanese reference and research materials in the field of Political Science. Ann Arbor, University of Michigan Press, 1950. 104p. (B92)

Washington University. St. Louis. Libraries. Guide to research material in political science, by Joseph M. Thom. St. Louis, 1952. 2 pts. (B93)

Wynar, Lubomyr R. Social sciences general references; political science, a selective and annotated bibliographical guide. Boulder, Social Sciences Library, University of Colorado Libraries, 1962. 66p. (B94)

Terminology

Lasswell, Harold Dwight. Language of politics; studies in quantitative semantics. With Nathan Leits and associates. New York, G.W. Stewart, 1949. 398p. (Bibliographical references included in "Notes" p. 382-398) (B95)

Salisbury, Franklin Cary. Speaking of politics. New York, Vantage Press, 1956. 294p. (Bibliography: p. 285-286) (B96)

Weldon, Thomas Dewar. Vocabulary of politics. Baltimore, Penguin Books, 1953. 199p. (B97)

General Works

The field of political science is as old as man himself. The literature has reached such formidable proportions that it is difficult to select works that will significantly indicate the general trends and tendencies exhibited by the field. This section is designed to give some idea of the general direction and orientation of the literature to serve as a useful guide in selection of meaningful material for study purposes. Many of the works cited contain excellent bibliographies, some of which are indicated at the end of the citation.

Collections

Bains, J.S., ed.   Studies in political science.   New York,
Asia Pub. House, 1961. 488p.   (B98)

Curtis, Michael, ed.   The nature of politics.   New York,
Avon Book Division, Hearst Corp., 1962. 672p.   (B99)

Durham, George Homer, ed.   Introductory readings in political science.   Salt Lake City, Bookcraft, 1948. 247p.
                                                        (B100)
Flechtheim, Ossip Kurt, ed.   Fundamentals of political science.   New York, Ronald, 1952. 587p.   (B101)

Gould, Lyman Jay, ed.   People, power, and politics; an introductory reader, edited with E. William Steele.   New
York, Random House, 1961. 710p.   (B102)

Hamilton, Howard Devon, ed.   Political institutions; readings in political science.   Boston, Houghton Mifflin, 1962.
359p.   (B103)

Laslett, Peter, ed.   Philosophy, politics and society. (Second series); a collection.   Edited with W.G. Runciman.
New York, Barnes & Noble, 1962. 229p.   (B104)

Morgenthau, Hans Joachim.   Dilemmas of politics.   Chicago,
University of Chicago Press, 1958. 389p.   (B105)

Review of Politics.   Image of man; a Review of politics
reader.   Edited by M.A. Fitzsimons, Thomas T. McAvon
and Frank O'Malley.   Notre Dame, Ind., University of
Notre Dame Press, 1959. 451p.   (B106)

Rubinstein, Alvin Z., comp.   The challenge of politics; ideas
and issues, with Garold W. Thumm.   Englewood Cliffs,
N.J., Prentice-Hall, 1962, c1961. 359p.   (B107)

Sciaky, Isacco.   Introductory essays on political science.
Jerusalem, 1952. 180p.   (B108)

Snyder, Richard Carlton, ed.   Roots of political behavior;
introduction to government and politics, with H. Hubert
Wilson.   New York, American Book Co., c1949. 694p.
                                                        (B109)

Compends

Huszar, George Bernard de. Political science. With Thomas H. Stevenson. Rev. ed. Ames, Iowa, Littlefield, Adams, 1955. 226p.   (B110)

Jacobsen, Gertrude Ann. Political science, with M. H. Lipman. 13th ed. New York, Barnes & Noble, 1955. 244p.
                                                                (B111)

Miscellanea

Nomand, Max. A skeptic's political dictionary and handbook for the disenchanted. New York, Bookman Associates, 1953. 171p.   (B112)

Monographs

Adam, Thomas Ritchie. Elements of government; an introduction to political science. New York, Random House, 1960. 468p.   (B113)

Appadorai, Angadipuram. The substance of politics. 7th ed. London, Oxford University Press, 1954. 546p. (B114)

Arnold, Thurman Wesley. The folklore of capitalism. New Haven, Yale University Press, 1937. 400p.   (B115)

Aruego, Jose Maminta. Principles of political science. 3d ed. Manila, University Pub. Co., 1947. 365p.   (B116)

Baldwin, Armand Jean. Christian principles of political science; an introduction to political science. Latrobe, Pa., Archabbey Press, 1957. 160p.   (B117)

Banerjea, Benoyendra Nath. Introduction to politics. 8th ed. Calcutta, Jijnasa, 1962. 152p.   (B118)

Batria, Puran. Studies in political science. Agra, Nauyug Sahitya Sadan, 1956. 204p.   (B119)

Baxter, Garrett. Government. Norfolk, Va., The Economic Press, 1926. 104p.   (B120)

Berle, Adolf Augustus. Natural selection of political forces. Lawrence, University of Kansas Press, 1950. 103p. (B121)

Bowman, Eric Fisher. An introduction to political science.

London, Methuen, 1927.   327p. (Bibliography: p. 321-323)
(B122)

Brookes, Edgar Harry.   The relationship between history and
political science; an inaugural lecture delivered at Pieter-
maritzburg on 1st Sept., 1959.   Natal, University Press,
1959.   19p.   (B123)

Burgess, John William.   Political science and comparative
constitutional law.   Boston, Binn, 1890-91. 2v.   (B124)

Caldwell, Lynton Keith, ed.   Politics and public affairs.
Assisted by Glenna Ryan.   Bloomington, Institute of Train-
ing for Public Service, Department of Government, Indiana
University, 1962.   188p.   (B125)

Catlin, George Edward Gordon.   Political theory: what is it?
... Together with Politics in theory and practice... Montreal,
McGill University Bookshop, 1959.   43p.   (B126)

---- ----.   Preface to action.   New York, Macmillan, 1934.
319p.   (B127)

---- ----.   A study of the principles of politics, being an
essay toward political rationalization... New York, Macmillan, 1930.   469p.   (B128)

---- ----.   Systematic politics; elementa politica et socio-
logica.   Toronto, University of Toronto Press, 1962.
434p.   (B129)

Center for the Study of Democratic Institutions.   Tragedy and
the new politics; a discussion by Scott Buchanan and others.
Santa Barbara, Calif., c1960.   23p.   (B130)

Cobban, Alfred.   The crisis of civilization.   London, J.
Cape, 1941.   272p.   (B131)

Cole, George Douglas Howard.   A guide to modern politics,
with Margaret Cole.   New York, Knopf, 1934.   454p.
(Bibliography: p. 449-454)   (B132)

Cowling, Maurice.   The nature and limits of political science.
Cambridge, Eng., University Press, 1963.   213p. (B133)

Crick, Bernard R.   In defense of politics.   Chicago, University of Chicago Press, 1962.   156p.   (B134)

DeGrazia, Alfred.   Politics and government; the elements of
political science.   New rev. ed.   New York, Collier Books,
1962.   2v.   (B135)

Dillon, Conley Hall.   Introduction to political science.
Princeton, N. J. , Van Nostrand, c1958. 298p.   (B136)

Eliot, Thomas Stearnes.   The literature of politics; a lecture delivered at a C. P. C. literary luncheon.   London,
Conservative Political Centre, 1955.   22p.   (B137)

Exline, Frank.   Politics... New York, Dutton, c1927. 226p.
                                                     (B138)
Friedrich, Carl Joachim.   Die politische Wissenschaft. Frei-
burg, K. Alber, 1961.   450p.   (B139)

Friedwald, Eugene Marie.   Man's last choice, a survey of
political creeds and scientific realities.   New York, Viking
Press, 1948. 128p.   (B140)

Garner, James Wilford.   Introduction to political science; a
treatise on the origin, nature, functions, and organization
of the state.   New York, American Book Co. , c1910.
616p.   (B141)

---- ----.   Political science and government.   Indian ed.
Calcutta, World Press, 1951.   832p.   (B142)

Gemayel, Sleiman M.   Cours d'introduction à la science
politique.   Beyrouth, Polycopié par Bureau ''Manndia,''
1961.   64p.   (B143)

Gettell, Raymond Garfield.   Introduction to political science.
Boston, New York, Ginn, c1910. 421p.   (B144)

Gilchrist, Robert Niven.   Principles of political science. 7th
ed.   New York, Longmans, Green, 1953. 844p.   (B145)

Halle, Louis Joseph.   Men and nations.   Princeton, N. J. ,
Princeton University Press, 1962.   228p.   (B146)

Hauptman, Jerzy.   The dilemmas of politics.   Parkville, Mo. ,
1957.   48p.   (B147)

Heckscher, August.   Pattern of politics.   New York, Reynal
& Hitchcock, 1947.   244p. (Notes and bibliography: p.
237-244)   (B148)

Hermens, Ferdinand Aloys.   Introduction to modern politics.
Notre Dame, Ind., University of Notre Dame Press, 1959,
c1958.   242p.   (B149)

Hitchner, Dell Gillette.   Modern government; a survey of
political science.   With William Henry Harbold.   New York,
Dodd, Mead, 1962.   718p.   (B150)

Jouvenel, Bertrand de.   The pure theory of politics.   New
Haven, Yale University Press, 1963.   220p.   (B151)

Kaeley, S. L.   A simple study of political science.   Delhi,
Jiwan Prakashan, 1957.   362p.   (B152)

Kellar, P. H.   The better state.   New York, Comet Books,
1960.   147p.   (B153)

Laski, Harold Joseph.   A grammar of politics.   New Haven,
Yale University Press, 1931.   672p.   (B154)

---- ----.   An introduction to politics.   New York, Barnes
& Noble, 1962.   91p.   (B155)

Lasswell, Harold Dwight.   Politics; who gets what, when,
how.   New York, McGraw-Hill, c1936. 264p.   (B156)

Leacock, Stephen Butler.   Elements of political science.
New and enl. ed.   Boston, Houghton Mifflin, 1921. 415p.
                                                        (B157)
Lilly, William Samuel.   First principles in politics.   New
York, Putnam, 1899.   322p.   (B158)

Lipson, Leslie.   The great issue of politics; an introduction
to political science.   2d ed.   Englewood Cliffs, N. J.,
Prentice-Hall, 1960.   431p.   (B159)

---- ----.   What is political science?   London, Whitcombe
& Tombs, 1939.   24p.   (B160)

MacLeod, William Christie.   The origin and history of politics.   New York, Wiley, 1931.   504p. (References; p.
470-481, 495-496)   (B161)

Merriam, Charles Edward.   Prologue to politics.   Chicago,
University of Chicago Press, c1939.   118p.   (B162)

---- ----.   The role of politics in social change.   New York,

New York University Press, 1936.   149p.   (B163)

---- ----.   Systematic politics.   Chicago, University of
Chicago Press, 1945.   348p.   (B164)

Micklem, Nathaniel.   Theology of politics.   New York, Oxford University Press, 1941.   163p.   (B165)

Miller, John Donald Bruce.   The nature of politics.   London, G. Duckworth, 1962.   296p.   (Bibliography: p. 288-
291)   (B166)

Morgenthau, Hans Joachim.   Scientific man vs. power poli-
tics.   Chicago, University of Chicago Press, 1946. 244p.
                                                       (B167)
Nandi, A.   Introduction to political science.   Calcutta,
Bookland ltd., 1955.   526p.   (B168)

Partridge, Percy Herbert.   Thinking about politics, an inaugural lecture...Canberra, Australian National University,
1956.   23p.   (B169)

Peel, Roy Victor, ed.   Introduction to politics.   New York,
Crowell, 1941.   587p.   (B170)

Pickles, Dorothy Maud.   Introduction to politics.   London,
Sylvan Press, 1951.   224p.   (B171)

Prelot, Marcel.   La science politique.   Paris, Presses universitaires, de France, 1961.   126p.   (B172)

Raj, M. Joseph.   Dynamics of politics (in principle and
practice)   Konni, India, Venus Press, 1950. 326p. (B173)

Raleigh, Thomas.   Elementary politics.   London, H. Frowde,
1886.   163p.   (B174)

Ranney, Austin.   The governing of men; an introduction to
political science.   New York, Holt, 1958. 628p.   (B175)

Read, Herbert Edward.   The politics of the unpolitical. London, Routledge, 1946.   160p.   (B176)

Riesman, David.   Faces in the crowd; individual studies in
character and politics.   With Nathan Glazer.   New Haven,
Yale University Press, 1952.   751p.   (B177)

Rodee, Carlton Clymer.   Introduction to political science.
With J. Anderson and C.Q. Christol.   New York, Mc-
Graw-Hill, 1957.   655p.   (B178)

Rogow, Arnold A.   Power, corruption, and rectitude.   With
Harold D. Lasswell.   Englewood Cliffs, N.J. , Prentice-
Hall, 1963.   138p.   (B179)

Rood, John Romain.   A political science primer.   Detroit,
Detroit Lawbook Co. , 1947.   238p.   (B180)

Roucek, Joseph Slabey, ed.   Classics in political science.
New York, Philosophical Library, 1963.   378p.   (B181)

---- ----.   Introduction to political science.   With George
B. DeHuszar and associates.   New York, Crowell, 1950.
696p.   (B182)

Santayana, George.   Dominations and powers; reflections on
liberty, society and government.   New York, Scribner,
1951.   431p.   (B183)

Schmandt, Henry J.   Fundamentals of government.   With
Paul G. Steinbicker.   2d ed.   Milwaukee, Bruce Pub. Co. ,
1963.   444p.   (B184)

Shaw, George Bernard.   Everybody's political what's what.
New York, Dodd, Mead, 1944.   380p.   (B185)

---- ----.   The future of political science in America.   New
York, Dodd, Mead, 1933.   43p.   (B186)

Sidgwick, Henry.   The development of European polity.
New York, Macmillan, 1920.   454p.   (B187)

---- ----.   The elements of politics.   4th ed.   London,
Macmillan, 1919.   665p.   (B188)

Sinha, H.N   Outlines of political science.   Bombay, Asia
Pub. House, 1959.   247p.   (B189)

Soltau, Roger Henry.   An introduction to politics.   New
York, Longmans, Green, 1951.   328p.   (Bibliography: p.
324-328)   (B190)

Tuckey, Edson Newton.   The best political system for our
complex world, containing many different nations, races,

civilizations, interests and goals.   Minneapolis, The author, 1945.   116p.   (B191)

Wallace, William Kay.   Passing of politics.   New York, Macmillan, 1924.   328p.   (B192)

Weldon, Thomas Dewar.   States and morals; a study in political conflicts.   London, J. Murray, 1962.   302p. (B193)

Wright, Quincy.   Political science and politics.   The Hague, International Political Science Association, 1952.   7p. (Mimeo)   (B194)

Approaches to the Study of Politics

The study of politics and the political process in the last several decades has taken on a greater depth of introspection and analysis through variances of approach and method.   Three of the basic approaches are covered below with a number of concomitant works.

General

Young, Roland Arnold, ed.   Approaches to the study of politics; twenty-two contemporary essays exploring the nature of politics and methods by which it can be studied.   Evanston, Ill., Northwestern University Press, 1958. 382p.
(B195)

Behavioral

The study of political phenomena from the behavioral point of view attempts to discover the extent and nature of the uniformities in the actual behavior of men and groups of men in the political process.   The objectives of analyzing political behavior are to identify the recurring patterns of political activity and the formulation of meaninful generalizations concerning political action.   The behavioral approach is interdisciplinary in nature; consequently it is extremely complex and requires rigorous ordering of evidence to reach valid conclusions.

Bennett, Edward M.   Emotional aspects of political behavior: the woman voter, With H. M. Gordon... Provincetown, Mass., Journal Press, 1958.   159p.   (B196)

Butler, David E.   The study of political behavior.   London,

Hutchinson, c1958, 1959.   128p.   (B197)

Eulau, Heinz.   The behavioral persuasion in politics.   New
    York, Random House, 1963.   141p.   (B198)

---- ----.   Political behavior; a reader in theory and re-
    search.   Edited with Samuel J. Eldersveld and Morris
    Janowitz.   Glencoe, Ill., Free Press, 1956. 421p. (B199)

---- ----.   Recent developments in the behavioral study of
    politics.   Stanford?   c1961.   36p.   (B200)

Fuchs, Lawrence H.   The political behavior of American
    Jews.   Glencoe, Ill., Free Press, 1956. 220p.   (B201)

Huntington, Samuel P., ed.   Changing pattern of military
    politics.   New York, Free Press of Glencoe, 1962. 272p.
                                                         (B202)
Janowitz, Morris, ed.   Community political systems.   Glen-
    coe, Ill., Free Press, 1961.   259p.   (Bibliography: p.
    251-255)   (B203)

Kent, Frank Richardson.   Political behavior; the heretofore
    unwritten laws, customs and principles of politics as prac-
    ticed in the United States.   New York, W. Morrow, 1928.
    342p.   (B204)

Lasswell, Harold Dwight.   The analysis of political behavior,
    an empirical approach.   New York, Oxford University
    Press, 1949.   314p.   (B205)

The limits of behavioralism in political science, a symposium
    sponsored by the American Academy of Political and Social
    Science.   Edited by James C. Charlesworth.   Philadelphia,
    American Academy of Political and Social Science, 1962.
    123p.   (B206)

Martin, Everett Dean.   Some principles of political behavior.
    New York, The Graduate School of Banking, American
    Bankers Association, c1939.   98p. (Suggested reading:
    p. 99)   (B207)

North, Robert Carver.   Content analysis; a handbook with
    applications for the study of international crisis.   Evans-
    ton, Northwestern University Press, 1963.   182p. (B208)

Pinner, Frank A.   Old age and political behavior; a case

study. With Paul Jacobs and Philip Selznick. Berkeley,
University of California Press, 1959. 352p.   (B209)

Polsby, Nelson W., ed. Politics and social life; an intro-
duction to political behavior. With Robert A. Dentler and
Paul A. Smith. Boston, Houghton Mifflin, c1963. 879p.
(B210)

Ranney, Austin, ed. Essays on the behavioral study of politics. Edited for the International Political Science Association. Urbana, University of Illinois Press, 1962. 251p.
(B211)

Shubik, Martin, ed. Readings in game theory and political
behavior. Garden City, N.Y., Doubleday, 1954. 74p.
(B212)

Tingsten, Herbert Lars Gustaf. Political behavior; studies
in election statistics. Totowa, N.J., Bedminster Press,
1963. 231p.   (B213)

Ulmer, S. Sidney, ed. Introductory readings in political behavior. Chicago, Rand, McNally, 1961. 465p.   (B214)

U.S. Dept. of State. Bureau of Intelligence and Research.
External Research Staff. Political behavior; a list of current studies. Washington, 1963. 60p.   (B215)

Verba, Sidney. Small groups and political behavior; a study
of leadership. Princeton, N.J., Princeton University
Press, 1961. 273p.   (B216)

Decision Making

Considered by some political scientists a misnomer,
the decision-making or decision-process approach seeks to
analyze the factors influencing political decision makers in
solving the problems and issues considered within a political
framework.

Downs, Anthony. An economic theory of government decision-making in a democracy. Stanford, Calif., Dept. of
Economics, Stanford University, 1956. 347p. (Bibliography: leaves, 342-347)   (B217)

Lasswell, Harold Dwight. The decision process; seven categories of functional analysis. College Park, Bureau of
Governmental Research, College of Business and Public Administration, University of Maryland, 1956. 23p.   (B218)

Marvick, Dwaine, ed.   Political decision-makers.   New York,
    Free Press of Glencoe, 1961.   347p. (Bibliography: p.
    334-343)   (B219)

Snyder, Richard Carlton, ed.   Foreign policy decision-mak-
    ing; an approach to the study of international politics.
    Ed. with H.W. Bruck and Burton Sapin.   New York, Free
    Press of Glencoe, 1962.   274p.   (B220)

Wasserman, Paul.   Decision-making; an annotated bibliogra-
    phy.   With Fred S. Silander.   Ithaca, N.Y., Graduate
    School of Business and Public Administration, Cornell Uni-
    versity, 1958.   111p.   (B221)

Scientific and Quantitative

        For many years political scientists have tried to apply
the scientific method to the study of politics.   Although the
field lacks many of the attributes of the pure sciences, many
scientific techniques have proved useful in the understanding
of political phenomena.

Amos, Sheldon.   The science of politics.   New York, D.
    Appleton, 1883.   490p.   (B222)

Bagehot, Walter.   Physics and politics; or, Thoughts on the
    application of the principles of "natural selection" and "in-
    heritance" to political society. New York, Knopf, 1948.
    230p.   (B223)

Born, Max.   Physics and politics.   New York, Basic Books
    Pub. co. 1962.   86p.   (B224)

Catlin, George Edward Gordon.   The science and method of
    politics.   New York, Knopf, 1927.   360p.   (B225)

Esslinger, William.   Politics and science.   New York,
    Philosophical Library, 1955.   167p.   (B226)

Pollock, Sir Frederick.   An introduction to the history of the
    science of politics.   Boston, Beacon Press, 1960. 138p.
                                                                    (B227)
Rice, Stuart Arthur.   Quantitative methods in politics.   New
    York, Knopf, 1928.   331p.   (B228)

Roy, Manabendra Nath.   Scientific politics.   2d ed.   Cal-
    cutta, Renaissance Publishers, 1947.   315p.   (B229)

Storing, Herbert J., ed.   Essays on the scientific study of
politics.   New York, Holt, Rinehart and Winston, 1962.
333p.   (B230)

Voegelin, Eric.   The new science of politics, an introduction.   Chicago, University of Chicago Press, 1952. 193p.
(B231)

Miscellaneous Aspects of Politics

The sociological and psychological, as well as the
other aspects of politics have received varying degrees of
emphasis over the years by political scientists.   The literature referred to here reflects the interdisciplinary nature of
politics in scholarly inquiry and underlines the importance of
studying the political process from several perspectives.

Political Economy

After having been relegated to an unimportant position
for some time now, political economy is beginning to show
some resurgence to its former place.   This approach dealt
primarily with the economic relationships inherent in the
study of politics in which the importance of political conditions and social institutions were stressed.   Originally the
term signified the application of "household management" to
the body politic.

Reference Materials

McCulloch, John Ramsay.   The literature of political economy: a classified catalogue of select publications in the
different departments of that science.   London, Longmans.
Reprinted by the London School of Economics & Political
Science, University of London, 1938.   407p.   (B232)

Palgrave, Sir Robert Harry Inglis, ed.   Palgrave's Dictionary of political economy.   Edited by Henry Higgs...Lon-
don, Macmillan, 1926.   3v.   (B233)

General Works

Beard, Charles Austin.   The economic basis of politics, and
related writing.   Compiled and annotated by William Beard.
New York, Vintage Books, 1961, c1957. 263p.   (B234)

Bladen, Vincent Wheeler.   Introduction to political economy.
3d ed.   Toronto, University of Toronto Press, 1956.

319p.   (B235)

Bonar, James. Elements of political economy. London, J.
Murray, 1904. 247p.   (B236)

Bonn, Moritz Julius. Economics and politics. Boston,
Houghton Mifflin, 1932. 36p.   (B237)

Cannan, Edwin. Elementary political economy. 2d ed. London, H. Milford, 1903. 152p.   (B238)

Carver, Thomas Nixon. Principles of political economy.
New York, Ginn, c1919. 588p.   (B239)

Chapman, Sydney John. Political economy. New York, Oxford University Press, 1945. 255p.   (B240)

Dobb, Maurice Herbert. Political economy and capitalism:
some essays in economic tradition. New York, International Publishers, 1945. 357p.   (B241)

Eaton, John. Political economy: a Marxist textbook. Rev.
ed. London, Lawrence & Wishart, 1953. 235p. (B242)

George, Henry. The science of political economy. New
York, Doubleday and McClure, 1898. 545p.   (B243)

Jevons, William Stanley. Theory of political economy. 5th
ed. New York, Kelley & Millman, 1957. 342p.   (B244)

The Journal of Political Economy. Landmarks in political
economy, selections from the Journal of Political economy.
Edited by Earl J. Hamilton, Albert Rees, and Harry G.
Johnson. Chicago, University of Chicago Press, 1962.
622p.   (B245)

Leontev, Lev Abramovich. Political economy; a beginner's
course. New York, International Publishers, 1934?
282p.   (B246)

Malthus, Thomas Robert. Principles of political economy
considered with a view to their practical application. 2d
ed. New York, A.M. Kelley, 1951. 446p.   (B247)

Robbins, Lionel Charles Robbins. Politics and economics;
papers in political economy. New York, St. Martin's
Press, 1963. 230p.   (B248)

Political Geography

As a separate discipline political geography is relatively new. It is concerned with the political implications
and relationships embodied in the study of geography. In
focusing on man's political activities it draws upon other social sciences as history, sociology, and economics as well
as political science. When considering the modern nation
state, political geography describes and analyzes the physical
aspects of the area, the degree of political homogeneity of
the state and its external relations. Although more properly
concerned with the study of international relations, it is included here because of its general nature.

Alexander, Lewis M. World political patterns. Chicago,
Rand McNally, c1957. 516p.   (B249)

Carlson, Lucile. Geography and world politics. Englewood
Cliffs, N.J., Prentice-Hall, 1958. 534p.   (B250)

Cohen, Saul Bernard. Geography and politics in a world
divided. New York, Random House, 1963. 347p (B251)

Fitzgerald, Walter. The new Europe, an introduction to its
political geography. New York, Harper, c1946. 298p.
                                                        (B252)
Fitzgibbon, Russell Humke, ed. Global politics. Berkeley,
University of California Press, 1944. 189p.   (B253)

Goblet, Yann Morvran. Political geography and the world
map. New York, Praeger, 1955. 291p.   (B254)

Jones, Stephen Barr. Geography and world affairs. With
Marian F. Murphy. 2d ed. New York, Rand McNally,
1962. 532p.   (B255)

McGovern, William Montgomery. Strategic intelligence and
the shape of tomorrow. Chicago, Regnery, 1961. 191p.
                                                        (B256)
Mattern, Johannes. Geopolitik: national self-sufficiency
and empire. Baltimore, The Johns Hopkins Press, 1942.
139p.   (B257)

Moodie, A.E. Geography behind politics. New York, Hutchinson's University Library, 1949. 178p.   (B258)

Pearcy, George Etzel. World political geography. 2d ed.

New York, Crowell, 1957. 734p.   (B259)

Pounds, Norman John Grenville. Political geography. New
   York, McGraw-Hill, c1963. 422p.   (B260)

Spykman, Nicholas John. The geography of peace. Edited
   by Helen R. Nicholl. New York, Harcourt, Brace, c1944.
   66p.   (B261)

Strausz-Hupé, Robert. Geopolitics; the struggle for space
   and power. New York, Putnam's, 1942. 274p.   (B262)

U.S. Air Force Reserve Officers' Training Corps. Military
   aspects of world political geography. Montgomery, Alabama, Air Force Reserve Officers' Training Corps, Air
   University, 1954. 2v.   (B263)

Van Valkenburg, Samuel. Elements of political geography.
   2d ed. With Carl L. Statz. New York, Prentice-Hall,
   1954. 400p. (Bibliography: p. 379-387)   (B264)

Weigert, Hans Werner. Principles of political geography.
   New York, Appleton-Century-Crofts, 1957. 723p. (B265)

Whittlesey, Derwent Stainthorpe. The earth and the state; a
   study of political geography. New York, Holt, 1944. 618p.
   (Bibliography: p. 595-596)   (B266)

Political Psychology

        The basic elements and processes of human behavior
such as temperament, abilities, motivation, learning, emo-
tion, attitudes and personality are closely related to the study
of the political process. Political psychology attempts to
analyze these factors and their relationship to political behavior.

Almond, Gabriel Abraham. The civic culture; political atti-
   tudes and democracy in five nations. With Sidney Verba.
   Princeton, N.J., Princeton University Press, 1963. 562p.
                                                          (B267)
The Authoritarian personality, by T.W. Adorno and others.
   New York, Harper, 1950. 990p. (Bibliography: p. 977-
   982)   (B268)

Cantril, Hadley. Human nature and political systems. New
   Brunswick, N.J., Rutgers University Press, 1961.

112p.   (B269)

Davies, James C.   Human nature in politics; the dynamics of
political behavior.   New York, Wiley, c1963. 403p. (B270)

DeGrazia, Sebastian.   Status as a political motive.   Chicago,
1947. 101p.   (B271)

Dewe, Joseph Adalbert.   Psychology of politics and history.
New York, Longmans, Green, 1910. 269p.   (B272)

Eysenck, Hans Jurgen.   The psychology of politics.   New
York, Praeger, 1955, c1954. 317p. (Bibliography:
p. 285-311)   (B273)

Haynes, Edmund Didney Pollock.   Religious persecution; a
study in political psychology.   London, Duckworth, 1904.
208p.   (B274)

Hyman, Herbert Hiram.   Political socialization; a study in
the psychology of political behavior.   Glencoe, Ill., Free
Press, 1959. 175p.   (B275)

Lane, Robert Edwards.   Political life; why people get involved in politics.   Glencoe, Ill., Free Press, 1959.
374p.   (B276)

Lasswell, Harold Dwight.   Psychopathology and politics.
Chicago, University of Chicago Press, 1930. 285p. (B277)

Lindzey, Gardner, ed.   Handbook of social psychology.
Cambridge, Mass., Addison-Wesley Pub. Co., 1954. 2v.
                                                   (B278)
Money-Kyrle, Roger Ernle.   Psychoanalysis and politics, a
contribution to the psychology of politics and morals. London, G. Duckworth, 1951. 182p.   (B279)

Reichardt, Martin.   Psychologie und Politik.   Munchen, J. F.
Lehman Vorwort, 1935. 66p.   (B280)

Rivers, William Halse Rivers.   Psychology and politics, and
other essays.   New York, Harcourt, Brace, 1923. 180p.
                                                   (B281)
Stanton, Alfred H., ed.   Personality and political crisis;
new perspectives from social science and psychiatry for
the study of war and politics.   Edited with Stewart E. Perry.
Glencoe, Ill., Free Press, 1951. 260p.   (282)

Wallas, Graham.   Human nature in politics.   3d ed.   New
   York, Knopf, 1921.   313p.   (B283)

Political Sociology

The study of political sociology seeks to analyze the
political process within a sociological frame of reference.
Particular attention is placed upon the dynamics of political
action as it is affected by various social processes, such as
cooperation, competition, conflict, and social mobility.   It is
also concerned with public opinion formation and shifts in
power of various groups, as well as all of those processes
which ultimately affect political behavior.

Bramson, Leon.   The political context of sociology.   Princeton, N. J., Princeton University Press, 1961.   164p.
                                                         (B284)
Eisenstadt, S. N.   Essays on sociological aspects of political
   and economic development.   London, Mouton, 1961.   88p.
                                                         (B285)
Lipset, Seymour Martin.   Political man; the social basis of
   politics.   Garden City, N.Y., Doubleday, 1960.   432p.
                                                         (B286)
Michels, Robert.   First lectures in political sociology; translated by Alfred deGrazia.   Minneapolis, University of Minnesota Press, 1949.   173p.   (B287)

Speier, Hans.   Social order and the risks of war: papers in
   political sociology.   New York, G.W. Stewart, 1952.   497p.
                                                         (B288)
Titus, Charles Hickman.   Government and society; a study
   in conflict.   With V.H. Harding.   New York, F. S. Crofts,
   1929.   250p.   (B289)

Political Statistics

A precise understanding of certain political processes
(e. g. voting behavior) could not be obtained without the use of
basic statistical methods.   There are several works in this
area that are specifically geared to the field of political science.

Davis, Harold Thayer.   Political statistics.   Evanston,
   Principia Press of Illinois, c1954.   364p.   (B290)

Florence, Philip Sargant.   The statistical method in economics and political science; a treatise on the quantitative and

institutional approach to social and industrial problems.
New York, Harcourt, Brace, 1929. 521p.   (B291)

Key, Vladimer Orlando. A primer of statistics for political
scientists. New York, Crowell, 1954. 209p.   (B292)

CHAPTER IV

Comparative Government

Government is primarily the mechanism of the state, and as a social organization it is dynamic and ever changing. It is also a man-made institution which reflects the existence of social problems and the need of man to take action with respect to them. Thus government becomes the chief means by which man resolves conflicts, gains protection, maintains social order and satisfies certain material wants. Since the time when Plato and Aristotle were inquiring into the nature and function of the state, three basic types of governmental structures; (1) the rule of one, (2) the rule of the few and (3) the rule of the many, have been recognized. Nearly all of the governments in the world today are ramifications or enlargements of these three primary governmental prototypes.

Emphasized in this chapter are monographs and reference materials on contemporary national and regional governments. Since governmental structures are always in a state of development or flux, works dealing with specific governments are dated quickly although many are valuable for historical study.

Government and the Study of Comparative Government

General Works

Allen, Stephen Haley. Evolution of government and laws. Princeton, N.J., Princeton University Press, 1922. 2v.
(C1)

Almond, Gabriel Abraham, ed. The politics of developing areas. Edited with James S. Coleman. Princeton, N.J., Princeton University Press, 1960. 591p. (C2)

Arnold, Thurman Wesley. The symbols of government. New Haven, Yale University Press, 1935. 278p. (C3)

Barker, Ernest. Reflections on government. New York, Oxford University Press, 1943, 1953. 424p. (C4)

Bentley, Arthur Fisher. The process of government; a
   study in social pressures. Bloomington, Ind. , Principia
   Press, 1949, c1935. 501p.   (C5)

Blachly, Frederick Frank. Introduction to comparative
   government. With Miriam E. Oatman. New York, Ronald Press Co., c1938. 465p.   (C6)

Brewster, Robert Wallace. Government in modern society,
   with emphasis on American institutions. 2d ed. Boston,
   Houghton Mifflin, 1963. 619p.   (C7)

Brogan, Denis William. Political patterns in today's world.
   With Douglas V. Verney. New York, Harcourt, Brace &
   World, 1963. 274p.   (C8)

Brown, Bernard Edward. New directions in comparative
   politics; issued under the auspices of the Indian Institute
   of Public Administration. New York, Asia Pub. House,
   1963, c1962. 91p.   (C9)

Brown, Delbert Franklin. The growth of democratic government. Washington, Public Affairs Press, 1959. 117p.
                                                          (C10)

Bryce, James Bryce. Modern democracies. New York,
   Macmillan, 1921. 2 v.   (C11)

Buck, Philip Wallenstein. The government of foreign
   powers. With John W. Masland. Rev. ed. New York,
   Holt, 1950. 948p.   (C12)

Carter, Gwendolen Margaret. Government and politics in
   the twentieth century. With John H. Herz. New York,
   Praeger, 1961. 218p.   (C13)

Cassinelli, C.W. The politics of freedom; an analysis of
   the modern democratic state. Seattle, University of Washington Press, 1961, i.e. 1962. 214p.   (C14)

Corry, James Alexander. Elements of democratic government. With Henry J. Abraham. 4th ed. , rev. & enl.
   New York, Oxford University Press, 1964. 827p. (C15)

Eckstein, Harry, ed. Comparative politics, a reader. Ed.
   with David E. Apter. New York, Free Press of Glencoe,
   1963. 746p.   (C16)

Eisenstadt, Samuel Noah. The political systems of empires.
New York, Free Press of Glencoe, 1963. 524p. (C17)

Field, George Lowell. Governments in modern society.
New York, McGraw-Hill, 1951. 554p.   (C18)

Finer, Herman. Theory and practice of modern government.
Rev. ed. New York, Holt, 1949. 978p.   (C19)

Foreign governments, the dynamics of politics abroad, by
Mario Einandi and others. Ed. by Fritz M. Marx. New
York, Prentice-Hall, 1949. 713p.   (C20)

Friedrich, Carl Joachim. Constitutional government and
democracy; theory and practice in Europe and America.
Rev. ed. Boston, Ginn, 1950. 687p. (Bibliography: p.
579-667)   (C21)

Hankey, Maurice Pascal Alers Hankey. The science and
art of government. Oxford, Clarendon Press, 1951.
34p.   (C22)

Heckscher, Gunnar. The study of comparative government
and politics. London, Allen & Unwin, 1957. 172p. (C23)

Kelly, Edmond. Government or human evolution. New York,
Longmans, Green, 1900-01. 2v.   (C24)

Larsen, Jakob Aall Ottesen. Representative government in
Greek and Roman history. Berkeley, University of California Press, 1955. 249p.   (C25)

Lowell, Abbott Lawrence. Essays on government. New
York, Houghton Mifflin, 1889. 229p.   (C26)

MacIver, Robert Morrison. The web of government. New
York, Macmillan, 1947. 498p.   (C27)

Macridis, Roy C. , ed. Comparative politics; notes and
readings. Edited with Bernard E. Brown. Homewood,
Ill. , Dorsey Press, 1961. 577p.   (C28)

---- ----., ed. Modern political systems. Englewood
Cliffs, N. J. , Prentice-Hall, 1963-64. 2v. (Europe and
Asia)   (C29)

---- ----. The study of comparative government. New

York, Random House, c1955. 77p. (Bibliography & footnotes: p. 73-77)   (C30)

McWhinney, Edward. Comparative federalism; states' rights
and national power. Toronto, University of Toronto Press,
c1962. 103p.   (C31)

Munro, William Bennett. The invisible government. New
York, Macmillan, 1928. 169p.   (C32)

Ogg, Frederic Austin. Modern foreign governments. With
Harold Zink. Rev. ed. New York, Macmillan, 1953.
1005p.   (C33)

Roche, John Pearson. The dynamics of democratic government. With Murray S. Stedman Jr. New York, McGraw-
Hill, 1954. 445p.   (C34)

Roucek, Joseph Slabey, ed. Governments and politics
abroad. 2d ed. New York, Funk & Wagnalls Co., 1948.
585p.   (C35)

Sait, Edward McChesney. Political institutions, a preface.
New York, Appleton-Century Co., c1936. 548p. (C36)

Schapera, Isaac. Government and politics in tribal societies. London, Watts, 1956. 238p.   (C37)

Shannon, Jasper Berry, ed. The study of comparative government, an appraisal of contemporary trends; essays
written in honor of Frederic Austin Ogg. New York, Appleton-Century-Crofts, 1949. 338p.   (C38)

Simon Yves. Philosophy of democratic government. Chicago, University of Chicago Press, 1951. 324p. (C39)

Spiro, Herbert J. Government by constitution, the political
systems of democracy. New York, Random House, 1959.
496p.   (C40)

Stewart, Michael. Modern forms of government: a comparative study. New York, Praeger, 1961, c1959. 284p.
                                                       (C41)
Swabey, Marie Taylor (Collins). Theory of the democratic
state. Cambridge, Harvard University Press, 1937.
234p.   (C42)

U.S. Military Academy, West Point. Dept. of Social Science. Contemporary foreign governments. By associates in government, Dept. of Social Sciences, U.S. Military Academy, Hermon Benkem and others. Rev. ed. New York, Rinehart, 1949. 482p. (Bibliography: p. 440-457)
(C43)

Von Mises, Ludwig. Omnipotent government, the rise of total state and total war. New Haven, Yale University Press, 1944. 291p. (C44)

Wheare, Kenneth Clinton. Federal government. 2d ed. New York, Oxford University Press, 1951. 278p. (Bibliography: p. 261-267) (C45)

Wit, Daniel. Comparative political institutions; a study of modern democratic and dictatorial systems. New York, Holt, 1953. 534p. (C46)

Witman, Shepherd Luther. Comparative government, visualized. With John J. Wurst. Paterson, N.J., Littlefield, Adams, 1959. 260p. (C47)

Zink, Harold. Modern governments. 2d ed. Princeton, N.J., Van Nostrand, 1962. 804p. (C48)

Reference Materials

The Europa yearbook. London, Europa Publications, 1959+ (Formerly: Europa, the encyclopedia of Europe)

Beginning in 1960, it is issued in 2 vols. V.1 covering international organizations and Europe; v.2 covering non-European countries, thus superseding Orbis (C135). Contains such material as: administration, constitutions, statistical surveys, etc. (C49)

Political handbook and atlas of the world; parliaments, parties and press. Ed. by Walter H. Mallory. New York, Harper, 1927+ (Annual)

Usually includes chief government officials, party programs and leaders, political events, and the press (names of newspapers, with political affiliation, and proprietors or editors, and in some cases the circulation.) Now contains an atlas section in the back. Changed title in 1963.
(C50)

The Statesman's yearbook; statistical and historical annual

of the states of the world.   London and New York, Macmillan, 1864+

This work is a concise and reliable manual of descriptive
and statistical information about the governments of the
world.   Information concerning rulers, constitutions, governments, area, population, etc. is given for each country.   (C51)

United Nations who's who in government and industry.
London, Allied Publications, 1941+

Arrangement is by country, giving under each, government
officials, diplomatic representatives, biographical notes and
brief information about trade and industrial organizations
and statistics.   (C52)

National and Regional Governments

African Region

Carter, Gwendolen Margaret.   The politics of inequality;
South Africa since 1948.   Rev. ed.   New York, Praeger,
1962, c1959.   541p.   (Bibliography: p. 497-524)   (C53)

Cookson, John.   Before the African storm.   Indianapolis,
Bobbs-Merrill, 1954.   279p.   (C54)

Datta, Ansu Kamar.   Tanganyika: a government in a plural
society.   Leiden, 1955?   147p.   (Bibliography: p. 144-
145)   (C55)

Elias, Taslim Olawale.   Government and politics in Africa.
2d ed.   New York, Asia Pub. House, 1963.   288p.(C56)

Fortes, Meyer, ed.   African political systems.   Edited with
E.E. Evans-Prichard.   London, Pub. for the International
African Institute by the Oxford University Press, 1958,
c1940.   301p.   (C57)

Taylor, James Clagett.   The political development of Tanganyika.   Stanford, Calif., Stanford University Press, 1963.
254p.   (C58)

Tingsten, Herbert Lars Gustaf.   The problem of South Africa.   Translated from the Swedish by Daniel Viklund.

London, Gollancz, 1955. 159p.   (C59)

American Region

Canada

Brady, Alexander.   Democracy in the Dominions; a comparative study in institutions.   3d ed.   Toronto, University of Toronto Press, 1958.   614p.   (C60)

Brown, George William.   Canadians and their government. With Allwin S. Merritt.   Toronto, J. M. Dent, 1961. 113p.   (C61)

Dawson, Robert MacGregor.   The government of Canada. 4th ed. rev. by Norman Ward.   Toronto, University of Toronto Press, 1963.   610p.   (C62)

Ward, Norman.   Government in Canada.   Toronto, W. J. Gage, 1960.   326p.   (C63)

Latin America

Christensen, Asher Norman, ed.   The evolution of Latin American government: a book of readings.   New York, Holt, 1951. 747p.   (C64)

Davis, Harold Eugene, ed.   Government and politics in Latin America.   New York, Ronald Press Co. , 1958. 539p.
                                                  (C65)
Gomez, Rosendo Adolfo.   Government and politics in Latin America.   New York, Random House, 1960. 128p. (C66)

Jorrin, Miguel.   Government of Latin America.   New York, Van Nostrand, 1953.   385p.   (C67)

Needler, Martin C.   Latin American politics in perspective. Princeton, N.J. , Van Nostrand, 1963.   192p.   (C68)

Pierson, William Whatley.   Governments of Latin America. With Frederico G. Gil.   New York, McGraw-Hill, 1957. 514p.   (C69)

Porter, Charles Orlando.   The struggle for democracy in Latin America.   With Robjert J. Alexander.   New York, Macmillan, 1962.   215p.   (C70)

Schmitt, Karl Michael. Evolution or chaos; dynamics of
Latin American government and politics. With David D.
Burks. New York, Praeger, 1963. 308p. (Bibliography:
p. 277-301) (C71)

Scott, Robert Edwin. Mexican government in transition.
Urbana, University of Illinois Press, 1959. 333p. (Bibliography: p. 307-316) (C72)

Silvert, Kalman H. A study in government: Guatemala.
Editor: Robert Wauchope. New Orleans, Middle Ameri-
can Research Institute, Tulane University, 1954. 239p.
(Bibliography: p. 95-96) (C73)

Stokes, William Sylvane. Latin American politics. New
York, Crowell, 1959. 538p. (C74)

United States

General Works

Burns, James MacGregor. Government by the people; the
dynamics of American national government. With Jack W.
Peltason. 5th ed. Englewood Cliffs, N.J., Prentice-Hall,
1963. 768p. (C75)

Caldwell, Gaylon L. American government today. New
York, Norton, 1963. 432p. (C76)

Coyle, David Cushman. The United States political system
and how it works. Rev. ed. New York, New American
Library, 1963. 160p. (C77)

Ferguson, John Henry. The American federal government.
With Dean E. McHenry. 7th ed. New York, McGraw-
Hill, 1963. 650p. (C78)

Froman, Lewis Acrelius. People and politics; an analysis
of the American political system. Englewood Cliffs,
N.J., Prentice-Hall, 1963. 114p. (C79)

Hermens, Ferdinand Aloys. The representative republic.
Notre Dame, University of Notre Dame Press, 1958. 578p.
(C80)

MacDonald, H. Malcolm, ed. Readings in American government. 4th ed. New York, Crowell, 1963. 835p. (C81)

Mitchell, William C.   The American polity, a social and cultural interpretation.   New York, Free Press of Glencoe,
1962.   434p.   (C82)

Nelson, William H., ed.   Theory and practice in American
politics.   Chicago, University of Chicago Press, 1964.
149p.   (C83)

Powell, Norman John.   Major aspects of American government.   With Daniel P. Parker.   New York, McGraw-Hill,
c1963.   369p.   (C84)

White, Robert.   American government: democracy at work.
2d ed.   Princeton, N.J., Van Nostrand, 1963.   707p.
                                                       (C85)

Reference Materials

American men in government, a biographical dictionary and
directory of federal officials.   Edited by Jerome M. Ro-
sow; Lillie Levine and Virginia Miller, associate editors.
Washington, Public Affairs Press, 1949.   472p.

A biographical dictionary of federal employees who hold the
top administrative, diplomatic, military, professional, scientific and technical positions.   Now long out of date.
                                                       (C86)
American statesmen's yearbook, from official reports of the
United States government, state reports, consular advices
and foreign documents...New York, McBride, Nast & Co.,
c1912+   (C87)

Cyclopedia of American government.   Ed. by Andrew C. Mc-
Laughlin...and Albert Bushnell Hart...New York, D. Appleton, 1914.   3v.

Although out of date, it is still a useful work.   Many topics are covered in theory or philosophy of political society,
forms of political organization and government, international and constitutional law, history of political parties and
other American political topics.   Included are many short
biographies.   It is arranged alphabetically by small subjects, with an analytical index.   There are signed articles
by specialists and bibliographies.   (C88)

Ewing, Cortez Arthur Milton, comp.   Documentary source
book in American government and politics.   With Royden

J. Dangerfield. New York, D.C. Heath, c1931. 823p.

Contains many useful documentary sources in American
government and politics but is greatly out of date. (C89)

Holt, Solomon. The dictionary of American government.
New York, MacFadden, c1964. 284p.

Alphabetical listing of statutes, laws, acts, agencies, offices, and other data relating to federal state, and city
government.   (C90)

McCarthy, Eugene J. The crescent dictionary of American
politics. New York, Macmillan, 1962. 182p.

A fairly brief alphabetical arrangement of terms on American government and politics. Contains many cross references and several supplements on government seals, territories, etc. It does not have an index.   (C91)

Mitchell, Edwin Valentine, comp. An encyclopedia of American politics. Garden City, New York, Doubleday, 1946.
338p.

Contains short articles on the presidents, states, parties,
political terms and slogans, along with texts of the constitution, Declaration of Independence and the United Nations
charter, inter alia. Articles are popular in style and usually without definite reference or citation.   (C92)

Plano, Jack C. The American political dictionary. With
Milton Greenberg. New York, Holt, Rinehart and Winston,
1962. 383p.

Terms in American politics are arranged under subject
chapters alphabetically. It is also intended as a study
guide where a chapter will provide basic information in a
specific area. Has good coverage and an excellent index.
                                                       (C93)
Smith, Edward Conrad, ed. Dictionary of American politics.
Edited with Arnold John Zurcher. New York, Barnes &
Noble, 1955. 437p.

Covers over 3500 terms. It attempts to incorporate all
leading ideas and institutions in each of the special areas
of American government and politics. Also included are
slogans, political slang, nicknames, etc. It give summa-

ries of documents and charters, not full texts, except for
the Constitution and the Declaration of Independence.
                                                            (C94)

Sperber, Hans.   American political terms; an historical dictionary. With Travis Trittschuh. Detroit, Wayne State
University Press, 1962. 516p. (Bibliography: p. 499-516)

A detailed dictionary of American political and governmental terms. Contains sources of terms, also a bibliography.
There is no index.   (C95)

Tallman, Marjorie. Dictionary of American government;
with the complete text of the Constitution of the United
States. Ames, Iowa, Littlefield, Adams, 1957. 324p.

This work is a reliable compendium of political, economic,
sociological and educational concepts and terminology associated with American governmental institutions.   (C96)

Tompkins, Dorothy Louise (Campbell) Culver. Materials for
the study of federal government. Chicago, Public Administration Service, 1948. 338p. (Issued by the Bureau
of Public Administration, University of California)

Treats government publications dealing with federal administration, covering the constitution, laws and codes,
publications of the legislative, executive and judicial
branches of the federal government and many other items.
                                                            (C97)

Who's who in United States politics and American political
almanac. Chicago, Capitol House, 1950+

Contains biographical sketches of politicians listed by
party; persons affiliated with no parties are excluded, and
there is no index. The almanac section gives current and
historical data on federal and state governments, lists of
officers, etc. Includes a great deal of miscellaneous information.   (C98)

Asian Region

General Works

Kahin, George McTurnan, ed. Major governments of Asia.
2d ed. New York, Cornell University Press, c1958,
1963. 719p.   (C99)

Linebarger, Paul Myron Anthony.   Far Eastern governments
and politics: China and Japan.   With Dgang Chu and Ardath W. Burke.   2d ed.   Princeton, N.J., Van Nostrand,
1956.   643p.   (C100)

Reference Materials

Asian annual; the "Eastern World" handbook.   London,
Eastern World, 1954+

With an alphabetical arrangement by country, this work
gives for each, brief information on geography and climate, population, government, with names of administrative officers, agriculture, industries, etc.   (C101)

China

General Works

Tang, Sheng-hao.   Communist China today; domestic and
foreign policies.   New York, Praeger, 1957-58.   2v.
Bibliography: p. 505-516)   (C102)

Thomas, S.B.   Government and administration in Communist
China.   New York, International Secretariat, Institute of
Pacific Relations, 1953.   150p.   (C103)

Reference Materials

Perleberg, Max.   Who's who in modern China.   Hong Kong,
Ye Olde Printerie, 1954.   426p.

Includes information on government organization and personnel for both Nationalist and Communist China. (C104)

India

General Works

Palmer, Norman Dunbar.   The Indian political system.
Boston, Houghton Mifflin, 1961.   277p.   (C105)

Srinivasan, N.   Democratic government in India.   Calcutta,
World Press, 1954.   404p. (References: p. 387-396)
                                                      (C106)

Reference Materials

India; a reference annual.   Delhi, Ministry of Information
and Broadcasting, 1953+

A general yearbook containing governmental data comprising considerable directory type, statistical and textual information on the principal services of the national government, and the activities of the country as a whole. (C107)

Japan

Burks, Ardath W.   The government of Japan.   New York,
   Crowell, 1961.   269p.   (C108)

Ike, Nobutaka.   Japanese politics, an introductory survey.
   New York, Knopf, 1957.   300p. (Works consulted: p.
   289-300)   (C109)

McNelly, Theodore.   Contemporary government of Japan.
   Boston, Houghton Mifflin, 1963.   288p.   (C110)

Maki, John McGilvrey.   Government and politics in Japan;
   the road to democracy.   New York, Praeger, 1962.
   275p.   (C111)

Quigley, Harold Scott.   The new Japan: government and
   politics.   With John E. Turner.   Minneapolis, University
   of Minnesota Press, 1956.   456p.   (C112)

Reischauer, Robert Karl.   Japan, government-politics.   New
   York, T. Nelson, 1939.   221p.   (Bibliography: p. 205-
   214)   (C113)

Yanaga, Chitoshi.   Japanese people and politics.   New York,
   Wiley, 1956.   408p.   (C114)

Pakistan

Callard, Keith B.   Pakistan: a   political study.   New York,
   Macmillan, c1957.   355p.   (C115)

Metz, William S.   Pakistan: government and politics.
   Berkeley, Human Relations Area Files, South Asia Project,
   University of California, 1956.   294p.   (Bibliography:
   p. 283-294)   (C116)

Southeast Asia

Emerson, Rupert. Representative government in southeast
Asia. Cambridge, Harvard University Press, 1955. 197p.
(C117)

Kahin, George McTurnan, ed. Governments and politics of
Southeast Asia. Ithaca, N.Y., Cornell University Press,
1959. 531p. (C118)

European Region

General Works

Andrews, William George, ed. European political institutions; a comparative government reader. Princeton, N.J.,
Van Nostrand, c1962. 387p. (C119)

Beer, Samuel Hutchinson. Patterns of government; the
major political systems of Europe. With Adam B. Ulam
and others. 2d ed. New York, Random House, c1962.
780p. (C120)

Buck, Philip Wallenstein. The governments of foreign
powers. With John W. Masland. Rev. ed. New York,
Holt, 1950. 948p. (C121)

Cole, Taylor, ed. European political systems. 2d ed.
New York, Knopf, 1959. 837p. (C122)

Dragnich, Alex N. Major European governments. Homewood, Ill., Dorsey Press, 1961. 454p. (C123)

Finer, Herman. Governments of greater European powers;
a comparative study of the governments and political culture of Great Britain, France, Germany, and the Soviet
Union. New York, Holt, 1956. 931p. (C124)

Hill, Norman Llewellyn, ed. Background of European government: Readings and documents. 3d ed. With Harold
W. Stoke and Carl J. Schneider. New York, Rinehart,
1951. 584p. (C125)

Laing, Lionel Hassell, ed. Source book in European government. New York, Sloane, 1950. 437p. (C126)

Muller, Steven, ed. Documents on European government.
New York, Macmillan, 1963. 266p. (C127)

Munro, William Bennett.   Governments of Europe.   4th ed.
With Morley Ayearst.   New York, Macmillan, 1954.
796p.   (C128)

Neumann, Robert G.   European and comparative government.
3d ed.   New York, McGraw-Hill, 1960. 886p.   (C129)

Nova, Fritz.   Contemporary European governments.   Baltimore, Helicon, 1963.   720p.   (C130)

Ranney,   John Calyer.   The major foreign powers: the
governments of Great Britain, France, the Soviet Union
and China.   With Gwendolen M. Carter.   New York, Harcourt, Brace, 1949.   865p.   (Bibliography: p. xxxi-xxxix.)
                                                             (C131)
Rich, Clifford A. L. , ed.   European politics and government;
a comparative approach.   New York, Ronald Press Co. ,
1962.   78p.   (C132)

Shotwell, James Thompson, ed.   Governments of continental
Europe.   Rev. ed.   New York, Macmillan, 1952. 881p.
                                                             (C133)

Reference Materials

Aids to the study of European governments; brief readings,
reprints of constitutions, chronologies, diagrams, questions, and topics for special study (with references) prepared for use in Government 1 at Harvard University.
Cambridge, Harvard Co-operative Society, 1926. 251p.
                                                             (C134)
Orbis; encyclopedia of extra-European countries; a survey
and directory of political, industrial, financial, cultural
and scientific organizations in the countries of Africa,
America, Asia and Australasia.   London, Europa Publications, 1938-1959.   1v.

Was the companion volume to Europa which now supersedes it.   Included much of the same information.
                                                             (C135)
France

Bertier de Sauvigny, Guillaume de.   Some historical clues to
French politics.   Yellow Springs, Ohio, Antioch Press,
1958.   29p.   (C136)

Duverger, Maurice.   The French political system.   Trans-

lated by Barbara and Robert North. Chicago, University
of Chicago Press, 1958. 227p.   (C137)

Godfrey, Edwin Drexel. The government of France. 2d ed.
New York, Crowell, 1963. 197p.   (C138)

Macridis, Roy C. The DeGaulle republic: quest for unity.
With Bernard E. Brown. Homewood, Ill. , Dorsey Press,
1960. 400p.   (C139)

Pickles, Dorothy Maud. The Fifth French Republic. New
York, Praeger, 1960. 222p.   (C140)

Germany

Almond, Gabriel Abraham, ed. The struggle for democracy
in Germany. Chapel Hill, University of North Carolina
Press, 1949. 345p.   (C141)

Golay, John Ford. The founding of the Federal Republic of
Germany. Chicago, University of Chicago Press, 1958.
299p. (Bibliography: p. 276-286)   (C142)

Heidenheimer, Arnold J. The governments of Germany.
New York, Crowell, 1961. 224p.   (C143)

Litchfield, Edward Harold, ed. Governing postwar Germany.
Ithaca, N. Y. , Cornell University Press, c1953. 661p.
                                                       (C144)
Plischke, Elmer. Contemporary government of Germany.
Boston, Houghton Mifflin, 1961. 248p.   (C145)

Great Britain & Australia

General Works

Curtis, M. R. Central government, an introduction. London, Pitman, 1956. 140p.   (C146)

Marshall, Geoffrey. Parliamentary sovereignty and the Commonwealth. Oxford, Clarendon Press, 1957. 277p.
(Bibliography: p. 267-272)   (C147)

Mathiot, Andre. The British political system. Translated
by Jennifer S. Hines. Stanford, Calif. , Stanford University Press, 1958. 352p. (Bibliography: p. 337-342)
                                                       (C148)

Moodie, Graeme C.   The government of Great Britain.
New York, Crowell, 1964.   213p.   (Bibliography: p. 200-
207)   (C149)

Saer, Geoffrey.   Australian government today.   Parkville,
Melbourne University Press, 1961.   107p.   (C150)

Stout, Hiram Miller.   British government.   New York, Oxford University Press, 1953.   433p.   (Bibliography: p.
419-423)   (C151)

Toch, Henry.   British political and social institutions.
London, Pitman, 1962.   149p.   (C152)

Reference Materials

Empire and Commonwealth year book.   London, Empire
Economic Union, 1952+

This work contains general and statistical information concerning the British Empire and the Commonwealth of Nations.   (C153)

Spaull, Hebe.   The new ABC of civics; a dictionary of terms
used in connection with Parliament, local authorities,
courts of law, diplomacy and the United Nations.   London,
Rockcliff, 1957.   127p.   (C154)

Italy

Adams, John Clarke.   The government of republican Italy.
With Paolo Barile.   Boston, Houghton Mifflin, 1961. 245p.
                                                                 (C155)
Kogan, Norman.   The government of Italy.   New York,
Crowell, 1962.   225p.   (C156)

The Soviet Union

Armstrong, John Alexander.   Ideology, politics, and government in the Soviet Union, an introduction.   New York,
Praeger, 1962.   160p.   (C157)

Fainsod, Merle.   How Russia is ruled.   Cambridge, Mass.,
Harvard University Press, 1963.   684p.   (C158)

Gripp, Richard C.   Patterns of Soviet politics.   Homewood,
Ill., Dorsey Press, 1963.   366p.   (C159)

Hazard, John Newbold.   The Soviet system of government.
Chicago, University of Chicago Press, 1960. 256p. (Bibliography: p. 241-248)   (C160)

Hendel, Samuel, ed.   The Soviet crucible; the Soviet system in theory and practice.   2d ed.   Princeton, N.J.,
Van Nostrand, 1963.   706p.   (C161)

Schuman, Frederick Lewis.   Government of the Soviet Union.
New York, Crowell, 1961.   190p.   (C162)

Other European Governments

Andren, Nils Bertel Einar.   The government of Sweden.
From the Swedish manuscript by Sarah V. Thorell and
Milton Williams. Stockholm, Swedish Institute, 1955. 110p.
                                                    (C163)
Codding, George Arthur.   The federal government of Switzer-
land.   Boston, Houghton Mifflin, 1961.   174p.   (C164)

Middle Eastern Region

General Works

Harari, Maurice.   Government and politics of the Middle
East.   Englewood Cliffs, N.J., Prentice-Hall, 1962. 179p.
                                                    (C165)
Kirk, George Eden.   Contemporary Arab politics; a concise
history.   New York, Praeger, 1961.   231p.   (C166)

Kraines, Oscar.   Government and politics in Israel.   Boston,
Houghton Mifflin, 1961.   246p.   (C167)

Royal Institute of International Affairs.   Information Dept.
The Middle East: a political and economic survey.   3d
ed.   Edited by Reader Bullard.   New York, Oxford University Press, 1958.   569p. (Bibliography: p. 547-555)
                                                    (C168)
Sharabi, H.R.   Governments and politics in the Middle East
in the twentieth century.   Princeton, N.J., Van Nostrand,
1962.   296p.   (C169)

Reference Materials

Middle East; a survey and directory of the countries of the
Middle East.   London, Europe Publications, 1948+

Covers many of the countries in this region. Information
for each country includes an outline map, geography,
peoples and religions, history, government (with names of
officials), communications, economic life, education,
places of interest, press, bibliography, etc.   (C170)

The Functions of Government

Government has two basic functions; (1) service and
(2) regulation. It renders some of those services which civi-
lized man expects and demands but cannot obtain by his own
individual efforts. The continuous clash of man, as all men
need to advance their interests in a complex society, makes
necessary a considerable measure of regulation if individual
and collective rights and interests are to be safeguarded, or,
in other words, to be kept in balance. These two categories
can be further subdivided into five more definitive or specific functions; (1) Legislative, (2) Executive, (3) Judicial,
(4) Administrative, and (5) Electoral. The first three are
treated in this section, and the last two, because of their
importance are included in separate chapters.

Legislative Function

General Works

Alden, Edmund K.   The world's representative assemblies
of today: a study in comparative legislation.   Baltimore,
The Johns Hopkins Press, 1893.   50p.   (C171)

Bentham, Jeremy.   Bentham's handbook of political fallacies.
Baltimore, The Johns Hopkins Press, 1952.   269p.
                                                      (C172)
Galloway, George Barnes.   Congress and Parliament: their
organization and operation.   Washington, National Planning Association, 1953.   105p.   (C173)

Inter-parliamentary Union.   Parliaments: a comparative
study on the structure and functioning of representative institutions in forty-one countries.   New York, Praeger,
1963, c1962.   321p.   (C174)

The Legislative system; explorations in legislative behavior.
By John C. Whalke and others.   New York, Wiley, 1962.
517p.   (C175)

Wahlke, John C., ed. Legislative behavior; a reader in theory and research. Edited with Heinz Eulau. Glencoe, Ill., Free Press, c1959. 413p. (C176)

Wheare, Kenneth Clinton. Legislatures. New York, Oxford University Press, 1963. 247p. (C177)

France

Gooch, Robert Kent. Parliamentary government in France; revolutionary origins, 1789-1791. Ithaca, N.Y., Cornell University Press, 1960. 253p. (Bibliographical note: p. 243-247) (C178)

Lidderdale, D.W.S. The Parliament of France. New York, Praeger, 1952. 296p. (C179)

Great Britain

General Works

Bailey, Sydney Dawson, ed. The House of Lords; a symposium. New York, Praeger, 1954. 180p. (C180)

Boardman, Harry. The glory of Parliament. Edited by Francis Boyd. New York, Taplinger Pub. Co., 1961. 208p. (C181)

Campion, Gilbert Montrion Campion. An introduction to the procedure of the House of Commons. 2d ed. London, Macmillan, 1950. 348p. (Bibliography: p. xvii) (C182)

Forsey, Eugene Alfred. The royal power of dissolution of Parliament in the British Commonwealth. Toronto, Oxford University Press, 1943. 316p. (Bibliography: p. 299-304) (C183)

Gordon, Strathern. The British Parliament. New York, Praeger, 1952. 247p. (C184)

Illingworth, Frank. British Parliament. London, S. Robinson, 1948. 249p. (C185)

Taylor, Eric. The House of Commons at work. 3d ed. Harmondsworth, Middlesex, Penguin Books, 1958. 256p. (Bibliography: p. 251-252) (C186)

Reference Material

Abraham, Louis Arnold. A parliamentary dictionary. With
S. C. Hawtray. London, Butterworth, 1956. 224p.

This is a brief encyclopedia of British parliamentary terms
and concepts, giving definitions and in some instances
longer articles. It has many cross references and a good
index.   (C187)

Wilding, Norman W. An encyclopedia of Parliament. With
Philip Laundy. New York, Praeger, 1958. 705p. (Bibliography: p. 681-705)

An encyclopedia, arranged alphabetically, of parliamentary
history and procedure. Has many brief articles, some
longer ones. Covers colonial parliaments as well as the
parliament at Westminster.   (C188)

United States

General Works

Barth, Alan. Government by investigation. New York,
Viking Press, 1955. 231p.   (C189)

Clark, Joseph S. The Senate establishment. New York,
Hill and Wang, 1963. 138p.   (C190)

Conaway, Orrin Bryte, ed. Legislative-executive relationships in the government of the United States. Washington,
Graduate School of the U. S. Dept. of Agriculture, 1954.
64p.   (C191)

DeGrazia, Alfred. Apportionment and representative government. New York, Praeger, 1963. 180p.   (C192)

Galloway, George Barnes. History of the House of Representatives. New York, Crowell, 1961. 334p.   (C193)

---- ----. The legislative process in Congress. New York,
Crowell, 1953. 689p.   (C194)

---- ----. Next steps in congressional reform. Urbana,
University of Illinois, Institute of Government and Public
Affairs, 1952. 32p. (Bibliography: p. 31-32)   (C195)

Griffith, Ernest Stacey. Congress: its contemporary role.
3d ed. New York, New York University Press, 1961.
244p.   (C196)

Gross, Bertram Myron. The legislative struggle, a study
in social combat. New York, McGraw-Hill, 1953. 472p.
                                                           (C197)
Horn, Stephen. The Cabinet and Congress. New York,
Columbia University Press, 1960. 310p.   (C198)

Lowi, Theodore J., ed. Legislative politics U.S.A.; Congress and the forces that shape it. Readings. Boston,
Little, Brown, 1962. 326p.   (C199)

McGeary, Martin Nelson. The development of congressional
investigative power. New York, Columbia University
Press, 1940. 172p. (Bibliography: p. 161-165) (C200)

Murphy, Walter F. Congress and the Court; a case study
in the American political process. Chicago, University
Press, 1962. 307p.   (C201)

Pritchett, Charles Herman. Congress versus the Supreme
Court, 1957-1960. Minneapolis, University of Minnesota
Press, 1961. 168O. (Bibliography: p. 160-162) (C202)

Walker, Harvey. The legislative process; lawmaking in the
United States. New York, Ronald Press Co., 1948. 482p.
(Bibliography: p. 459-467)   (C203)

White, William Smith. Citadel, the story of the U.S. Senate.
New York, Harper, c1957. 274p.   (C204)

Wilson, Woodrow. Congressional government; a study in
American politics. New York, World Pub. Co., 1961,
c1956. 222p.   (C205)

Young, Roland Arnold. The American Congress. New
York, Harper, 1958. 333p.   (C206)

Reference Materials

C Q Weekly report. Washington, Congressional Quarterly
News Features, 1946+

Issued weekly, The Report digests Congressional and political activity for the current week. This includes full

texts of Presidential press conferences, major statements, messages and speeches.   (C207)

U.S. Congress. Biographical directory of the American Congress, 1774-1961. Rev. ed. Washington, U.S. Govt. Print. Off., 1961. 1863p.

Contains a list of executive officers 1789-1960, the continental Congress, Representatives under each apportionment, members of each congress arranged by states and biographies in an alphabetical manner.   (C208)

---- ----. Congressional index. Chicago, Commerce Clearing House, 1952+

The Congressional index gives quick contact with all legislation pending in Congress. All public bills and resolutions are listed and indexed, and their progress is followed until a final disposition is made. Includes composition of Congress and voting records. Is valuable because of its factual and current information.   (C209)

U.S. Congress. House. Constitution, Jefferson's Manual and rules of the House of Representatives. Washington, Govt. Print. Off., 1824+

This is the House Manual which is issued for each session of Congress.   (C210)

U.S. Congress. Senate. Senate manual, containing the standing rules, orders, and resolutions affecting the business of the United States Senate; Jefferson's Manual; Declaration of Independence, Articles of Confederation; Constitution of the United States, etc. Washington, Govt. Print. Off., 1820+

Issued for each session of Congress.   (C211)

---- ----. Senate procedure: precedents and practices, by Charles L. Watkins and Floyd M. Riddick. Washington, 1958. 674p. (85th Cong., 2d sess., Senate Doc. no. 93)

A compilation of the rules of the Senate, portions of laws affecting Senate procedure, rulings, the presiding officers and established practices of the Senate. It is divided into chapters and arranged alphabetically with a detailed index. Includes much, but not all, of the information contained in

the Senate Manual and has a different arrangement.
                                                        (C212)
Congressional quarterly almanac; a service for editors and
   commentators. Washington, Congressional Quarterly News
   Features, 1945+ (Quarterly, 1945/47 - annual 1948+)

   Published annually, The Almanac digests, reorganizes and
   cross-indexes the full year in Congress, politics and
   lobbying.   (C213)

The Congressional digest. Washington, Congressional Digest
   Corporation, 1921+

   A timely publication on congressional happenings with pro
   and con discussions of measures pending in Congress as
   well as other useful information.   (C214)

Congressional staff directory. Indianapolis, New Bobbs-
   Merrill, 1959+ (Various publishers)

   A current directory of congressional staff members and
   administrative staffs.   (C215)

Other Legislative Bodies

Bailey, Sydney Dawson. Parliamentary government in
   southern Asia; a survey of developments in Burma, Ceylon, India and Pakistan, 1847-1952. New York, International Secretariat, Institute of Pacific Relations, 1953.
   100p. (Bibliography: p. 96-97)   (C216)

King-Hall, Stephen. German parliaments: a study of the
   development of representative institutions in Germany.
   With Richard K. Ullmann. New York, Praeger, 1954.
   162p. (Bibliography: p. 143)   (C217)

Morris-Jones, Wyndraeth Humphreys. Parliament in India.
   London, New York, Longmans, Green, 1957. 417p.
   (Bibliography: p. 407-412)   (C218)

Parliamentary Procedure

Bridge, Lawrence Wilford. The Funk & Wagnalls book of
   parliamentary procedure; a guide to democratic practice
   in meetings. New York, Funk & Wagnalls, 1954. 180p.
                                                        (C219
Cushing, Luther Stearns. Cushing's manual of parliament-

ary practice; rules of procedure and debate in delibera-
tive assemblies. New ed. by Albert S. Balles. Philadelphia, J.L. Winston, 1947. 252p. (C220)

Robert, Henry Martyn. Rules of order, revised. 75th anni-
versary ed. Chicago, Scott, Foresman, 1951. 326p.
(C221)
Sturgis, Alice Fleenor. Standard code of parliamentary procedure. New York, McGraw-Hill, 1950. 268p. (C222)

Executive Function

Great Britain

Barker, Ernst. British constitutional monarchy. London,
Central Office of Information, 1958. 32p. (C223)

Carter, Byrum E. The office of Prime Minister. Princeton, N.J., Princeton University Press, 1956. 362p.
(C224)
Jennings, William Ivor. Cabinet government. 3d ed. Cambridge, Eng., University Press, 1959. 586p. (C225)

Morrah, Dermot. The work of the Queen. London, W.
Kimber, 1958. 191p. (C226)

Schwartz, Bernard. Law and the executive in Britain, a
comparative study. New York, New York University
Press, 1949. 388p. (C227)

United States

Corwin, Edward Samuel. The President, office and powers,
1787-1957; history and analysis of practice and opinion.
4th ed. New York, New York University Press, 1957.
519p. (C228)

Freeman, John Leiper. The political process: executive
bureau-legislative committee relations. Garden City,
N.Y., Doubleday, 1955. 72p. (Bibliography: p. 71-72)
(C229)
Grundstein, Nathan D. Presidential delegation of authority
in wartime. Pittsburgh, University of Pittsburgh Press,
1961. 106p. (C230)

Koenig, Louis William. The invisible presidency. New
York, Rinehart, 1960. 438p. (C231)

Laski, Harold Joseph.   The American presidency, an interpretation.   New York, Grosset & Dunlap, c1940.   278p.
(C232)

Lasswell, Harold Dwight.   The comparative study of elites,
an introduction and bibliography.   With Daniel Lerner and
C. Easton Rothwell.   Stanford, Stanford University Press,
1952.   72p.   (Bibliography: p. 43-72)   (C233)

Longaker, Richard P.   The Presidency and individual liberties.   Ithaca, N.Y., Cornell University Press, 1961.
239p.   (C234)

MacLean, Joan Coyne, ed.   President and Congress: the
conflict of powers.   New York, H.W. Wilson, 1955.
218p.   (Bibliography: p. 207-218)   (C235)

May, Ernest Richard.   The ultimate decision: the President
as Commander in Chief.   New York, G. Braziller, 1960.
290p.   (Bibliographical notes: p. 259-269)   (C236)

Neustadt, Richard E.   Presidential power, the politics of
leadership.   New York, Wiley, 1960.   224p.   (C237)

Patterson, Caleb Perry.   Presidential government in the
United States; the unwritten constitution.   Chapel Hill, University of North Carolina Press, 1947.   301p. (Bibliography: p. 281-296)   (C238)

Rossiter, Clinton Lawrence.   The American presidency. 2d
ed.   New York, Harcourt, Brace, 1960. 281p.   (C239)

Tugwell, Rexford Guy.   The enlargement of the Presidency.
Garden City, N.Y., Doubleday, 1960. 508p.   (C240)

Warner, William Lloyd.   The American Federal executive; a
study of the social and personal characteristics of the ci-
vilian and military leaders of the United States Federal
Government.   New York, Yale University Press, 1963.
405p.   (C241)

Judicial Function

General Works

Abraham, Henry Julian.   The judicial process; an introductory analysis of the courts of the United States, England,
and France.   New York, Oxford University Press, 1962.

381p.   (Bibliography: p. 329-360)   (C242)

Gooch, George Peabody.   Courts and cabinets.   New York,
    Knopf, 1946.   372p. (Bibliographical note: p. 366-372)
                                                        (C243)

Schubert, Glendon A. , ed.   Judicial decision-making.   Con-
    tributors: Villhelm Aubert and others.   New York, Free
    Press of Glencoe, 1963.   278p.   (C244)

Latin America

Clagett, Helen (Lord).   The administration of justice in Lat-
    in America.   New York, Oceana Publication, 1952. 160p.
    (Bibliography: p. 143-156)   (C245)

The Soviet Union

Berman, Harold Joseph.   Justice in the U.S.S.R., an inter-
    pretation of Soviet law.   Rev. ed.   New York, Random
    House, c1950, 1963.   450p.   (C246)

Hazard, John Newbold.   Settling disputes in Soviet society;
    the formative years of legal institutions.   New York,
    Columbia University Press, 1960.   534p. (Bibliography:
    p. 492-508)   (C247)

Morgan, Glenn Guy.   Soviet administrative legality; the role
    of the attorney general's office.   Stanford, Calif. , Stan-
    ford University Press, 1962.   281p. (Bibliography: p.
    267-276)   (C248)

United States

Acheson, Patricia C.   The Supreme Court, America's judi-
    cial heritage.   New York, Dodd, Mead, c1961, 1962.
    270p.   (C249)

Bickel, Alexander M.   The least dangerous branch; the Su-
    preme Court at the bar of politics.   Indianapolis, Bobbs-
    Merrill, c1962.   303p.   (C250)

Jackson, Robert Haughwout.   The Supreme Court in the
    American system of government.   New York, Harper and
    Row, 1963, c1955.   92p.   (C251)

McCloskey, Robert Green.   The American Supreme Court.

Chicago, University of Chicago Press, 1960. 260p. (Bibliographical essay: p. 236-252)   (C252)

Peltason, Jack Walter.   Federal courts in the political proc-
ess.   New York, Random House, 1962, c1955. 81p.
                                                      (C253)
Starr, Isadore.   The Federal judiciary.   New York, Oxford
Book Co. , 1957.   92p.   (C254)

CHAPTER V

State and Local Government

A distinguishable feature of most political systems is the variable division of authority among several levels of government. This is particularly noticeable in the United States where, besides the federal government, there are 50 state governments, approximately 3,000 counties, 17,000 municipalities and the same number of townships with separate governmental units. The basis of the study of state and local government lies in the development of the degree of authority and the interrelationships between the various governmental units within the modern nation state. The scope of this section is enlarged to include foreign local governments for comparative study.

General Works

Adrian, Charles R. State and local governments, a study in the political process. New York, McGraw-Hill, 1960. 531p. (D1)

Alderfer, Harold Freed. American local government and administration. New York, Macmillan, 1956. 662p. (D2)

American Assembly. The forty-eight states: their tasks as policy makers and administrators...New York, American Assembly, Graduate School of Business, Columbia University, 1956? 147p. (D3)

Anderson, William. Government in the fifty states. With Clara Pennimen and Edward W. Weidner. New York, Holt, Rinehart and Winston, 1960. 509p. (D4)

Babcock, Robert S. State and local government & politics. 2d ed. New York, Random House, 1962. 425p. (D5)

Frost, Richard Theodore, ed. Cases in State and local government. Englewood Cliffs, N.J., Prentice-Hall, 1961. 862p. (D6)

Gosnell, Cullen Bryant.   State and local government in the
  United States.   With Lynwood M. Holland.   New York,
  Prentice-Hall, 1951.   619p.   (D7)

Grant, Daniel R.   State and local government in America.
  With H. C. Nixon.   Boston, Allyn and Bacon, 1963.   439p.
                                                            (D8)
Holloway, William Vernon.   State and local government in
  the United States.   New York, McGraw-Hill, 1951.   460p.
                                                            (D9)
International Union of Local Authorities.   Local government
  in the United States of America; recent trends and devel-
  opments.. The Hague, M. Nijhoff, for the International
  Union of Local Authorities, 1961.   133p.   (D10)

Inter-university Case Program.   State and local government;
  a case book.   Ed. by Edwin A. Bock.   University, Ala.,
  University of Alabama Press, 1963.   669p.   (D11)

Johnson, Claudius Osborne.   American state and local government.   With H. Paul Caltleburry and others.   3d ed.
  New York, Crowell, 1961.   396p.   (D12)

Kaufman, Herbert.   Politics and policies in state and local
  government.   Englewood Cliffs, N. J. , Prentice-Hall, 1963.
  120p.   (D13)

Lockard, Duane.   The politics of state and local government.
  New York, Macmillan, 1963.   566p.   (D14)

Maas, Arthur, ed.   Area and power; a theory of local government.   With Paul Ylvisker and others.   Glencoe, Ill. ,
  Free Press, 1959.   224p.   (D15)

Macdonald, Austin Faulks.   American state governement ad-
  ministration.   6th ed.   New York, Crowell, 1960. 702p.
                                                           (D16)
---- ----.   State and local government in the United States.
  New York, Crowell, 1955.   667p.   (D17)

Maddox, Russell Webber.   State and local government. With
  Robert F. Fuquay.   Princeton, N. J., Van Nostrand, 1962.
  712p.   (D18)

Morlan, Robert Loren, ed.   Capitol, courthouse, and city
  hall; readings in American state and local government.
  2d ed. Boston, Houghton Mifflin, 1960. 348p.   (D19)

Pate, James Ernest.   Local government and administration:
principles and problems.   New York, American Book Co.,
1954.   595p.   (D20)

Phillips, Jewell Cass.   State and local government in America.   New York, American Book Co., 1954 728p. (D21)

Riker, William H.   The study of local politics, a manual.
New York, Random House, 1959. 126p.   (D22)

Snider, Clyde Frank.   Local government in rural America.
New York, Appleton-Century-Crofts, 1957.   584p. (D23)

Swarthout, John M.   Principles and problems of state and
local government.   With Ernest R. Bartles.   New York,
Oxford University Press, 1958.   369p.   (D24)

Zimmerman, Joseph Francis.   State and local government.
New York, Barnes & Noble, 1962.   352p.   (D25)

Reference Materials

        A number of specialized reference tools dealing with
several aspects of state and local government provide useful
information, particularly of a short term or statistical nature.   In general, these works are revised periodically to include current or up to date material for quick reference.

Bibliographies

Council of State Governments.   State government: an annotated bibliography, containing periodically revised sources
of comparative data.   Compiled by Muriel Hoppes, Legislative reference librarian.   Chicago, 1959. 46p.   (D26)

Governmental Affairs Foundation.   Metropolitan communities:
a bibliography with special emphasis upon government and
politics.   Chicago, Public Administration Service, 1957,
c1956.   392p. (With supplement, 1955-57+)

        Includes 5120 numbered items in the main volume. Pt. 1,
comprises Government and politics in metropolitan areas
while pt. 2, incorporates socioeconomic background of
metropolitan areas.   (D27)

Graves, William Brooke.   American state government and
administration; a state by state bibliography of significant

general and special works.   Compiled with N.J. Small and
E.F. Dowell.   Chicago, Council of State Governments,
1949.   79p.   (D28)

Halasz, D.   Metropolis; a selected bibliography on administrative and other problems of metropolitan areas throughout the world.   The Hague, Nijhoff, 1961.   45p.   (D29)

Jonas, Frank H.   Bibliography on western politics; selected,
annotated, with introductory essays.   Salt Lake City, Institute of Government, University of Utah, 1958.   167p.
(Western political quarterly, v. 11, no. 4, December, 1958,
Supplement)

List a number of books, articles, documents, theses,
pamphlets, etc. under eleven western states.   There is no
index.   Deals primarily with state and local government.
                                                      (D30)
Munro, William Bennett.   Bibliography of municipal government in the United States.   2d ed.   Cambridge, Mass.,
Harvard University Press, 1915.   472p.   (D31)

Tompkins, Dorothy (Campbell) Culver.   State government and
administration; a bibliography.   Berkeley, Bureau of Public Administration, University of California, 1955, c1954.
269p.

Primarily an annotated list of books and articles issued
for the most part since 1930.   Arranged by large subject
field, with an author and title index.   (D32)

Other Reference Materials

Bishop, Warren A.   Sources of information on state and local government (with special reference to the state of
Washington).   Seattle, Bureau of Governmental Research
and Services, University of Washington, 1951. 64p.
                                                      (D33)
The Book of the States.   Chicago, Council of State Governments, 1935+   (Biennial)

A comprehensive manual on state activities and functions
that includes operations of state legislatures, administrative organ, etc.   (D34)

Hearle, Edward F.R.   A data processing system for state
and local governments.   With Raymond J. Muson.   Engle-

wood Cliffs, N.J., Prentice-Hall, 1963.   150p. (Bibliography: p. 141-142)

Shows how governmental agencies can effectively utilize the technology of data processing.   Concentrates primarily on developing new concepts of data handling.   (D35)

Municipal index; the purchasing guide for city officials.
   New York, American City Magazine Corp., 1924+

Incorporates a number of articles dealing with municipal subjects, directories of organizations, statistics, illustrations of machinery and bibliographies.   (D36)

The Municipal yearbook; an authoritative resume of activities and statistical data of American cities.   Chicago, International City Managers' Association, 1934+

Over the years the contents vary, but most always include two types of information, signed annual surveys by various writers and statistical tables.   The bibliographies are appended.   (D37)

Press, Charles.   State manuals, blue books, and election results.   With Oliver Williams.   Berkeley, Institute of Governmental Studies, University of California, 1962. 101p.

An excellent listing of state manuals and blue books and their uses.   Also includes election results.   (D38)

Schattschneider, Elmer Eric.   Local political surveys.
   With Victor Jones.   New York, Holt, Rinehart and Winston, 1962.   229p.

A basic guide on making surveys with respect to state and local politics.   Lists prime source materials on survey taking and prescribes methods of handling gathered data.
                                                           (D39)
U.S Bureau of the Census.   County and city data book.
   Washington, U.S. Govt. Print. Off., 1949+

This work gives the latest available census figures for each county and approximately 400 of the larger cities in the United States.   Also included are summary figures for states, geographical regions, and standard metropolitan areas.   (D40)

Aspects of State and Local Government

The functions of state and local governments can be broken down into specialized areas. A variety of these are included in this section, with additional bibliography to indicate the nature and scope of these areas.

National and State Relations

In the United States governmental power is divided between the National government and the State governments through the instrumentality of the constitution which forms the basis of the American federal partnership. This is accomplished by delegating certain powers to the National government with all other power to be exercised by the States or the people. Along with these, both National and State governments are prohibited from doing certain specific things to the detriment of each other or the people.

Anderson, William. The Nation and the States, rivals or partners? Minneapolis, University of Minnesota Press, 1955. 263p.   (D41)

---- ----. Intergovernmental relations in review. Minneapolis, University of Minnesota Press, 1960. 178p. (Bibliography: p. 167-171)   (D42)

Benson, George Charles Sumner. The new centralization, a study of intergovernmental relationships in the United States. New York, Farrar and Rinehart, c1941. 181p. (Bibliography: p. 170-175)   (D43)

Blundred, Robert Henry. Federal services to cities and towns; an alphabetical listing of services of the United States to cities, towns, boroughs, and villages, and to counties and other local governments. With Donoh W. Hanks, Jr. Chicago, American Municipal Association, 1950. 81p.   (D44)

Clark, Jane Perry. The rise of a new federalism; federal-state cooperation in the United States. New York, Columbia University Press, 1938. 347p. (Bibliography: p. 321-340)   (D45)

Macmahon, Arthur Whittier, ed. Federalism, mature and emergent. New York, Russell & Russell, 1962, c1955. 557p.   (D46)

Maxwell, James Ackley. The fiscal impact of federalism in
the United States. Cambridge, Mass., Harvard University
Press, 1946. 427p.   (D47)

Sady, Emil John. Research in federal-state relations, a report on recent developments and problems requiring further
study. Washington, Brookings Institution, 1957. 57p.
                                                                (D48)

White, Leonard Dupee. The States and the Nation. Baton
Rouge, Louisiana State University Press, 1953. 103p.
                                                                (D49)
Wisconsin University. Regionalism in America. Edited by
Merrill Jenson and others. Madison, University of Wis-
consin Press, 1951. 425p.   (D50)

Interstate Relations

Cooperation between the states is an important aspect
of American government. In the Constitution, Article I,
Section 10 governs compacts between the states; while Article III, Section 2 invests the powers of jurisdiction over
state controversies with the federal courts. Article IV,
which is commonly known as the "interstate article," regulates the relations of the states with respect to the full faith
and credit provision, the interestate citizenship provision
and the interstate rendition provision.

Bird, Frederick Lucien. A study of the Port of New York
Authority. New York, Dun & Bradstreet, 1949. 191p.
                                                                (D51)
Jackson, Robert Houghwout. Full faith and credit, the lawyer's clause of the constitution. New York, Columbia University Press, 1945. 69p.   (D52)

Thursby, Vincent V. Interstate cooperation, a study of the
interstate compact. Washington, Public Affairs Press,
1953. 152p.   (D53)

State Constitution

With respect to the boundaries of state activity, the
state consitution is the fundamental law that creates all state
offices and delimits their power. Each state can draft and
amend its own constitution within restrictions imposed by the
federal constitution.

Baker, Gordon E.   State constitutions: reapportionment.
New York, National Municipal League, 1960. 70p.   (D54)

Dealey, James Quayle.   Growth of American State constitutions from 1776 to the end of the year 1914.   New York,
Ginn, c1915.   308p.   (D55)

Hoar, Roger Sherman.   Constitutional conventions, their nature, powers, and limitations.   Boston, Little, Brown,
1917.   240p.   (D56)

Rankin, Robert Stanley.   State constitutions: the bill of
rights.   New York, National Municipal League, 1960. 20p.
                                                          (D57)
Sturm, Albert Lee.   Major constitutional issues in West
Virginia.   Morgantown, Bureau for Governmental Research, West Virginia University, 1961.   154p.   (D58)

---- ----.   Methods of State constitutional reform.   Ann
Arbor, University of Michigan Press, 1954. 175p. (D59)

Direct Legislation and Recall

     All governmental systems are faced with the problem of
keeping officials responsible for their actions.   Although the
automatic replacement of corrupt officials through the expira-
tion of terms and election of more trusted persons is a part
of the American political system, no method existed prior to
the twentieth century to remove office holders between regular terms.   Now through the initiative, the referendum, and
the recall there is an attempt to enforce continuous political
responsibility to the voters.

Bird, Frederick Lucien.   The recall of public officers; a
study of the operation of the recall in California.   With
Francis M. Ryan.   New York, Macmillan, 1930.   403p.
(Bibliography: p. 363-369)   (D60)

Crouch, Winston Winford.   The initiative and referendum in
California.   Los Angeles, Haynes Foundation, 1950. 56p.
                                                          (D61)
LaPalombra, Joseph G.   The initiative and referendum in
Oregon, 1938-1948.   Corvallis, Oregon State College,
1950.   137p.   (D62)

Pollock, James Kerr.   The direct primary in Michigan,
1909-1935.   Ann Arbor, University of Michigan Press,

1943.   81p.   (D63)

---- ----. The initiative and referendum in Michigan. Ann
Arbor, University of Michigan Press, 1940. 100p. (D64)

State Legislative Bodies

The primary policy-making branch of a state government is its legislature. In twenty-six states these bodies
are officially called "the legislature," and in nineteen they
are termed the "general assembly," the "general court" or
just "assembly." Along with the difference in name is a vari-
ance in composition. In New Hampshire's general court
there is a membership of 424; on the other hand, Nebraska,
with the only unicameral state legislature in the United
States, has a membership of only 43.

American Political Science Association. Committee on
American Legislatures. American state legislatures; report. Belle Zeller, editor. New York, Crowell, 1954.
294p. (Bibliography: p. 265-282)   (D65)

Baker, Gordon E. The politics of reapportionment in Washington State. New York, McGraw-Hill, c1960. 32p. (D66)

---- ----. Rural versus urban political power; the nature
and consequence of unbalanced representation. Garden
City, N.Y., Doubleday, 1955. 70p.   (D67)

Breckenridge, Adam Carlyle. One house for two; Nebraska's
unicameral legislature. Washington, Public Affairs Press,
1957. 98p. (Bibliography: p. 62-68)   (D68)

Buck, Arthur Eugene. Modernizing our state legislatures.
Philadelphia, American Academy of Political and Social Science, 1936. 45p. (Bibliographical notes: p. 43-45) (D69)

Chamberlain, Joseph Perkins. Legislative processes: national and state. New York, D. Appleton-Century, c1936.
369p. (Bibliography: p. 355-357)   (D70)

Council of State Governments. American legislatures: structure and procedure: summary and tabulations of a 1959
survey. Chicago, 1959. 63p.   (D71)

Fordham, Jefferson Barnes. The state legislative institution. Philadelphia, University of Pennsylvania Press,

1959.   109p.   (D72)

Greenfield, Margaret.   Legislative reapportionment: California in national perspective.   With Pamela S. Ford and
Donald R. Emery.   Berkeley, Bureau of Public Administration, University of California, 1956.   102p. (Bibliography:
p. 100-102)   (D73)

Jewell, Malcolm Edwin.   The state legislature; politics and
practice.   New York, Random House, 1962. 146p. (D74)

Neuberger, Richard Lewis.   Adventures in politics; we go to
the Legislature.   New York, Oxford University Press,
1954.   210p.   (D75)

Sears, Kenneth Craddock.   Methods of reapportionment.
Chicago, University of Chicago Law School, c1952. 89p.
                                                       (D76)
Siffin, William J.   The legislative council in the American
states.   Bloomington, Indiana University Press, 1959.
266p.   (D77)

Weeks, Oliver Douglas.   Research in the American state
legislative process; need, scope, method and suggested
problems.   Ann Arbor, Mich., J.W. Edwards, 1947.
                                                       (D78)

The Governor

    The most important elected officer in state government
is the governor.   His is a dignified position of influence in
which he acts in a ceremonial capacity both within and outside the state.   In most cases the governor wields a considerable amount of power with respect to legislation and state
administration.

Brooks, Glenn E.   When governors convene; the Governors'
conference on national policies.   Baltimore, Johns Hopkins Press, 1961.   186p.   (D79)

Council of State Governments.   The American governors:
their backgrounds, occupations, and governmental experience.   Chicago, 1961.   unpaged.   (D80)

Jensen, Christen.   The pardoning power in the American
states.   Chicago, University of Chicago Press, c1922.
143p. (Bibliography: p. 131-136)   (D81)

Lipson, Leslie.   The American governor from figurehead
   to leader.   Chicago, University of Chicago Press, c1939.
   282p. (Bibliography: p. 269-275)   (D82)

Ransone, Coleman Bernard.   The office of governor in the
   United States.   University, Ala., University of Alabama
   Press, 1956.   417p.   (D83)

Rich, Bennett Milton.   State constitutions: the governor.
   New York, National Municipal League, 1960. 33p. (D84)

Smith, Alfred Emanuel.   Up to now; an autobiography. New
   York, Viking Press, 1929.   439p.   (D85)

State Judicial Organization

      If organized society is to exist, law and courts are
essential to authoritatively settle disputes.   There is little
doubt that state court systems handle the majority of litiga-
tion in the United States.   State courts are an independent
judicial system and are in no way dependent on the federal
court system.

Aumann, Francis Robert.   The instrumentalities of justice;
   their forms, functions and limitations.   Columbus, Ohio
   State University Press, 1956.   137p. (Bibliography: p.
   123-131)   (D86)

Frank, Jerome.   Courts on trial; myth and reality in American justice.   Princeton, N.J., Princeton University Press,
   1949.   441p.   (D87)

Haynes, Evan.   The selection and tenure of judges.   Newark,
   N.J., The National Conference of Judicial Councils, 1944.
   308p.   (D88)

Keeney, Barnaby Conrad.   Judgment by peers.   Cambridge,
   Mass., Harvard University Press, 1949. 191p.   (D89)

Pound, Roscoe.   Criminal justice in America.   Cambridge,
   Mass., Harvard University Press, 1945. 226p.   (D90)

Vanderbilt, Arthur T.   Judges and juries; their functions,
   qualifications, and selection.   Boston, Boston University
   Press, 1956.   76p.   (D91)

---- ----.   Men and measures in the law.   New York,

Knopf, 1949. 156p.   (D92)

---- ----. Minimum standards of judicial administration...
New York, Published by the Law Center of New York University for the National Conference of Judicial Councils,
1949. 752p.   (D93)

Wendell, Mitchell. Relations between the Federal and state
courts. New York, Columbia University Press, 1949.
298p. (Select bibliography: p. 291-292)   (D94)

Rural Local Government

For reasons of administrative convenience, most governmental systems employ regional subdivisions. General
practice in the United States grants to these units a large
amount of autonomy; however, these subdivisions are creatures of the state, and in various ways their actions are limited. The most common unit of rural government in the
United States is the county.

Bollens, John Constantinus. Special district governments in
the United States. Berkeley, University of California
Press, 1957. 280p.   (D95)

Burchfield, Laverne. Our rural communities, a guidebook
to published materials on rural problems. Chicago, Public Administration Service, 1947. 201p.   (D96)

Lancaster, Lane W. Government in rural America. 2d ed.
New York, Van Nostrand, 1952. 375p.   (D97)

Snider, Clyde Frank. Local government in rural America.
New York, Appleton-Century-Crofts, 1957. 584p. (D98)

Wager, Paul Woodford, ed. County government across the
nation. Chapel Hill, University of North Carolina Press,
1950. 817p. (Bibliography: p. 809-811)   (D99)

Weidner, Edward W. The American county-patchwork of
boards. New York, National Municipal League, 1946.
24p. (Bibliography: p. 20-24)   (D100)

Municipal Government

Rapid urbanization has characterized the development
of the United States. This is evidenced by the accelerated

growth of urban population which, at the present time, is approximately 70 per cent of the population of the United States. The importance of municipal government to the average citizen is accentuated because of his dependence upon it for essential services.

Baker, Benjamin. Urban government. Princeton, N. J., Von Nostrand. 1957. 572p.   (D101)

Banfield, Edward C. City politics. With James Q. Wilson. Cambridge, Harvard University Press, 1963. 362p.
                                                    (D102)
---- ----. Urban government: a reader in politics and administration. New York, Free Press of Glencoe, 1961. 593p.   (D103)

Bromage, Arthur Watson. Councilmen at work. Ann Arbor, Mich., G. Wahr Pub. Co., 1954. 119p.   (D104)

Childs, Richard Spencer. Civic victories; the story of an unfinished revolution. New York, Harper, 1952. 350p.
                                                    (D105)
Derthick, Martha. City politics in Washington, D. C. Cambridge, Joint Center for Urban Studies of the Massachusetts Institute of Technology and Harvard University. Distributed by Harvard University Press, 1962. 239p. (D106)

Hobbs, Edward Henry. A manual of Mississippi municipal government. With Donald S. Vaughn. 2d ed. University, Miss., Bureau of Governmental Research, University of Mississippi, 1962. 196p.   (D107)

Huefner, Dixie S. A report on politics in Salt Lake City. Cambridge, Mass., Joint Center for Urban Studies of the Massachusetts Institute of Technology and Harvard University, c1961. 1v. (Looseleaf)   (D108)

MacCorkle, Stuart Alexander. The city manager's job. Austin, Institute of Public Affairs, University of Texas, 1958. 38p.   (D109)

Maddox, Russell Webber. Extra-territorial powers of municipalities in the United States. Corvallis, Oregon State College, 1955. 114p. (Bibliography: p. 110-114) (D110)

Owen, Wilfred. Cities in the motor age. New York, Viking Press, 1959. 176p. (Source material: p. 157-160) (D111)

Phillips, Jewell Cass. Municipal government and administration in America. New York, Macmillan, 1960. 648p.
(D112)

Polsby, Nelson W. Community power and political theory.
New Haven, Yale University Press, 1963. 144p. (D113)

Robson, William Alexander. Great cities of the world; their governments, politics, and planning. New York, Macmillan, 1955. 693p. (Bibliography: p. 643-658)   (D114)

Smith, Thelma E. Guide to the municipal government of the city of New York, 8th ed. New York, Record Press, 1960. 278p.   (D115)

Stewart, Frank Mann. A half-century of municipal reform; the history of the National Municipal League. Berkeley, University of California Press, 1950. 289p. (Bibliography: p. 248-277)   (D116)

Stone, Harold Alfred. City manager government in the United States; a review after twenty-five years. With Don K. Price and Kathryn H. Stone. Chicago, Published for the Committee on Public Administration of the Social Science Research Council by the Public Administration Service, 1940. 279p.   (D117)

Williams, Oliver P. Four cities, a study in comparative policy making. With Charles R. Adrian. Philadelphia, University of Pennsylvania Press, 1963. 334p. (D118)

Woodbury, Coleman, ed. The future of cities and urban redevelopment. By Catherine Bauer and others. Chicago, University of Chicago Press, 1953. 764p.   (D119)

---- ----. Urban redevelopment: problems and practices.
By Charles S. Ascher and others. Chicago, University of Chicago Press, 1953. 525p.   (D120)

State and Local Relations

The American tradition of local self-government is deeply rooted in the past. It is founded on the concept that local units of government can provide for their own needs in their own way. It is important to note, however, that the state delimits control over various areas such as budgeting affairs. There is no clear cut division of functions between state and local government which, in many cases, presents some perplexing problems.

Dillon, John Forest.   Commentaries on the law of municipal
   corporations.   5th ed.   Boston, Little, Brown, 1911.
   5v.   (D121)

McMillan, Thomas E.   State supervision of municipal finance.   Austin, Institute of Public Affairs, University of
   Texas, 1953.   100p.   (D122)

Mott, Rodney Loomer.   Home rule for America's cities.
   Chicago, American Municipal Association, 1949.   68p.
                                                         (D123)
Pontius, Dale.   State supervision of local government, its
   development in Massachusetts.   Washington, D.C., American Council on Public Affairs, 1942.   165p.   (D124)

Metropolitan Areas

          A standard metropolitan statistical area (SMSA) has
been defined by the United States Bureau of the Budget as
"a county or group of contiguous counties which contains at
least one city of 50,000 inhabitants or more or 'twin cities'
with a combined population of at least 50,000." The problems encountered by these areas range from conflicts of authority, duplication, inadequacy of services and lack of planning to financial and other problems.

Banfield, Edward C.   Political influence.   Glencoe, Ill.,
   Free Press, 1961.   354p.   (D125)

Bollens, John Constantinus.   The problem of government in
   the San Francisco Bay region.   Berkeley, Bureau of Public Administration, University of California, 1948.   162p.
   (Select bibliography: p. 150-162)   (D126)

Fortune.   The exploding metropolis.   Garden City, N.Y.,
   Doubleday, 1958.   193p.   (D127)

Government Affairs Foundation.   Metropolitan communities:
   a bibliography with special emphasis upon government and
   politics.   Chicago, Public Administration Service, 1957,
   c1956.   392p.   (Supplement. 1955-57+ Issued in cooperation with the Bureau of Public Administration, University
   of California)   (D128)

Greer, Scott A.   Metropolitics: a study of political culture.

Advice and assistance of Norton E. Long. New York,
Wiley, 1963. 207p.   (D129)

Illinois. Northeastern Illinois. Northeastern Illinois Metropolitan Area Local Government Service Commission. Governmental problems in the Chicago metropolitan area; a
report. Edited by Leverett S. Lyon. Chicago, University
of Chicago Press, 1957. 288p.   (D130)

Jones, Victor. Metropolitan government. Chicago, University of Chicago Press, 1942. 364p. (Bibliography: p.
343-344)   (D131)

Kantor, Harry. Governing our metropolitan communities.
Gainesville, 1958. 24p. (Bibliography: p. 23)   (D132)

Los Angeles. Public Library. Municipal Reference Library.
The government of metropolitan areas, a bibliography.
Los Angeles, 1947. 42p.   (D133)

Owen, Wilfred. The metropolitan transportation problem.
Washington, Brookings Institution, 1956. 301p.   (D134)

Simon, Herbert Alexander. Fiscal aspects of metropolitan
consolidation. Berkeley. Bureau of Public Administration,
University of California, 1943. 67p.   (D135)

Sweeney, Stephen Binnington, ed. Metropolitan analysis, im-
portant elements of study and action. Assistant editor:
George S. Blair. Philadelphia, University of Pennsylvania
Press, 1958. 189p.   (D136)

Wood, Robert Coldwell. Metropolis against itself. New
York, Committee for Economic Development, 1959. 56p.
                                                       (D137)

---- ----. 1400 governments; the political economy of the
New York metropolitan region. With Vladimir V. Almen-
diner. Cambridge, Mass., Harvard University Press,
1961. 267p.   (D138)

---- ----. Suburbia, its people and their politics. Boston,
Houghton Mifflin, 1959, c1958. 340p.   (D139)

Public Protection, Health and Welfare

It can be stated with a great deal of accuracy that

among the most important functions of government in general are public protection, health and welfare. With a rapidly
developing society these governmental services face a great
number of complex problems. Many times these problems
can only be solved through the combined efforts of local,
state and federal governments.

American Public Welfare Association.   Public welfare administration.   By Marietta Stevenson... New York, Macmillan, 1938.   352p.   (Bibliography: p. 333-343) (D140)

Burns, Eveline Mabel (Richardson).   Social security and
   public policy.   New York, McGraw-Hill, 1956. 291p.
                                                        (D141)
Chute, Charles Lionel.   Crime, courts, and probation.
   With Margorie Bell.   New York, Macmillan, 1956. 268p.
                                                        (D142)
Corson, John Jay.   Economic needs of older people.   With
   John W. McConnell... New York, Twentieth Century Fund,
   1956.   533p.   (D143)

Crump, Irving.   Our state police.   New York, Dodd, Mead,
   1955.   238p.   (D144)

Drake, Joseph Turpin.   The aged in American society. New
   York, Ronald Press Co., 1956.   431p.   (D145)

Ehlers, Victor Marcus.   Municipal and rural sanitation.
   With Ernest W. Steel... 3d ed.   New York, McGraw-Hill,
   1943.   449p.   (D146)

Hiscock, Ira Vaughn.   Community health organization.   4th
   ed.   New York, Commonwealth Fund, 1950. 278p. (D147)

Lemkau, Paul Victor.   Mental hygiene in public health. New
   York, McGraw-Hill, 1949.   396p.   (D148)

Leonard, Vivian Anderson.   Police organization and management.   Brooklyn, Foundation Press, 1951. 507p. (D149)

Linford, Alton A.   Old age assistance in Massachusetts.
   Chicago, University of Chicago Press, 1949.   418p. (Bibliography: p. 416-418)   (D150)

Meyer, Harold Diedrich.   Community recreation, a guide to
   its organization.   With Charles K. Brightbill.   2d ed.
   Englewood Cliffs, N.J., Prentice-Hall, 1956.

525p.   (D151)

Mustard, Harry Stoll.   An introduction to public health. 3d
  ed. New York, Macmillan, 1953. 315p.   (D152)

Smith, Bruce.   Police systems in the United States. Rev.
  ed. New York, Harper, 1949. 351p.   (D153)

Straus, Nathan.   Two-thirds of a nation; a housing program.
  New York, Knopf, 1952, c1951. 291p.   (D154)

Wilson, Orlando Winfield.   Police administration. New York,
  McGraw-Hill, 1950. 540p.   (D155)

Wyatt, Laurence Reginald.   Intergovernmental relations in
  public health.   Minneapolis, University of Minnesota Press,
  1951. 212p. (Bibliography: p. 201-207)   (D156)

Schools, Libraries, and Museums

        The most expensive service that state and local gov-
ernments provide is education.   From its earliest beginnings
the concept of an educated electorate in the United States has
been a guiding force in governmental affairs.   Public schools
and universities are maintained in every state for formal
education, with libraries and museums providing additional opportunities for educational and cultural development.

Beach, Fred Francis.   The state and education; the struc-
  ture and control of public education at the state level.
  With Robert E. Will, in cooperation with the Study Com-
  mission of the Council of Chief State School Officers.
  Washington, U.S. Dept. of Health, Education and Welfare,
  Office of Education, 1957. 175p.   (D157)

Conant, James Bryant.   The American High School today; a
  first report to interested citizens. New York, McGraw-
  Hill, 1959. 140p.   (D158)

Garceau, Oliver.   The public library in the political process;
  a report of the Public Library Inquiry. With the assistance
  of C. Dewitt Hardy and others. New York, Columbia University Press, 1949. 254p. (Bibliography: p. 241-243)
                                                             (D159)
Hagman, Harlan L.   The administration of American public
  schools. New York, McGraw-Hill, 1951. 428p. (D160)

Joeckel, Carleton Burns.   The government of the American
  public library.   Chicago, University of Chicago Press,
  1935.   393p.   (D161)

Millett, John David.   Financing higher education in the
  United States... New York, Published for the Commission
  of Financing Higher Education by Columbia University
  Press, 1952.   503p.   (D162)

Morlan, Robert Loren.   Intergovernmental relations in education.   Minneapolis, University of Minnesota Press, 1950.
  220p.   (Bibliography: p. 207-215)   (D163)

Pittenger, Benjamin Floyd.   Local public school administration.   New York, McGraw-Hill, 1951.   512p.   (D164)

Reeves, Charles Everand.   School boards: their status,
  functions, and activities.   New York, Prentice-Hall, 1954.
  368p.   (D165)

Remmlein, Madaline (Kinter).   The law of local public school
  administration.   New York, McGraw-Hill, 1953.   271p.
                                                               (D166)
Public Works

        The term public works comprises a broad area that
includes such things as highways and other facilities for
transportation, water supply and other public utilities, public buildings, public parks, sewage and refuse disposal and
many other things.   Public works are chiefly characterized
by (1) improving public facilities, (2) building and maintain-
ing public facilities, with or without payment of a fee, and
(3) having their construction and maintenance an engineering
problem rather than primarily one of health, education or
other functions.

Gomez, Rosendo Adolfo.   Intergovernmental relations in highways.   Minneapolis, University of Minnesota Press, 1950.
  123p.   (Bibliography: p. 117-119)   (D167)

Hebden, Norman.   State-city relationships in highway affairs.
  With Wilbur S. Smith.   New Haven, Yale University Press,
  1950.   230p.   (D168)

Stone, Donald Crawford.   The management of municipal public works.   Chicago, Public Administration Service, 1939.
  344p.   (D169)

Land Policies and Planning

     In the early years of American history there were
abundant amounts of natural resources available. Over the
years, through mismanagement, many of these natural resources have been destroyed or greatly depleted. It has not
been until the twentieth century that Americans have become
aware of the need to conserve and carefully plan the future
use of agricultural and urban land, water, forest, and min-
eral resources.

Baker, Gladys. The county agent. Chicago, University of
    Chicago Press, c1939. 226p. (Select bibliography: p.
    214-215)   (D170)

Bartholomew, Harland. Land uses in American cities.
    Assisted by Jack Wood. Cambridge, Mass., Harvard Uni-
    versity Press, 1955. 196p.   (D171)

Branch, Melville Campbell. Aerial photography in urban
    planning and research. Cambridge, Mass., Harvard Uni-
    versity Press, 1948. 150p.   (D172)

Chapin, Francis Stuart. Urban land use planning. New
    York, Harper, 1957. 397p.   (D173)

Gallion, Arthur B. The urban pattern; city planning and de-
    sign. In collaboration with Simon Fisher. New York,
    Van Nostrand, 1950. 446p. (Bibliography: p. 419-437)
                                                        (D174)
Gulick, Luther Halsey. American forest policy, a study of
    government administration and economic control. New
    York, Published for the Institute of Public Administration
    by Duell, Sloan and Pearce, 1951. 252p.   (D175)

Hillman, Arthur. Community organization and planning.
    New York, Macmillan, 1950. 378p.   (D176)

Lewis, Harold MacLean. Planning the modern city. New
    York, Wiley, 1949. 2v.   (D177)

Parson, Ruben L. Conserving American resources. Engle-
    wood Cliffs, N.J., Prentice-Hall, 1956. 550p.   (D178)

Rodgers, Cleveland. American planning; past, present, fu-
    ture. New York, Harper, 1947. 290p.   (D179)

Smith, Guy Harold, ed.   Conservation of natural resources.
New York, Wiley, 1950.   552p.   (D180)

Walker, Robert Averill.   The planning function in urban
government.   2d ed.   Chicago, University of Chicago
Press, 1950.   410p.   (D181)

Webster, Donald Hopkins.   Urban planning and municipal
public policy.   New York, Harper, 1958.   572p.   (D182)

State Governments

The following list is a bibliography of works pertain-
ing to state governments in the United States.   This is not
meant to be a comprehensive listing but only an indicator of
the types of materials that have been printed concerning the
governments of the fifty states.

Alabama

Alabama.   University.   Bureau of Public Administration.
Alabama governmental manual.   University of Alabama,
1959.   219p.   (D183)

Ranson, Coleman Bernard.   The governments under which
we live;   Alabama civics.   Tuscaloosa, Ala., P.R. Ma-
lone, 1955.   420p.   (D184)

Alaska

Alaska.   Legislative Council.   Legislative handbook on Alaska State government.   Juneau, 1960+   (D185)

Arizona

Robinson, Dorothy Fulwiler.   The making of Arizona, a history and government of Arizona.   Tucson?, Ariz., c1962.
74p.   (D186)

Van Petten, Donald Robinson.   The Constitution and government of Arizona.   3d ed.   Phoenix?, Ariz., 1960. 239p.
                                                        (D187)
Arkansas

Alexander, Henry M.   Government in Arkansas; organization
and function at state, county, and municipal levels.   3d

printing with revisions.   Little Rock,   Pioneer Press,
1959.   264p.   (D188)

California

Crouch, Winston Winford.   California government and poli-
tics.   Englewood Cliffs, N. J., Prentice-Hall, 1956. 272p.
(D189)
Hyink, Bernard L.   Politics and government in California.
With S. Brown and E.W. Thacker.   3d ed.   New York,
Crowell, 1963.   287p.   (D190)

Colorado

Martin, Curtis.   Colorado politics.   2d ed.   Denver, Big-
Mountain Press, 1962.   89p.   (D191)

Connecticut

Buckley, William Edward.   Connecticut: the state and its
government... With Charles E. Perry.   New Ed.   New
York, Oxford Book Co., 1953.   141p.   (D192)

Delaware

Dolan, Paul.   The government and administration of Dela-
ware.   New York, Crowell, 1956.   396p.   (D193)

Florida

Morris, Allen Covington.   Our Florida government.   Chicago, Lyons and Carnahan, 1961. 234p.   (D194)

Georgia

Gosnell, Cullen Bryant.   The government and administration
of Georgia.   With C. David Anderson.   New York, Crowell,
1956.   403p.   (Bibliography: p. 386-389)   (D195)

Hawaii

Hawaii.   University, Honolulu.   Legislative Reference Bureau.   The Structure of the Hawaii state government.   Honolulu, 1960.   24p.   (D196)

Terauchi, Mildred.   Hawaiian politics, 1945-1961; a selected
bibliography.   With Daniel W. Tuttle, Jr.   Honolulu, Dept.

of Government, University of Hawaii, 1962.   7 leaves.
                                                            (D197)
Idaho

Davis, Deborah.   Idaho civics.   Boise, Ida. , Syms-York Co. ,
   c1941.   195p.   (D198)

Illinois

Garvey, Neil Ford.   The government and administration of
   Illinois.   New York, Crowell, 1958. 622p.   (D199)

Indiana

Malan, Clement Timothy.   An outline of Indiana civil government; a classroom text book.   Hillsdale, Mich., Hillsdale
   School Supply Co. , 1950, c1949.   164p.   (D200)

Iowa

Ross, Russell Marion.   The government and administration
   of Iowa.   New York, Crowell, 1957. 382p. (Bibliography:
   p. 365-372)   (D201)

Kansas

Drury, James Westbrook.   The government of Kansas.
   With associates.   Lawrence, University of Kansas Press,
   1961.   393p.   (D202)

Kentucky

Reeves, John Estill.   Kentucky government.   Lexington,
   Bureau of Government Research, University of Kentucky,
   1955. 87p.   (D203)

Louisiana

Havard, William C.   The Government of Louisiana. Baton
   Rouge, Bureau of Public Administration, Louisiana State
   University, 1958.   194p.   (D204)

Maine

Starkey, Glenn Wendell.   Maine, its history, resources, and
   government.   4th ed.   New York, Silver Burdett Co. ,
   1947.   263p.   (D205)

Maryland

Bard, Harry. Maryland today: the state, the people, the
   government. New York, Oxford Book Co., 1961. 188p.
                                                            (D206)

Massachusetts

League of Women Voters of Massachusetts. Massachusetts
   state government, a citizen's handbook. Cambridge,
   Mass., Harvard University Press, 1956. 399p.   (D207)

Mariner, Elwyn E. This is your Massachusetts government
   ...3d ed. Arlington Heights, Mass., Mariner Books,
   1962. 183p.   (D208)

Michigan

Carr, Robert. Government of Michigan under the 1962 Constitution. Ann Arbor, Mich., Ann Arbor Public Schools,
   1963. 96 leaves. (Bibliography: leaves 94-96)   (D209)

McHargue, Daniel S. Michigan government in brief. Prepared by the Institute of Public Administration. Rev. ed.
   Ann Arbor, University of Michigan Press, 1961. 76p.
                                                            (D210)

Minnesota

Kise, Joseph. Minnesota's government. New York, Winston,
   1961. 209p.   (D211)

Mississippi

Highsaw, Robert Baker. The government and administration
   of Mississippi. With Charles N. Fortenberry. New York,
   Crowell, 1954. 414p.   (D212)

Missouri

McCandless, Carl Albert. Government and administration in
   Missouri. Saint Louis, Educational Publishers, 1949.
   261p.   (D213)

Montana

Renne, Roland Roger. The government and administration of
   Montana. New York, Crowell, 1958. 508p.   (D214)

Nebraska

Sheldon, Addison Erwin.   Nebraska civil government. Lincoln, The University Publishing Co. , 1946. 386p. (D215)

Nevada

Mack, Effie Mona.   Nevada government: a study of the administration and politics of state, county, township, and cities.   With Idel Anderson and Beulah E. Singleton. Caldwell, Ida. , Caxton Printers, 1953. 384p.   (D216)

New Hampshire

Morrison, Leonard Samuel.   Government of New Hampshire. Rev. ed.   Mount Vernon, N.H. , 1952.   154p.   (D217)

New Jersey

Rich, Bennett Milton.   The government and administration of New Jersey.   New York, Crowell, 1957.   415p. (Bibliography: p. 404-408)   (D218)

New Mexico

Judah, Charles Burned.   The 47th state; an appraisal of its government.   With Frederick C. Irion.   Albuquerque, Division of Government Research, University of New Mexico, 1956, i.e. 1959. 70p.   (D219)

New York

Caldwell, Lynton Keith.   The government of New York. New York, Crowell, 1954.   506p.   (D220)

League of Women Voters of New York.   New York State; a citizen's handbook.   Marjorie G. Stein, editor.   New York, c1963.   112p. (Bibliography: p. 104-105)   (D221)

North Carolina

Rankin, Robert Stanley.   The government and administration of North Carolina. New York, Crowell, 1955. 429p. (Bibliography: p. 416-422)   (D222)

North Dakota

North Dakota. Legislative Reference Service. Legislative
handbook of state governmental agencies and their principal duties. Bismarck, 1960. 58 leaves.   (D223)

Ohio

Aumann, Francis Robert. The government and administration of Ohio. With Harvey Walker. New York, Crowell,
1956. 489p. (Bibliography: p. 479-482)   (D224)

Eells, William Hastings. Your Ohio government. 4th ed.
Columbus, Book Dept., Midwest Law Printers and Publishers, 1960. 154p.   (D225)

Greene, Alexander. Ohio government. Englewood Cliffs,
N.J., Prentice-Hall, 1961. 105p.   (D226)

Oklahoma

Thornton, Hurschell Vern. The government of Oklahoma.
With Gene Aldrich. Oklahoma City, Harlow Pub. Corp.,
1960. 366p.   (D227)

Oregon

Tucker, E. Bernice. Your government in Oregon. San
Francisco, H. Wagner Pub. Co., 1956. 60p.   (D228)

Pennsylvania

Alderfer, Harold Freed. Pennsylvania government: views-
reviews and previews. Mechanicsburg, Pa., Local Government Service, 1962. 109p.   (D229)

Branning, Rosalind Lorraine. Annotated bibliography on
Pennsylvania State government. Prepared for the Dept. of
Political Science, University of Pittsburgh, Pittsburgh,
1959. 42p.   (D230)

Rhode Island

Stitely, John O. An outline of Rhode Island state government.
Kingston, University of Rhode Island, Bureau of Government Research, 1961. 20p.   (D231)

South Carolina

Coleman, James Karl.   State administration in South Carolina.   New York, Columbia University Press, 1935. 299p.
(Bibliography: p. 285-292)   (D232)

South Dakota

Farber, William Ogden.   Government of South Dakota. With
Thomas C. Geary and William H. Cape.   Sioux Falls,
S. D. , Midwest Beach Co. , 1962.   211p.   (D233)

Tennessee

Greene, Lee Siefert.   Government in Tennessee.   With
Robert S. Avery.   Knoxville, University of Tennessee
Press, 1962.   368p.   (D234)

Texas

McCleskey, Clifton.   The government and politics of Texas.
With T. C. Sinclair and Pauline Yelderman.   Boston,
Little, Brown, 1963.   427p.   (D235)

MacCorkle, Stuart Alexander.   Texas government.   With
Dick Smith.   4th ed.   New York, McGraw-Hill, 1960.
518p.   (D236)

Utah

Utah Foundation.   State and local government in Utah; a description of the structure, operations, function and finances
of all branches of state and local government in Utah-their
departments, commissions and agencies.   Rev. ed.   Salt
Lake City, 1962.   233p.   (D237)

Vermont

Vermont.   Commission to Study State Government.   The
operation of Vermont state government.   Report to the
General Assembly by the Commission to Study State Government on the results of its study and its recommendations.   Montpelier, 1959.   115p.   (D238)

Virginia

Hemphill, William Edwin.   Cavalier Commonwealth; history

and government of Virginia. With Marvin W. Schlegel and
Sadie E. Engelberg. New York, McGraw-Hill, 1957.
686p.   (D239)

Washington

Avery, Mary Wilhamson. History and government of the
State of Washington. Seattle, University of Washington
Press, 1961. 583p.   (D240)

Webster, Donald Hopkins. Washington state government;
administrative organization and functions. With Ernest H.
Campbell and George D. Smith. Rev. by David W. Stevens.
Seattle, University of Washington Press, 1962. 254p.
                                                             (D241)

West Virginia

Davis, Claude J. West Virginia state and local government.
Morgantown, Bureau for Governmental Research, West Virginia University, 1963. 277p.   (D242)

Wisconsin

Epstein, Leon D. Politics in Wisconsin. Madison, University of Wisconsin Press, 1958. 218p.   (D243)

Wisconsin Taxpayers Alliance. The framework of your Wisconsin government. 3d ed. Madison, 1960. 69p. (D244)

Wyoming

Trachsel, Herman Henry. The government and administration of Wyoming. With Ralph M. Wade. New York,
Crowell, 1952. 381p.   (D245)

Comparative Local Government

There is a fairly substantial number of works in the
English language on local governments in foreign nations. A
selective list of these is presented below to show the types
of materials available for comparative study of local government.

Alderfer, Harold Freed. Local government in developing
countries. New York, McGraw-Hill, c1964. 251p.
                                                             (D246)

Chapma.i, Brian.   Introduction to French local government.
London, Allen & Unwin, 1953.   238p.   (D247)

Ch'u, Tung-tsu.   Local government in China under the Chin.
Cambridge, Mass., Harvard University Press, 1962.
366p.   (Bibliography: p. i-xiv)   (D248)

Cowan, Laing Gray.   Local government in West Africa.
New York, Columbia University Press, 1959, c1958.
292p.   (D249)

Cross, Charles Albert.   Principles of local government.
2d ed.   London, Sweet, 1962.   492p.   (D250)

Finer, Herman.   English local government. 4th ed., rev.
London, Methuen, 1950.   561p. (Bibliography: p. 547-549)
                                                       (D251)
Green, L. P.   History of local government in South Africa,
an introduction.   Cape Town, Juta, 1957. 113p.   (D252)

Harris, George Montagu.   Comparative local government.
London, New York, Hutchinson's University Library, 1948.
207p.   (Bibliography: p. 198-200)   (D253)

Humes, Samuel.   The structure of local governments throughout the world.   With Eileen M. Martin.   The Hague, M.
Nijhoff, 1961.   449p.   (D254)

Jackson, William Eric.   The structure of local government
in England and Wales.   4th ed.   London, Longmans, 1960.
253p.   (D255)

Jessup, Frank.   Problems of local government in England
and Wales.   Cambridge, Eng., University Press, 1949.
134p.   (D256)

Retzlaff, Ralph Herbert.   Village government in India; a
case study.   Bombay, New York, Asia Pub. House, c1962.
140p.   (D257)

Wang, Kan-yu.   The local government of China; a study of
the administrative nature of local units.   Chungking, China,
China Institute of Pacific Relations, 1945. 50p.   (D258)

Zink, Harold.   Rural local government in Sweden, Italy, and
India: a comparative study.   London, Stevens, 1957. 147p.
(Bibliography: p. 135-137)   (D259)

CHAPTER VI

Political Parties, Public Opinion
and Electoral Processes

Political parties, public opinion and electoral processes are so closely related that they can readily be treated together. Source material concerning these topics is as numerous as it is varied. Although this section is skewed largely toward American experience, practice and party structure, an attempt has been made to include works printed in the English language about foreign countries to provide source material for comparative study. None of these topics has extensive bibliographic coverage; consequently, the student will find the sources in the General Research Materials chapter of particular value. Many works in this section include good bibliographies which will also serve to alleviate the absence of adequate treatment.

Political Parties

Political events have always been accompanied by dissensus, factions, cliques and lobbies. A political party is a group of individuals, usually bound together by some guiding theme or cause, who are attempting by various means, to gain governmental control. Source materials dealing with political parties are primarily comprised of party literature, histories, pamphlets, addresses and scholarly monographs. McDonald's study is particularly helpful in defining the problem areas in the study of political parties. Some other useful reference works include the Statesman's yearbook (C51), the World Almanac (A92), the Political handbook and atlas of the world (C50), and the Europa yearbook (C49).

McDonald, Neil A. Study of political parties. New York, Random House, 1955. 97p. (Selected Readings: p. 95-97)
(E1)

General Works

Duverger, Maurice. Political parties, theory, organization and activity in the modern state. Tr. by Barbara and

Robert North.   New York, Wiley, 1954. 439p.   (E2)

Leiserson, Avery.   Parties and politics, an institutional and
behavioral approach.   New York, Knopf, 1958. 379p. (E3)

Michels, Robert.   Political parties; a sociological study of
the oligarchial tendencies of modern democracy.   Tr. by
Eden & Ceda Paul.   New York, Dover Publications, 1959.
416p.   (E4)

Neumann, Sigmund, ed.   Modern political parties; approaches
to comparative politics.   Contributor: Frederick C. Borg-
hoorn.   Chicago, University of Chicago Press, 1956. 460p.
(Bibliography: p. 425-446)   (E5)

Ostrogorskii, Moisei Iakovlevich.   Democracy and the organization of political parties.   Tr. by Frederick Clarke.
New York, Macmillan, 1908. 2v.   (E6)

Regional Works

African Region

Ashford, Douglas E.   Political change in Morocco. Princeton, N.J., Princeton University Press, 1961. 432p. (E7)

Hodgkin, Thomas Lionel.   African political parties, an introductory guide.   Harmondsworth, Middlesex, Penguin
Books, 1962, c1961. 217p.   (E8)

Kruger, D.W., ed.   South African parties and policies,
1910-1960; a select source book.   Cape Town, South Africa, Humon & Rousseau, 1960. 471p.   (E9)

Landau, Jacob M.   Parliaments and parties in Egypt. New
York, Praeger, 1954. 212p. (Bibliography: p. 195-208)
                                                    (E10)
Segal, Ronald.   Political Africa; a who's who of personali-
ties and parties.   In collaboration with Catherine Hoskyns
and Roselynde Ainslie.   New York, Praeger, 1961. 475p.
                                                    (E11)
American Region

Canada

Knowles, Stanley.   The new party.   Toronto, McClelland
and Steward, c1961. 136p.   (E12)

Thorburn, Hugh Garnet, ed.   Party politics in Canada.
Englewood Cliffs, N. J., Prentice-Hall, c1963. 172p. (E13)

Latin America

Alexander, Robert.   Labor parties in Latin America.   New
York, League for Industrial Democracy, 1942. 47p.
(Bibliographical note: p. 47)   (E14)

Gil, Frederico Guillermo.   Genesis and modernization of
political parties in Chile.   Gainesville, University of Florida Press, 1962.   55p.   (E15)

United States

Bibliography

New York Public Library.   Political parties in the United
States, 1800-1914; a list of references.   New York, New
York Public Library, 1915.   74p.   (E16)

U.S. Library of Congress.   Division of Bibliography.   Brief
list of books on political parties before 1865.   November
30, 1921.   Washington, 1921.   4p. (Typewritten)   (E17)

---- ----.   List of references on party government. March
29, 1920.   Washington, 1920.   6p. (Typewritten)   (E18)

---- ----.   List of references on the national committees of
political parties.   January 31, 1924.   Washington, 1924.
7p. (Typewritten)   (E19)

---- ----.   ...List of works relating to political parties in
the United States.   Washington, Govt. Print. Off., 1907.
29p.   (E20)

---- ----.   Selected list of references on the convention
system.   October 8, 1927.   Washington, 1927.   8p.
(Mimeographed)   (E21)

---- ----.   Short list of references to recent writings on
American politics and political parties.   February 5,
1925.   3p. (Typewritten)   (E22)

Historical and Analytical Works

Agar, Herbert.   Price of union.   Boston, Houghton Mifflin,

1950. 750p. (Bibliography: p. 717-726)   (E23)

Binkley, Wilford Ellsworth.   American political parties,
their natural history.   4th ed.   New York, Knopf, 1962.
486p.   (E24)

Bone, Hugh Alvin.   American politics and the party system.
2d ed.   New York, McGraw-Hill, 1955. 670p.   (E25)

---- ----.   Party committees and national politics.   Seattle,
University of Washington Press, 1958.   256p. (Bibliography: p. 245-249)   (E26)

Brooks, Robert Clarkson.   Political parties and electoral
problems.   3d ed.   New York, Harper, c1933. 645p.
                                                          (E27)
Bruce, Harold Rozelle.   American parties and politics, history and role of political parties in the United States.   3d
ed.   New York, Holt, 1937.   608p.   (E28)

Burns, James MacGregor.   The deadlock of democracy;
four-party politics in America.   Englewood Cliffs, N.J.,
Prentice-Hall, 1963.   388p.   (E29)

Charles, Joseph.   Origins of the American party system;
three essays.   Williamsburg, Va., Institute of Early
American History and Culture, 1956. 147p.   (E30)

Eulau, Heinz.   Class and party in the Eisenhower years;
class roles and perspectives in the 1952 and 1956 elections.   New York, Free Press of Glencoe, 1962. 162p.
                                                          (E31)
Ewing, Cortez Arthur Milton.   Congressional elections,
1896-1944; the sectional basis of political democracy in
the House of Representatives.   Norman, University of
Oklahoma Press, 1947.   110p.   (E32)

Goodman, William.   Two-party system in the United States.
2d ed.   Princeton, N.J., Van Nostrand, 1960. 681p.(E33)

Graper, Elmer Diedrich.   A brief course of ten lectures
and bibliography on party government in the United States.
With John W. Oliver and Benjamin H. Williams.   Pittsburgh, c1942.   76p.   (Bibliography: p. 73-76)   (E34)

Greenstein, Fred I.   The American party system and the
American people.   Englewood Cliffs, N.J., Prentice-Hall,

c1963. 115p.   (E35)

Hinderaker, Ivan Henrik. Party politics. New York, Holt,
    1956. 694p.   (E36)

Holcombe, Arthur Norman. The new party politics. New
    York, Norton, c1933. 148p.   (E37)

Jacobs, Milton C. Political parties; election law provisions
    and digest of cases. New York, 1951. 149p.   (E38)

Key, Vladimer Orlando. Politics, parties, and pressure
    groups. 4th ed. New York, Crowell, 1958. 783p. (E39)

Lewis, Stuart. Party principles and practical politics. New
    York, Prentice-Hall, 1928. 523p.   (E40)

---- ----, ed. Readings in party principles and practical
    politics. New York, Prentice-Hall, 1928. 702p.   (E41)

Lubell, Samuel. The future of American politics. New
    York, Harper, 1952. 285p.   (E42)

McKean, Dayton David. Party and pressure politics. Bos-
    ton, Houghton Mifflin, 1949. 712p.   (E43)

Merriam, Charles Edward. The American party system; an
    introduction to the study of political parties in the United
    States. With Harold F. Gosnell. 4th ed. New York,
    Macmillan, 1949. 530p.   (E44)

Potter, David Morris, ed. Party politics and public action,
    1877-1917. Rev. by Howard R. Mamar. New York,
    Holt, 1960. 84p.   (E45)

Ranney, Austin. Democracy and the American party system.
    With Willmoore Kendall. New York, Harcourt, Brace,
    1956. 550p.   (E46)

Ray, Perley Orman. An introduction to political parties and
    practical politics. 3d ed. New York, Scribner, c1924.
    691p. (Bibliography: p. 513-640)   (E47)

Rossiter, Clinton Lawrence. Parties and politics in Amer-
    ica. Ithaca, N.Y., Cornell University Press, 1960.
    205p.   (E48)

Sait, Edward McChesney. Sait's American parties and elections. 5th ed. By Howard R. Denniman. New York,
Appleton-Century-Crofts, 1952. 574p.   (E49)

Schattschneider, Elmer Eric. Party government. New
York, Farrar and Rinehart, c1942. 219p. (Select bibliography: p. 211-214)   (E50)

Smith, Thomas Vernor. The promise of American politics.
2d ed. Chicago, University of Chicago Press, c1936.
307p.   (E51)

Truman, David Bicknell. The Congressional party, a case
study. New York, Wiley, 1959. 336p.   (E52)

Turner, Henry A., ed. Politics in the United States; readings in political parties and pressure groups. New York,
McGraw-Hill, 1955. 436p.   (E53)

Vorees, Edith. Political parties in the United States. New
York, Pageant Press, 1960. 68p.   (E54)

Westerfield, Bradford. Foreign policy and party politics;
Pearl Harbor to Korea. New Haven, Yale University
Press, 1955. 488p. (Bibliography: p. 429-435)   (E55)

Woodburn, James Albert. American politics. Political
parties and party problems in the United States. 3d ed.
New York, Putnam, 1924. 542p.   (E56)

Improvement of Party Politics

American Political Science Association. Committee on Political Parties. Toward a more responsible two-party system, a report. New York, Rinehart, 1950. 99p.   (E57)

Ranney, Austin. The doctrine of responsible party government; its origins and present state. Urbana, University
of Illinois Press, 1962. 176p. (Bibliography: p. 165-172)
                                                        (E58)

Major Parties, Histories and Politics

Acheson, Dean Gooderham. A Democrat looks at his party.
New York, Harper, 1955. 199p.   (E59)

Bowles, Chester. Coming political breakthrough. New
York, Harper, 1959. 209p.   (E60)

Burdette, Franklin L. , ed.   Readings for Republicans.   New
York, Oceana Publications, 1960.   256p.   (E61)

Clancy, Herbert John.   The Democratic party; Jefferson to
Jackson.   New York, Fordham University Press, 1962.
240p.   (E62)

Cohn, David Lewis.   The fabulous Democrats; a history of
the Democratic Party in text and pictures.   New York,
Putnam, 1956.   192p.   (E63)

Crandall, Andrew Wallace.   The early history of the Republican party.   Boston, R. G. Badger, c1930. 313p. (Bibliography: p. 289-305)   (E64)

Cunningham, Noble E.   Jeffersonian Republicans: the term-
ination of party organization, 1789-1801.   Chapel Hill,
University of North Carolina Press, c1957. 279p. (Note:
p. 264-266)   (E65)

DeSantis, Vincent P.   Republicans face the Southern ques-
tion; the new departure years, 1877-1897.   Baltimore,
The Johns Hopkins Press, 1959. 275p.   (E66)

Holcombe, Arthur Norman.   The political parties of to-day;
a study in Republican and Democratic politics.   New York,
Harper, 1924.   399p.   (E67)

Kent, Frank Richardson.   The Democratic party, a history.
New York, Century, c1928.   568p. (Bibliography: p. 519)
                                                            (E68)
Minor, Henry Augustine.   The story of the Democratic party.
New York, Macmillan, 1928. 501p. (Bibliography: p. 469-
475)   (E69)

Moos, Malcolm Charles.   The Republicans; a history of
their party.   New York, Random House, 1956. 564p. (E70)

Myers, William Starr.   The Republican party, a history.
Rev. ed.   New York, Century, c1931.   517p.   (E71)

Reed, Edward, ed.   Readings for Democrats.   New York,
Oceana Publications, 1960.   256p.   (E72)

Schnapper, Morris Bartel.   Grand Old Party; the first hundred years of the Republican Party, a pictorial history.
Washington, Public Affairs Press, 1955. 520p.   (E73)

Schriftgiesser, Karl. This was normalcy, an account of
party politics during the Republican years: 1920-1932.
Boston, Little, Brown, 1948. 325p. (Bibliography: p.
299-306)   (E74)

Tinkcom, Harry Marlin. Republicans and federalists in
Pennsylvania, 1790-1801; a study in national stimulus and
local response. Harrisburg, Pennsylvania Historical and
Museum Commission, 1950. 354p. (Bibliography: p. 329-
338)   (E75)

Party Economics

Harris, Seymour Edwin. The economics of the political
parties, with special attention to Presidents Eisenhower
and Kennedy. New York, Macmillan, 1962. 382p.   (E76)

Heard, Alexander. Money and politics. New York, Public
Affairs Committee, 1956. 28p.   (E77)

State and Local Party Politics

Benson, Lee. Concept of Jacksonian democracy, New York
as a test case. Princeton, N.J., Princeton University
Press, 1961. 351p.   (E78)

Carlisle, Douglas. Party loyalty; the election process in
South Carolina. Washington, Public Affairs Press, 1963.
156p. (References: p. 135-151)   (E79)

Cresap, Dean Russell. Party politics in the Golden State.
Los Angeles, Haynes Foundation, 1954. 126p.   (E80)

Fisher, Marguerite J. Parties and politics in the local community; analysis of the problem. Washington, Pub. for
the Maxwell Graduate School of Citizenship and Public Affairs, Syracuse University, by the National Council for the
Social Sciences, 1951. 144p. (Bibliography: p. 139-148)
                                                                       (E81)

Gosnell, Harold Foote. Machine politics; Chicago model.
Chicago, University of Chicago Press, c1937. 229p.
(Bibliography: p. 214-219)   (E82)

Hamilton, Joseph Greyore de Roulhec. Party politics in
North Carolina, 1835-1860. Durham, N.C., The Seman
Printery, 1916. 212p. (Bibliography: p. 211-212)   (E83)

Heard, Alexander. A two-party South? Chapel Hill, University of North Carolina Press, 1952. 334p. (Notes: p. 281-
318)   (E84)

Huthmacher, J. Joseph. Massachusetts people and politics,
1919-1933. Cambridge, Belknap Press of Harvard University Press, 1959. 328p.   (E85)

Lockard, Duane. New England state politics. Princeton,
N. J. , Princeton University Press, 1959. 374p.   (E86)

Millspaugh, Arthur Chester. Party organization in Michigan
since 1890. Baltimore, The Johns Hopkins Press, 1917.
189p.   (E87)

Montgomery, Horace. Cracker parties. Baton Rouge, La. ,
Louisiana State University Press, 1950. 278p. (Bibliography: p. 252-261)   (E88)

Sarasohn, Stephen Beisman. Political party pattern in
Michigan. Detroit, Wayne State University Press, 1957.
76p.   (E89)

Wagstaff, Henry McGilbert. State rights and parties in
North Carolina, 1776-1831. Baltimore, The Johns Hopkins Press, 1906. 155p.   (E90)

Third Party Movements

Fine, Nathan. Labor and farmer parties in the United
States, 1828-1928. New York, Russell & Russell, 1961,
c1928. 445p.   (E91)

Hesseltine, William Best. Third-party movements in the
United States. Princeton, N. J. , Van Nostrand, c1962.
192p.   (E92)

Nash, Howard Pervear. Third parties in American politics.
Washington, Public Affairs Press, 1959. 326p.   (E93)

Odegard, Peter H. Pressure politics, the story of the Anti-
saloon league. New York, Columbia University Press,
1928. 299p.   (E94)

Whitman, Alden. Labor parties, 1827-1844. New York,
International Publishers, c1943. 64p. (Selected bibliography: p. 64)   (E95)

Asian Region

India

Hull, William Isaac.   India's political crisis.   Baltimore,
   The Johns Hopkins Press, 1930.   190p. (Sources: p. 182-
   183)   (E96)

Weiner, Myron.   Party politics in India; the development of
   a multi-party system.   Princeton, N.J., Princeton University Press, 1957.   319p. (Bibliography: p. 293-312) (E97)

Japan

Scalapino, Robert A.   Democracy and the party movement in
   prewar Japan;   the failure of the first attempt.   Berkeley,
   University of California Press, 1953.   471p. (Bibliography:
   p. 420-442)   (E98)

---- ----.   Parties and politics in contemporary Japan.
   With Junnosuke Masumi.   Berkeley, University of California Press, 1962.   190p.   (E99)

Australian Region

Burns, Creighton.   Parties and people; a survey based on
   the LaTrohe electorate.   Parkville, Melbourne University
   Press, 1961.   173p.   (E100)

Overacker, Louise.   The Australian party system.   New
   Haven, Published for Wellesley College by Yale University
   Press, 1952.   373p. (Bibliography: p. 342-359)   (E101)

European Region

Lowell, Abbott Lawrence.   Governments and parties in continental Europe.   New York, Houghton Mifflin, 1900. 2v.
                                                            (E102)

France

Barron, Richard William.   Parties and politics in modern
   France.   Washington, Public Affairs Press, 1959. 213p.
                                                            (E103)

Laponce, J.A.   The government of the Fifth Republic;
   French political parties and the constitution.   Berkeley,
   University of California Press, 1961.   415p. (Bibliography:
   p. 387-400)   (E104)

Leites, Nathan Constantin. On the game of politics in
France. Stanford, Calif., Stanford University Press,
1959. 190p.   (E105)

Taylor, Owen R. The Fourth Republic of France; constitution and political parties. New York, Royal Institute of
International Affairs, 1951. 221p. (Bibliography: p. 216)
                                                    (E106)

Germany

Pollock, James Kerr, ed. German democracy at work; a
selective study. University of Michigan Press, 1955.
208p.   (E107)

Great Britain

Bailey, Sydney D., ed. Political parties and the party system in Britain; a symposium. New York, Praeger, 1952.
211p. (Bibliography: p. 203-207)   (E108)

Bulmer-Thomas, Ivor. The party system in Great Britain.
London, Phoenix House, 1953. 328p. (Bibliography: p.
311-323)   (E109)

Jennings, Sir William Ivor. Party politics. Cambridge,
Eng., University Press, 1960+   (E110)

McKenzie, Robert Trelford. British political parties; the
distribution of power within the Conservative and Labour
Parties. New York, St. Martin's Press, 1955. 623p.
(Bibliography: p. 602-608)   (E111)

Trevelyan, George Macaulay. The two-party system in English political history. Oxford, Clarendon Press, 1926.
27p.   (E112)

Italy

Adams, John Clarke. The government of Republican Italy.
With Paolo Barile. Boston, Houghton Mifflin, 1961.
245p.   (E113)

Taylor, Lily Ross. Party Politics in the age of Caesar.
Berkeley, University of California Press, 1949. 255p.
                                                    (E114)

Soviet Union

Almond, Gabriel Abraham.   Appeals of Communism.   With
   Herbert E. Krugman, Elsbeth Lewin and Howard Wriggins.
   Princeton, N.J., Princeton University Press, 1954. 415p.
                                                        (E115)

Armstrong, John Alexander.   Politics of totalitarianism; the
   Communist Party of the Soviet Union from 1934 to the
   present.   New York, Random House, 1961. 458p. (Bibliography: p. 349-427)   (E116)

Cantril, Hadley.   Politics of despair.   New York, Basic
   Books, 1959.   269p.   (E117)

Meyer, Frank S.   Moulding of Communists; the training of
   the Communist cadre.   New York, Harcourt, Brace, 1961.
   214p.   (E118)

Reshetar, John Stephen.   Concise history of the Communist
   Party of the Soviet Union.   New York, Praeger, 1960.
   331p.   (E119)

Schapiro, Leonard Bertram.   Communist Party of the Soviet
   Union.   New York, Random House, 1960, c1959. 631p.
   (Bibliographical note: p. 591-603)   (E120)

Sweden

Rustow, Dankwart A.   The politics of compromise; a study
   of parties and cabinet government in Sweden.   Princeton,
   N.J., Princeton University Press, 1955. 257p.   (E121)

Turkey

Karpat, Kemal H.   Turkey's politics: the transition to a
   multi-party system.   Princeton University Press, 1959.
   522p.   (Bibliography: p. 461-497)   (E122)

Public Opinion

      Although very illusive, public opinion can be con-
sidered as a belief held by a number of individuals regarding
political as well as other issues.   Public opinion formulation
cannot be divorced from the activities of pressure groups;
consequently, the literature is concerned to a large extent,
with their influence in moulding the opinions of the body

politic.

Collections

Berelson, Bernard, ed.   Reader in public opinion and communication.   Edited with Morris Janowitz.   Enl. ed.
Glencoe, Ill., Free Press, 1953. 611p. (Bibliography:
p. 603-611)   (E123)

Christenson, Rea Millard, comp.   Voice of the people;
readings in public opinion and propaganda.   With Robert
O. McWilliams.   New York, McGraw-Hill, 1962. 585p.
                                                         (E124)

General Works

Albig, William.   Modern public opinion.   New York, Mc-
Graw-Hill, 1956. 518p.   (E125)

American Society for Political and Legal Philosophy.   The
public interest.   Edited by Carl J. Friedrich.   New York,
Atherton Press, 1962. 256p.   (E126)

Angell, Sir Norman.   The public mind; its disorders: its
exploitation.   New York, Dutton, c1927. 232p.   (E127)

Bogardus, Emory Stephen.   The making of public opinion.
New York, Association Press, 1951. 265p. (Bibliography:
p. 246-260)   (E128)

Buchanan, William.   How nations see each other, a study in
public opinion.   With Hadley Cantril and others.   Urbana,
University of Illinois Press, 1953. 220p.   (E129)

Cantril, Hadley.   Gauging public opinion.   Princeton, N.J.,
Princeton University Press, 1944. 318p. (Bibliography:
p. 310-315)   (E130)

Conference on Communication and Political Development,
Dobbs Ferry, N.Y., 1961.   Communication and political
development.   Ed. by Lucian W. Pye.   Princeton, N.J.,
Princeton University Press, 1963. 381p. (Selected bibliography: p. 351-368)   (E131)

Doob, Leonard William.   Public opinion and propaganda.
New York, Holt, 1948. 600p. (References: p. 559-586)
                                                         (E132)

Irion, Frederick Clarence.   Public opinion and propaganda.

New York, Crowell, 1950. 782p.   (E133)

Katz, Elihu.   Personal influence; the part played by people
in the flow of mass communication.   With Paul F. Lazarsfeld.   Glencoe, Ill., Free Press, 1955.   400p. (Bibliography: p. 381-393)   (E134)

Key, Vladimer Orlando.   Public opinion and American democracy.   New York, Knopf, 1961.   566p.   (E135)

Lasswell, Harold Dwight.   Democracy through public opinion.
Menasha, Wis., Banta, c1941.   176p.   (E136)

Lippmann, Walter.   Public opinion.   New York, Harcourt,
Brace, c1922.   427p.   (E137)

Lowell, Abbott Lawrence.   Public opinion in war and peace.
Cambridge, Harvard University Press, 1923. 302p. (E138)

McPhee, William N., ed.   Public opinion and congressional
elections.   Ed. with William A. Glaser.   New York, Free
Press of Glencoe, 1962.   326p.   (E139)

Markel, Lester.   Public opinion and foreign policy.   New
York, Harper, 1949.   227p.   (E140)

Ogle, Marbury Bladen.   Public opinion and political dynamics.   Boston, Houghton Mifflin, 1950.   361p. (Bibliography: p. 333-353)   (E141)

Rosenau, James N.   Public opinion and foreign policy, an
operational formulation.   New York, Random House,
c1961.   118p.   (E142)

Schettler, Clarence Henry.   Public opinion in American society.   New York, Harper, 1960.   534p.   (E143)

Society for the Psychological Study of Social Issues.   Public
opinion and propaganda, a book of readings.   New York,
Dryden Press, 1954.   779p.   (E144)

Truman, David Bicknell.   The governmental process; political interests and public opinion.   New York, Knopf, 1951.
544p.   (Bibliography: p. 537-544)   (E145)

Reference Works

Blum, Eleanor.   Reference books in the mass media, an annotated, selected booklist covering book publishing, magazines, and advertising.   Urbana, University of Illinois
   Press, 1962.   103p.

   Covers a great number of reference works dealing with
   public opinion and propaganda.   (E146)

Bureau of Social Science Research, Washington, D. C.   Inter-
   national communication and political opinion; a guide to the
   literature.   By Bruce Lannes Smith and Chiltra M. Smith.
   Prepared for the Rand Corporation by the Bureau of Social
   Science Research, Washington, D. C.   Princeton, N. J.,
   Princeton University Press, c1956.   325p.

   This is a classified, annotated bibliography of 2563 num-
   bered items with author and subject index.   As a continuation of B. L. Smith's Propaganda, communication and public opinion (E150) this work covers from 1943 to 1956.

   'It concentrates on materials dealing with international
   propaganda, communication, and opinion, and cites works
   on internal matters only when they are of more than general reference to international politics.   It deals primarily
   with political propaganda and promotional activities." --
   Introd.   (E147)

Childs, Harwood Lawrence.   A reference guide to the study
   of public opinion.   Princeton, N. J., Princeton University
   Press, 1934.   105p.

   Contains a variety of useful bibliographies but without the
   aid of annotations.   It is primarily limited by its cut-off
   date of 1934.   (E148)

The Gallup political almanac.   Compiled by the American
   Institute of Public Opinion.   Princeton, N. J., 1946+

   Designed to aid in analyzing national political trends of recent years, this work gives election information for federal elections by state; for state governors; special election information; voting turnout; totals of city, state, and
   national vote percentages, etc.   (E149)

Smith, Bruce Lannes.   Propaganda, communication, and public opinion; a comprehensive reference guide. With Harold D. Lasswell, and Ralph Casey. Princeton, N.J., Princeton University Press, 1946. 435p.

Included in this work are four essays on the Science of mass communication which are followed by an annotated, selective bibliography of about 3000 titles in a classified arrangement. It also contains books, periodicals and articles which appeared between the middle of 1934 and early 1943 with a few titles of earlier dates. 150 titles have been starred as "outstanding" and given somewhat fuller annotations than most of the others. Some materials receive only brief annotations, and the whole work is well indexed.
(E150)

Electoral Processes

When the electorate of a state chooses those who will govern them, the means of this choice is termed an election. The literature in this area is expansive, particularly with regard to elections in the United States. Statistics and area analyses form an important factor in establishing electoral behavior. Special attention should be paid to the various forms of suffrage and their effect on the electoral process. Many works in this area are included for quick reference.

General Works

Bean, Louis Hyman. How to predict elections. New York, Knopf, 1948. 196p. (References: p. 196)   (E151)

Bone, Hugh Alvin. Politics and voters. With Austin Ranney. New York, McGraw-Hill, 1963. 138p.   (E152)

Gosnell, Harold Foote. Getting out the vote; an experiment in the stimulation of voting. Chicago, University of Chicago Press, c1927. 129p.   (E153)

Mackenzie, William James Millar. Free elections, an elementary textbook. New York, Rinehart, 1958. 184p.
(E154)

Merriam, Charles Edward. Non-voting causes and methods of control. With Harold Foote Gosnell. Chicago, University of Chicago Press, c1924. 287p.   (E155)

Robinson, Claude Everett. Straw votes; a study of political

prediction. New York, Columbia University Press, 1932.
203p.   (E156)

Reference Works

America votes; a handbook of contemporary American election statistics. New York, Macmillan, 1956+

With an alphabetical arrangement by states, this work
gives for each; election statistics for President and latest
vote for governor, state senators, congress, etc. (E157)

Bain, Richard C. Convention decision and voting records.
Washington, Brookings Institution, 1960. 327p.

A very useful compilation of informational and statistical
data on political convention developments.   (E158)

Burnham, Walter Dean. Presidential ballots, 1836-1892.
Baltimore, The Johns Hopkins Press, 1955. 956p.

This work contains a historical introduction that is followed
by tables showing distribution of votes by county, section
and state. It is a very useful compilation which precedes
in time Robinson's work. (E165)   (E159)

The electoral process. Durham, N.C., School of Law,
Duke University, 1962+

This publication deals basically with the problems in-
curred in election law.   (E160)

McKee, Thomas Hudson. The national conventions and platforms of all political parties, 1789-1905; convention, popular, and electoral vote. Also the political complexion of
both houses of Congress at each biennial period. 6th ed.,
rev. and enl. Baltimore, The Friedenwald Company, 1906.
418p.   (E161)

Petersen, Svend. A statistical history of the American presidential elections. New York, Ungar, c1963. 247p.

A new and valuable statistical record of American presidential elections with much informational data.   (E162)

Political party platforms. In presidential campaigns 1840 to
1904. Washington, D.C., Globe, 1904. 184p.   (E163)

Porter, Kirk Harold, comp.   National party platforms,
1840-1956.   Urbana, University of Illinois Press, 1960.
573p.

A collection of "authenticated copies of all the platforms of
the major parties, and of the principle minor parties."--
pref.   (E164)

Robinson, Edgar Eugene.   The presidential vote. 1896-1932.
Stanford, Calif., Stanford University Press, c1934.   403p.
(Sources: p. 379-399)   (E165)

---- ----.   The presidential vote, 1936.   Supplementing The
Presidential vote, 1896-1932.   Stanford, Calif., Stanford
University Press, c1940.   91p.   (E166)

Scarrow, Howard A.   Canada votes; a handbook of Federal
and Provincial election data.   New Orleans, Hauser Press,
1962.   238p.   (E167)

Elections

United States

Bean, Louis Hyman.   Ballot behavior; a study of presidential
elections.   Washington, D.C., American Council on Public
Affairs, c1940.   102p.   (E168)

Beman, Lamar Taney, comp.   Proportional representation.
New York, Wilson, 1925.   149p. (Bibliography: p. 15-24)
                                                            (E169)
Blanchard, Robert.   Presidential elections, 1948-1960.
With Richard Meyer and Blane Morley.   Salt Lake City,
Institute of Government, University of Utah, 1961. 58p.
(Bibliography: p. 53-58)   (E170)

Berelson, Bernard.   Voting; a study of opinion formation in
a presidential campaign.   With Paul F. Lazarsfeld and
William N. McPhee.   Chicago, University of Chicago
Press, 1954.   395p.   (E171)

Campbell, Angus.   The voter decides.   With Gerald Garin
and Warren E. Miller, with the assistance of Sylvia Eber-
hart and Robert O. McWilliams.   Evanston, Ill., Row,
Peterson, 1954.   242p.   (E172)

David, Paul Theodore.   Presidential nominating politics in

1952.   Prepared with Malcolm Moos and Ralph M. Gold-
man.   Baltimore, Johns Hopkins Press, 1954. 5v. (E173)

Gammon, Samuel Rhea.   Presidential campaign of 1837.
Baltimore, Johns Hopkins Press, 1922. 180p. (Bibliography: p. 171-174)   (E174)

Gosnell, Harold Foote.   Grass roots politics; national voting
behavior of typical states.   Washington, American Council
on Public Affairs, 1942.   195p. (References: p. 159-186)
                                                        (E175)
Jonas, Frank H., ed.   Western politics and the 1956 elections.   With essays by Frank H. Jonas and others.   Institute of Government, University of Utah, 1957. 95p. (E176)

Kornhauser, Arthur William.   When labor votes, a study of
auto workers.   With Harold L. Sheppard and Albert J.
Meyer.   New York, University Books, 1956. 352p. (E177)

Lazarsfeld, Paul Felix.   The people's choice; how the
voter makes up his mind in a presidential campaign.   With
Bernard Berelson and Hazel Gaudet.   2d ed.   New York,
Columbia University Press, c1948.   178p. (Bibliographical
references included in "footnotes" p. 159-173)   (E178)

Overacker, Louise.   The presidential primary.   New York,
Macmillan, 1926.   308p. (Bibliography: p. 277-294)
                                                        (E179)

Election Laws

Harris, Joseph Pratt.   Registration of voters in the United
States.   Washington, Brookings Institution, 1929. 390p.
(Select bibliography: p. 383-385)   (E180)

Jacobs, Milton C.   Political parties; election law provisions
and digest of cases.   New York, 1951. 149p.   (E181)

Smith, Constance E.   Voting and election laws; laws for
voters.   New York, Oceana Publications, 1960. 100p.
                                                        (E182)
U.S. Library of Congress. Legislative Reference Service.
Election law guidebook; summary of Federal and State laws
regulating the nomination of United States Senators. Washington, U.S. Govt. Print. Off., 1952+   (E183)

Money in Elections

Overacker, Louise.   Money in elections... largely from material collected by Victor J. West.   New York, Macmillan, 1932.   476p.   (Bibliography: p. 419-439)   (E184)

Shannon, Jasper Barry.   Money and politics.   New York, Random House, 1959.   126p.   (E185)

Suffrage

McCulloch, Albert Johnston.   Suffrage and its problems. Baltimore, Warwick and York, 1929.   185p. (References: p. 178-180)   (E186)

McGovney, Dudley Odell.   The American suffrage medley; the need for a national uniform suffrage.   Chicago, University of Chicago Press, 1949.   201p.   (E187)

Miller, George Frederick.   Absentee voters and suffrage laws.   Washington, Daylion, 1948.   224p. (References: p. 215-218)   (E188)

Foreign

Black, Duncan.   The theory of committees and elections. Cambridge, Eng., University Press, 1958. 211p.   (E189)

Butler, David E., ed.   Elections abroad.   By Philip M. Williams and others.   New York, St. Martin's Press, 1959.   280p.   (E190)

---- ----.   The electoral system in Britain; 1918-1951. Oxford, Clarendon Press, 1953.   222p. (Bibliography: p. 212-214)   (E191)

Degras, Henry Ernest.   How people vote; a study of electoral behaviour in Greenwich.   By Mark Benney, pseud., A. P. Gray and R. H. Dear.   London, Routledge & Paul; New York, Grove Press, 1956.   227p.   (E192)

Gosnell, Harold Foote.   Why Europe votes.   Chicago, University of Chicago Press, c1930.   247p.   (E193)

Gwyn, William B.   Democracy and the cost of politics in Britain.   London, University of London, Athlone Press, 1962.   256p.   (E194)

Smith, T. E.   Elections in developing countries; a study of
   electoral procedures used in tropical Africa, Southeast
   Asia and the British Caribbean.   New York, St. Martin's
   Press, 1960.   278p.   (E195)

CHAPTER VII

Political Theory

Political theory is basically concerned with the collective body of doctrines or principles related to man in a political context and the origin, form, behavior, and purpose of the state. The literature of political theory is largely in the form of essays or monographs setting forth individual concepts or complex doctrines related to observed or perceived political phenomena. Concomitant to individual concepts and doctrines has been a large body of literature dealing with criticism or historical analysis of aspects of political theory. This has been accompanied by descriptions and analyses of ideologies applied in actual practice. Although political theory is not a well-integrated body of doctrine, it does exhibit an evolutionary trend toward diversity as well as complexity. Two special works are particularly useful in their identification of the problems involved in the study and analysis of political theory.

Jenkin, Thomas Paul. The study of political theory. New York, Random House, 1961, c1955. 99p. (F1)

Miwa, Ralph M. Problems in political theory. With Jerzy Hauptman and Mulford Q. Sibley. Columbia, Bureau of Government Research, University of Missouri, 1961. 57p. (F2)

Classification of Political Theory

Smith and Zurcher, in their Dictionary of American Politics (C94), set up a somewhat arbitrary five-fold classification which will be useful here for the purpose of identification. This work also provides many excellent definitions of political concepts and doctrines.

Ethical

This class includes what is considered political philosophy or ethics and is fundamentally a branch of ethics.

144

Through the method of systematic analysis of common-sense notions and relevant data it is concerned with what ought to be in terms of political phenomena.

Speculative

Dealing with imaginative constructions of ideal or utopian states, this grouping includes such works as Plato's Republic, More's Utopia, and Campanella's City of the Sun.

Sociological

Belonging to a larger theory of society, sociological political theory deals with the state as a form of social organization or institution. As such, it utilizes analytical and empirical methods to determine the relation of the state to other aspects of society.

Legal

Legal political theory is largely concerned with the nature of law, the concept of sovereignty, and various legal situations that arise out of the institutions that distribute and conduct the exercise of political coercion or power.

Scientific

Through the empirical observation of political phenomena, this class of political theory attempts to ascertain probable trends, generalizations or laws which govern or regulate political behavior.

General Works

Collections

Abbott, Leonard Dalton, ed.   Masterworks of government; digests of 13 great classics.   Garden City, N.Y., Doubleday, 1947.   754p.   (F3)

Barker, Ernest, ed.   From Alexander to Constantine; passages and documents illustrating the history of social and political ideas, 336 B.C. to A.D. 337.   Oxford, Clarendon Press, 1956.   505p.   (F4)

Coker, Francis William.   Readings in political philosophy. New York, Macmillan, 1914.   573p. (Bibliography: p. 561-

566)   (F5)

Curtis, Michael, ed.   The great political theories.   New
    York, Avon Book Division, 1961-63.   2v.   (F6)

Leslie, Thomas Edward Cliffe.   Essays in political and mor-
    al philosophy.   Dublin, Hodges, Foster & Figgis, 1879.
    483p.   (F7)

Masters of political thought... Edited by Edward McChesney
    Sait.   Boston, New York, Houghton Mifflin, c1941+   (v.1.
    Plato to Machiavelli, v.2.   Machiavelli to Bentham, v.3.
    Hegel to Dewey)   (F8)

Utley, Thomas Edwin, ed.   Documents of modern political
    thought.   Edited with J. Stuart Maclure.   Cambridge, Eng.,
    University Press, 1957.   276p.   (F9)

Histories

Abbo, John A.   Political thought: men and ideas.   West-
    minster, Md., Newman Press, 1960.   452p.   (F10)

Bowle, John.   Western political thought.   New York, Oxford
    University Press, 1949+   (Bibliography: v.1, p. 454-461)
                                                                      (F11)
Brecht, Arnold.   Political theory; the foundations of twenti-
    eth-century political thought.   Princeton, Princeton Univer-
    sity Press, 1959.   603p.   (F12)

Catlin, George Edward Gordon.   The story of the political
    philosophers.   New York, McGraw-Hill, c1939.   802p.
                                                                      (F13)
Cook, Thomas Era.   History of political philosophy from
    Plato to Burke.   New York, Prentice-Hall, 1936.   725p.
                                                                      (F14)
Dunning, William Archibald.   A history of political theories,
    ancient and medieval.   New York, Macmillan, 1902.
    360p.   (F15)

---- ----.   A history of political theories from Luther to
    Montesquieu.   New York, Macmillan, 1905.   459p. (Bibli-
    ography: p. 435-448)   (F16)

---- ----.   A history of political theories from Rousseau to
    Spencer.   New York, Macmillan, 1920.   446p. (Bibliogra-
    phy: p. 425-436)   (F17)

Ebenstein, William, ed.   Great political thinkers, Plato to
   the present.   New York, Rinehart, 1951.   903p.   (F18)

---- ----, ed.   Modern political thought, the great issues.
   New York, Rinehart, 1954.   806p.   (F19)

Engelmann, Geza.   Political philosophy from Plato to Jeremy Bentham.   New York, Harper, 1927.   398p. (Bibliographical note: p. 384-386)   (F20)

Farrell, Henry Percy.   Introduction to political philosophy.
   New York, Longmans, Green, 1917.   220p.   (Bibliography:
   p. 204-205)   (F21)

Field, Guy Cromwell.   Political theory.   New York, Barnes
   & Noble, 1956?   297p.   (F22)

Gierke, Otto Friedrich von.   The development of political
   theory.   New York, Norton, c1939.   364p.   (F23)

Greaves, Harold Richard Goring.   The foundations of political theory.   London, Allen & Unwin, 1958.   208p.   (F24)

Grimes, Alan Pendleton, ed.   Modern political ideologies.
   Edited with Robert H. Horwitz.   New York, Oxford University Press, 1959.   535p.   (F25)

Hacker, Andrew.   Political theory: philosophy, ideology,
   science.   New York, Macmillan, 1961.   612p.   (F26)

Hallowell, John Hamilton.   Main currents in modern political thought.   New York, Holt, c1950.   759p.   (F27)

Harmon, Mont Judd.   Political thought, from Plato to the
   present.   New York, McGraw-Hill, c1964.   469p.   (F28)

Hearnshaw, Fossey John Cobb.   The development of political ideas.   New York, T. Nelson, 1937.   151p. (Bibliography: p. 147-149)   (F29)

Heater, Derek Benjamin.   Political ideas in the modern
   world.   New York, Barnes & Noble, 1962, c1960.   (F30)

Herz, John H.   Political realism and political idealism, a
   study of theories and realities.   Chicago, University of
   Chicago Press, 1951.   275p.   (F31)

Hsiao, Kung-Chuan.   Political pluralism; a study in contemporary political theory.   New York, Harcourt, Brace,
1927.   271p.   (Bibliography: p. 264-271)   (F32)

Joad, Cyrin Edwin Mitchinson.   Introduction to modern political theory.   Oxford, Clarendon Press, 1924.   127p. (Bibliography: p. 124-127)   (F33)

Lane, Robert Edwards.   Political ideology: why the American common man believes the way he does.   New York,
Free Press of Glencoe, 1962. 509p.   (F34)

McCoy, Charles Nicholas Reiten.   The structure of political
thought, a study in the history of political ideas.   New
York, McGraw-Hill, 1963. 323p.   (F35)

McDonald, Lee Cameron.   Western political theory: the
modern age.   New York, Harcourt, Brace & World, 1962.
557p.   (F36)

McIlwain, Charles Howard.   The growth of political thought
in the West, from the Greeks to the end of the middle
ages.   New York, Macmillan, 193?.   417p.   (F37)

Maxey, Chester Collins.   Political philosophies.   2d ed.
New York, Macmillan, 1948. 712p.   (F38)

Merriam, Charles Edward, ed.   A history of political theories, recent times; essays on contemporary developments
in political theory... Ed. with Harry Elmer Barnes.   New
York, Macmillan, 1935.   597p.   (F39)

Morris, Charles Richard.   History of political ideas.   London, Christophers, 1924.   190p. (Bibliography: p. 185-187)
                                                     (F40)
Murray, Alexander Rainy Maclean.   An introduction to political philosophy.   New York, Philosophical Library, 1953.
240p.   (F41)

Parkinson, Cyril Northcote.   The evolution of political
thought.   Boston, Houghton Mifflin, 1958. 327p.   (F42)

Roucek, Joseph Slabey, ed.   Contemporary political ideologies.   New York, Philosophical Library, 1961. 470p.
                                                     (F43)
Sabine, George Holland.   A history of political theory.   3d
ed. New York, Holt, Rinehart and Winston, 1961.

948p.   (F44)

Srivastava, I. N.   A hand book of political science theory.
   Delhi, Malhotra Bros., 1951?   286p.   (F45)

Strauss, Leo, ed.   History of political philosophy.   Edited
   with Joseph Cropsey.   Chicago, Rand McNally, 1963.
   790p.   (F46)

Vaughn, Charles Edwin.   Studies in the history of political
   philosophy before and after Rousseau.   New York, Longmans, Green, 1925.   2v.   (F47)

Wasserman, Louis.   Handbook of political "isms."   New
   York, Association Press, 1941.   147p.   (Selected readings:
   p. 132-147)   (F48)

Wolin, Sheldon S.   Politics and vision; continuity and innovation in western political thought.   Boston, Little, Brown,
   1960.   529p.   (F49)

Regions

American Political Theory

Fiske, John.   American political ideas viewed from the
   standpoint of history.   New York, Houghton Mifflin, 1911.
   196p.   (F50)

Grimes, Alan Pendleton.   American political thought.   Rev.
   ed.   New York, Holt, Rinehart and Winston, 1960.   556p.
                                                               (F51)
Hartz, Louis.   The liberal tradition in America; an interpretation of American political thought since the revolution.
   New York, Harcourt, Brace, 1955.   329p.   (F52)

Jacobson, Jacob Mark.   Development of American political
   thought, a documentary history.   2d ed.   New York, Appleton-Century-Crofts, 1961.   659p.   (F53)

Jenks, Jeremiah Whipple.   Principles of politics from the
   viewpoint of the American citizen.   New York, Columbia
   University Press, 1909.   187p.   (Bibliography: p. xvii-
   xviii)   (F54)

Scott, Andrew MacKay.   Political thought in America.   New
   York, Rinehart, 1959.   668p.   (F55)

Wilson, Francis Graham. The American political mind; a textbook in political theory. New York, McGraw-Hill, 1949. 506p.   (F56)

Wright, Benjamin Fletcher, ed. A source book of American political theory. New York, Macmillan, 1929. 644p.(F57)

Chinese Political Theory

Lin, Mou-sheng. Men and ideas, an informal history of Chinese political thought. New York, John Day, c1942. 256p. (Bibliography: p. 239-244)   (F58)

Pott, William Sumner Appleton. Chinese political philosophy. New York, Knopf, 1925. 110p.   (F59)

Thomas, Elbert Duncan. Chinese political thought; a study based upon the theories of the principal thinkers of the Chou period. New York, Prentice-Hall, 1927. 317p. (Bibliography: p. 310)   (F60)

English Political Theory

Brinton, Clarence Crane. English political thought in the 19th century. New York, Harper, 1962. 318p.   (F61)

---- ----. Political ideas of the English romanticists. London, Oxford University Press, 1926. 242p.   (F62)

Davidson, William Leslie. Political thought in England; the Utilitarians from Bentham to J.S. Mill. New York, Holt, 1916. 256p. (Bibliography: p. 252-253)   (F63)

Hearnshaw, Fossey John Cobb, ed. The social & political ideas of some English thinkers of the Augustan age, 1650-1750. New York, Barnes & Noble, 1950. 246p.   (F64)

Laski, Harold Joseph. Political thought in England from Locke to Bentham. New York, Holt, c1920. 323p. (Bibliography: p. 317-320)   (F65)

Rockow, Lewis. Contemporary political thought in England. London, Parsons, 1925. 335p. (Bibliography: p. 319-323)   (F66)

French Political Theory

Hearnshaw, Fossey John Cobb, ed. The social & political
ideas of some great French thinkers of the Age of Reason.
New York, Barnes & Noble, 1950. 251p.   (F67)

Martin, Kingsley. French liberal thought in the eighteenth
century; a study of political ideas from Bayle to Condor-
cet. London, E. Benn, 1929. 313p. (Bibliographical
note: p. 307-308)   (F68)

Mayer, Jacob Peter. Political thought in France from the
Revolution to the Fifth Republic.   3d ed.   London, Routledge & Paul, 1961. 152p.   (F69)

Muret, Charlotte (Tonzalia) French royalist doctrines since
the Revolution. New York, Columbia University Press,
1937. 326p. (Bibliography: p. 305-320)   (F70)

Soltau, Roger Henry. French political thought in the nineteenth century. London, E. Benn, 1931. 500p. (Bibliographical foreword: p. xv-xvi)   (F71)

German Political Theory

Aris, Reinhold. History of political thought in Germany:
from 1789-1815. London, Allen & Unwin, 1936. 414p.
                                                (F72)
Butz, Otto. Modern German political theory. Garden City,
N.Y., Doubleday, 1955. 72p.   (F73)

Dewey, John. German philosophy and politics. New York,
Holt, 1915. 134p.   (F74)

Reiss, Hans Siegbert, ed. The political thought of the German romantics, 1793-1815. New York, Macmillan, 1955.
                                                (F75)

Hindu Political Theory

Brown, Donald Mackenzie. The white umbrella; Indian political thought from Manu to Gandhi. Berkeley, University of
California Press, 1953. 205p.   (F76)

Sarkar, Benoy Kumar. The political institutions and theories of the Hindus. Leipzig, Markert & Petters, 1922.
242p. (Authorities consulted: p. xiii-xxiv)   (F77)

Italian Political Theory

Villari, Luigi.   Development of political ideas in Italy in the
   nineteenth century.   London, Oxford University Press,
   1926.   30p.   (F78)

Concepts and Doctrines of Political Theory

   Concepts and doctrines form the basic substance of
political theory.   They are ideas concerning some aspect of
political phenomena that may or may not bear any relation
to fact.   Intrinsically a political concept is a mental tool
that will allow man to understand and exercise control over
the social universe of politics.   Political doctrines are carefully worked out principles which, in many cases, use com-
binations of political concepts.   This section will include the
major categories of political concepts and doctrines, accompanied by brief statements or definitions and followed by a
few representative works.

Concepts of Political Entities

   Political entities are the subjects that have been frequently conceptualized throughout the history of western political thought.   The most often treated of these subjects have
been MAN and the STATE.

Man

   The generic unit or element in all politics is man.
As a consequence of this, he has been the focal point of political theorists since before the time of the classical Greek
political philosophers.

Berggrav, Eivind Josef.   Man and the state; translated from
   the Norwegian by George Aus.   Philadelphia, Muhlenberg
   Press, 1951.   319p.   (F79)

Corbett, Thomas Albert, Sister.   People or masses: a comparative study in political theory.   Washington, Catholic
   University of America Press, 1956.   241p. (Bibliography:
   p. 217-237)   (F80)

Ebenstein, William, ed.   Man and the state; modern political ideas.   New York, Rinehart, 1947.   781p. (Bibliographical notes: p. 747-776)   (F81)

Hocking, William Ernest. Man and the state. New Haven,
    Yale University Press, 1926. 463p.   (F82)

Hoffman, Frank Sargent. Sphere of the state; or, the people
    as a body-politic. New York, Putnam, 1894. 275p. (F83)

Maritain, Jacques. Man and the state. Chicago, Univer-
    sity of Chicago Press, 1951. 219p.   (F84)

  Political Authority

    The concept of political authority implies legitimacy
of action. It consists of the legal coercive power usually
vested in the state or public agency to enable its officers to
execute its functions.

Friedrich, Carl Joachim, ed. Authority. Edited by Carl J.
    Friedrich for the American Society of Political and Legal
    Philosophy. Cambridge, Mass., Harvard University Press,
    1958. 234p.   (F85)

Green, Thomas Hill. Lectures on the principles of political
    obligation. New York, Longmans, Green, 1901. 252p.
                                                          (F86)
Hollister, William Wallace. Government and the arts of
    obedience. New York, King's Crown Press, 1948. 139p.
    (Bibliography: p. 131-134)   (F87)

Simon, Yves. Nature and functions of authority. Milwaukee,
    Marquette University Press, 1940. 78p.   (F88)

Willoughby, Westel Woodbury. The ethical basis of political
    authority. New York, Macmillan, 1930. 460p.   (F89)

  Political Community

    A political community consists of a group of people
who live together in the same locality, having orginated as
a family group or tribal village. From this type of organization, customs and rules finally resulted in the formation
of a governmental structure. Although each viewed the political community differently, Plato and Aristotle agreed that
man's reason made him capable of establishing the good
state or community.

DeGrazia, Sebastian. The political community, a study of
    anomie. Chicago, University of Chicago Press, 1948.

258p.   (F90)

Friedrich, Carl Joachim, ed.   Community.   New York,
  Liberal Arts Press, 1959.   243p.   (F91)

Gentile, Giovanni.   Genesis and structure of society.   Tr.
  by H.S. Harris.   Urbana, University of Illinois Press,
  1960.   228p.   (F92)

Holcombe, Arthur Norman.   The foundations of the modern
  commonwealth.   New York, Harper, 1923.   491p.   (F93)

Lipmann, Walter.   An inquiry into the principles of the good
  society.   Boston, Little, Brown, 1937.   402p.   (F94)

Strausz-Hupé, Robert.   Power and community.   New York,
  Praeger, 1956.   134p.   (F95)

Political Power

        Force and consent are the basic elements of political
power and are most always used in relation to authority and
the state.

Hook, Sidney.   Political power and personal freedom; critical studies in democracy, communism, and civil rights.
  New York, Criterion Books, 1959.   462p.   (F96)

Jouvenel, Bertrand de.   On power, its nature and the history of its growth.   New York, Viking Press, 1949, c1948.
  421p.   (F97)

Lasswell, Harold Dwight.   Power and society; a framework
  for political inquiry.   With Abraham Kaplan.   New Haven,
  Yale University Press, 1950.   295p. (Bibliography: p.
  285-286)   (F98)

Loewenstein, Karl.   Political power and the governmental
  process.   Chicago, University of Chicago Press, 1957.
  442p.   (F99)

Merriam, Charles Edward.   Political power, its composition and incidence.   New York, McGraw-Hill, c1934.
  331p.   (F100)

Mills, Charles Wright.   Power, politics and people: the
  collected essays of C. Wright Mills.   Ed. by Irving E.

Horowitz. New York, Oxford University Press, 1963.
657p.   (F101)

Moore, Barrington. Political power and social theory; six
studies. Cambridge, Harvard University Press, 1958.
215p.   (F102)

Russell, Bertrand Russell. Power, a new social analysis.
New York, Norton, c1938. 315p.   (F103)

A Study of power... Essays by Harold D. Lasswell, Charles
E. Merriam, and T. V. Smith. Glencoe, Ill., Free Press,
1950. 3v. in 1.   (F104)

The State

Second only to the consideration of man, the state
possesses none of man's physical qualities and is treated
primarily in conjunction with other political concepts. For
the most part, the state legally exists when a politically organized body of people occupy a definite territory and habitu-
ally obey the same government which is entirely or almost
completely free from external control, i. e. a government
that possesses both external and internal sovereignty.

Bosanquet, Bernard. The philosophical theory of the state.
New York, Macmillan, 1899. 342p.   (F105)

Botero, Giovanni. The reason of the state. Tr. by P. J.
and D. P. Weley: and The greatness of cities. Tr. by
Robert Peterson, 1606. New Haven, Yale University
Press, 1956. 298p.   (F106)

Cassirer, Ernst. The myth of the state. New Haven, Yale
University Press, c1946. 303p.   (F107)

Coker, Francis William. Organismic theories of the state;
nineteenth century interpretations of the state as organism
or as person. New York, Columbia University, Longmans,
Green, 1910. 209p. (Bibliography: p. 205-209)   (F108)

Dealey, James Quayle. Development of the state, its governmental organization and its activities. New York,
Silver, Burdett, c1909. 343p. (Bibliography: p. 315-326)
                                                        (F109)
Fabre d'Olivet, Antoine. Hermeneutic interpretation of the
origin of the social state of man and the destiny of the

Adamic race. New York, Putnam, 1915. 548p. (F110)

Ford, Henry Jones. Natural history of the state: an intro-
duction to political science. Princeton, N. J., Princeton
University Press, 1915. 188p. (Authorities: p. 179-182)
(F111)

Long, Norton E. The polity. Edited with and introd. by
Charles Press. Chicago, Rand McNally, 1962. 247p.
(F112)

Lowie, Robert Harry. The origin of the state. New York,
Harcourt, Brace, c1927. 117p.   (F113)

Mabbott, John David. The state and the citizen; an introduction to political philosophy. London, Hutchinson University Library, 1958. 183p.   (F114)

MacIver, Robert Morrison. The modern state. Oxford,
The Clarendon Press, 1926. 504p.   (F115)

Mattern, Johannes. Concepts of state, sovereignty and international law, with special reference to the juristic conception of the state. Baltimore, The Johns Hopkins Press,
1928. 200p. (Bibliography: p. 190-194)   (F116)

Neumann, Franz Leopold. The democratic and the authoritarian state; essays in political and legal theory. Ed. by
Herbert Marcuse. Glencoe, Ill., Free Press, 1957.
303p. (Bibliography: p. 301-303)   (F117)

Nock, Albert Jay. Our enemy the state. New York, Morrow, 1935. 209p.   (F118)

Oppenheimer, Franz. The state; its history and development viewed sociologically. Tr. by John M. Gitterman.
Indianapolis, Bobbs-Merrill, c1914. 302p.   (F119)

Pitamic, Leonid. A treatise on the state. Baltimore, J.H.
Furst, 1933. 301p. (Bibliography: p. 293-294)   (F120)

Watkins, Frederick Mundell. The state as a concept of political science. New York, Harper, 1934. 84p.   (F121)

Weldon, Thomas Dewar. States and morals, a study in political conflicts. London, J. Murray, 1962. 302p. (F122)

Wilde, Norman. Ethical basis of the state. Princeton,
N. J., Princeton University Press, 1924. 236p. (Bibliog-

graphy: p. 229-234)   (F123)

Willoughby, Westel Woodbury.   An examination of the nature
of the state.   A study in political philosophy.   New York,
Macmillan, 1896.   448p.   (F124)

Wilson, Woodrow.   The state.   Elements of historical and
practical politics.   A sketch of institutional history and administration.   Boston, D. C. Heath, 1889.   686p.   (F125)

Woolsey, Theodore Dwight.   Political science; or, the state
theoretically and practically considered.   New York, Scribner, 1905.   2v.   (F126)

Concepts and Doctrines Concerning Relationships Among Entities

Many individual political concepts are treated collectively with the interrelationships receiving major emphasis.
These relationships can take the form of (1) those defining
relationships in terms of coercion or power, (2) those dealing with distributive formulas, and (3) those concerned with
social change.   Political doctrine may be equated with ideology.   A system of political doctrine usually refers to a well
worked out or logical set of political principles or concepts
put into actual practice.   Contained in this section is a representative set of political concepts and doctrines accompanied by a short explanation or definition and followed by a
listing of works.

Anarchism

Anarchism is a political theory that opposes all forms
of government and governmental interference and supports
voluntary cooperation and free association of individuals and
groups in order to satisfy needs and desires.

Bakunin, Mikhail Aleksandrovich.   The political philosophy of
Bakunin: scientific anarchism.   Comp. and ed. by G. P.
Maximoff.   Glencoe, Ill. , Free Press, 1953.   434p. (F127)

Madariaga, Salvador de.   Anarchy or hierarchy.   London,
Allen & Unwin, 1937.   244p.   (F128)

Authoritarianism

Authoritarian thought deals with distribution of su-

preme authority without legal responsibility to the one or few
within a political system.

Hogben, Lancelot Thomas.   New authoritarianism.   London,
    Watts, 1949.   44p.   (F129)

Metz, Harold William.   Authoritarianism and the individual.
    With Charles A. H. Thompson.   Washington, Brookings In-
    stitution, 1950.   371p.   (F130)

Conservatism

    A political doctrine which opposes change and is based
on a strong awareness of tradition and social stability.   Conservatism stresses the importance of established institutions
and basic concepts.

Auerbach, M. Morton.   The conservative illusion.   New
    York, Columbia University Press, 1959.   359p.   (Bibliog-
    raphy: p. 333-337)   (F131)

Viereck, Peter Robert Edwin.   Conservatism: from John
    Adams to Churchill.   Princeton, N. J. , Van Nostrand,
    1956.   192p.   (F132)

Democracy

    Although democratic thought may exhibit many diverse
viewpoints, it is concerned mostly with participation by the
governed in the policy making process of the state.

Babbitt, Irving.   Democracy and leadership.   Boston and
    New York, Houghton Mifflin, 1924.   349p.   (Bibliography:
    p. 337-344)   (F133)

Bingham, Alfred Mitchell.   The techniques of democracy.
    New York, Duell, Sloan and Pearce, 1942.   314p.   (F134)

Burns, Cecil Delisle.   Democracy, its defects and advan-
    tages.   London, Allen & Unwin, 1929.   217p.   (Bibliogra-
    phy: p. 213)   (F135)

Dahl, Robert Alan.   A preface to democratic theory.   Chi-
    cago, University of Chicago Press, 1956. 155p.   (F136)

Giddings, Franklin Henry.   Democracy and empire; with
    studies of their psychological, economic, and moral foun-

dations. New York, Macmillan, 1900. 363p.   (F137)

Hobhouse, Leonard Trelawney. Democracy and reaction.
New York, Putnam, 1905. 244p.   (F138)

Lecky, William Edward Hortpole. Democracy and liberty.
New York, Longmans, Green, 1900. 2v.   (F139)

Madariaga, Salvador de. Democracy versus liberty? The
faith of a liberal heretic. London, Pall Mall Press, 1938.
124p.   (F140)

Smith, Thomas Vernor. The democratic way of life. Chicago, University of Chicago Press, c1926. 210p. (F141)

Distribution of Rights and Duties

A large portion of the literature has been concerned
with the concepts and interrelations of the distribution of
rights and duties. Included within this area are ideas of
status and contract, liberties and obligation, consent and
compromise and the distribution of material goods.

Abbott, Lyman. Rights of man; a study in twentieth century
problems. Boston, Houghton Mifflin, 1901. 375p. (F142)

Jellinck, Georg. Declaration of the rights of man and of
citizens. New York, Holt, 1901. 98p.   (F143)

Ritchie, David George. Natural rights, a criticism of some
political and ethical conceptions. New York, Macmillan,
1895. 304p.   (F144)

Fascism

An authoritarian political doctrine evolved and put into practice by Benito Mussolini and his followers in Italy
after 1922. Under this type of political system all social,
economic and political processes are subordinated to the
goals and purposes of the state, which maintains rigid control over them.

Ashton, E. B. The fascist: his state and his mind. New
York, Morrow, c1937. 320p.   (F145)

Ebenstein, William. The nazi state. New York, Farrar &
Rinehart, c1943. 355p.   (F146)

McGovern, William Montgomery.   From Luther to Hitler;
the history of fascist-nazi political philosophy.   Boston,
Houghton Mifflin, c1941.   683p.   (F147)

Schapiro, Jacob Salwyn.   Liberalism and the challenge of
fascism: social forces in England and France, 1815-1870.
New York, McGraw-Hill, 1949.   421p.   (Bibliography: p.
405-413)   (F148)

Schneider, Herbert Wallace.   Making the fascist state.   New
York, Oxford University Press, 1928.   392p. (Bibliography: p. 365-385)   (F149)

Internationalism

        A political doctrine that world peace can best be ob-
tained by the friendly cooperation of all nations on a basis of
equality without the sacrifice of national character for the se-
curing and maintenance of international justice is called internationalism.

Grinnell College, Grinnell, Iowa.   Internationalism and democracy.   Essays: personal, historical and political in
memory of Charles E. Payne.   Syracuse, N.Y., Syracuse
University Press, 1950, 1949.   185p.   (F150)

Strogoff, Stephen, pseud.   Escape from Moscow: the diary
of a Russian student.   Tr. from the French by Lancelot C.
Sheppard.   London, A. Barker, 1955.   172p.   (F151)

Liberty and Liberalism

        Although separate concepts, liberty and liberalism are
somewhat related in the sense that one's ability to make
choices within the sphere of politics can and often does involve change which is the basis of liberal thought.

American Society of Political and Legal Philosophy.   Liberty.
Ed. by Carl J. Friedrich.   New York, Atherton Press,
1962.   333p.   (F152)

Benett, William.   Freedom and liberty.   New York, Oxford
University Press, 1920.   367p.   (F153)

Bullock, Alan Louis Charles, ed.   The liberal tradition:
from Fox to Keynes.   Ed. with Maurice Shock.   Washington Square,   New York, New York University Press,

288p.   (F154)

Carlyle, Alexander James.   Political liberty, a history of
the conception in the middle ages and modern times. New
York, Barnes & Noble, 1963.   220p.   (F155)

Center for the Study of Democratic Institutions.   The power
of reason.   Santa Barbara, Calif., 1963.   93p.   (F156)

Kallen, Horace Meyer.   A study of liberty.   Yellow Springs,
Ohio, Antioch Press, 1959.   151p.   (F157)

Lieber, Francis.   On civil liberty and self-government. 3d
ed.   Philadelphia, Lippincott, 1874.   622p.   (F158)

Taylor, Overton H.   Classical liberalism, Marxism, and the
twentieth century.   Cambridge, Harvard University Press,
1960.   122p.   (F159)

Watkins, Frederick Mundell.   The political tradition of the
west; a study in the development of modern liberalism.
Cambridge, Harvard University Press, c 1948. 368p.
                                                   (F160)

Social Contract

        Social Contract is a political notion that man once ex-
isted in a state of nature and later, through mutual agree-
ment, organized society with certain rights that were to be
granted and protected by government.

Barker, Ernest, ed.   The social contract; essays by Locke,
Hume and Rousseau.   New York, Oxford University Press,
1962.   307p.   (F161)

Gough, John Wiedhofft.   The social contract; a critical study
of its development.   Oxford, Clarendon Press, 1936. 234p.
                                                   (F162)

Socialism

        The primary and utopian tenet of this type of political
doctrine is the concept of social ownership of the state's
productive mechanism and production for use instead of prof-
it.   There are a number of variations on this theme.   Marxism is predicated upon the concept of economic determinism
and of the idea that ownership and distribution of property
should have a controlling influence in formulating the nature
and purpose of human relationships and institutions.   Russian

communism and bolshevism are also derived from socialism
and are socio-political theories that advocate violent transition to social ownership of all means of production. Governmental power is to be entrusted to a dictatorship of the pro-
letariat and is eventually supposed to wither away. Actual
practice has shown that control is exercised by a closely
knit, oligarchically regulated class conscious party.

Almond, Gabriel. The appeals of communism. With Her-
bert E. Kingman, Elizabeth Lewin and Havord Wriggins.
Princeton, N. J., Princeton University Press, 1954. 415p.
(F163)

Anderson, Thornton. Masters of Russian Marxism. New
York, Appleton-Century-Crofts, 1963. 296p. (F164)

Bernstein, Eduard. Evolutionary socialism; a criticism and
affirmation. Tr. by Edith C. Harvey. New York,
Schocken Books, 1961. 224p. (F165)

Buber, Martin. Paths in Utopia. Tr. by R. F. C. Hull.
Boston, Beacon Hill, 1958, c1949. 152p. (F166)

Cohen, Carl, ed. Communism, fascism, and democracy,
the theoretical foundations. New York, Random House,
1962. 704p. (F167)

Dilas, Milovan. The new class; an analysis of the communist system. New York, Praeger, 1957. 214p. (F168)

Ebenstein, William. Today's isms. 4th ed. Englewood
Cliffs, N. J., Prentice-Hall, 1964. 243p. (F169)

Gay, Peter. The dilemma of democratic socialism: Eduard
Bernstein's challenge to Marx. New York, Columbia Uni-
versity Press, 1952. 334p. (Bibliography: p. 303-315)
(F170)

Hook, Sidney. Marx and the Marxists; the ambiguous leg-
acy. Princeton, N. J., Van Nostrand, 1955. 254p. (F171)

Hunt, Robert Nigel Carew. A guide to communist jargon.
New York, Macmillan, 1957. 169p. (F172)

---- ----. The theory and practice of communism. 5th ed.
New York, Macmillan, 1957. 286p. (F173)

Kelsen, Hans. The political theory of Bolshevism; a critical analysis. Berkeley, University of California Press,

1948.   60p.   (Select bibliography: p. 59)   (F174)

Leites, Nathan Constantin.   A study of Bolshevism.   Glencoe, Ill., Free Press, 1953.   639p.   (F175)

Marcuse, Herbert.   Soviet Marxism, a critical analysis.
New York, Columbia University Press, 1958. 271p. (F176)

Mills, Charles Wright.   The Marxists.   New York, Dell
Pub. Co., 1962.   480p.   (F177)

Ulam, Adam Bruno.   The unfinished revolution; an essay on
the sources and influence of Marxism and communism.
New York, Random House, 1960.   307p.   (F178)

Sovereignty

In its pristine sense, sovereignty refers to the highest or supreme power over citizens or individuals. With regard to politics this power is considered the legitimate pos-
session of the state or its agencies.

Jouvenel, Bertrand de.   Sovereignty; an inquiry into the political good.   Tr. by T. F. Huntington.   Chicago, University of Chicago Press, 1957.   319p.   (F179)

Laski, Harold Joseph.   The foundations of sovereignty, and
other essays.   New Haven, Yale University Press, 1931.
317p.   (F180)

Merriam, Charles Edward.   History of the theory of sovereignty since Rousseau.   New York, Columbia University
Press, 1900.   232p.   (Bibliography: p. 228-232)   (F181)

Riesenberg, Peter N.   Inalienability of sovereignty in med-
ieval political thought.   New York, Columbia University
Press, 1956, c1955.   204p.   (Bibliography: p. 179-193)
                                                       (F182)
Ward, Paul William.   Sovereignty, a study of a contempo-
rary political notion.   London, Routledge, 1928.   201p.
(Bibliography: p. 191-201)   (F183)

Syndicalism

This is a socio-political theory espoused by a number
of revolutionary labor movements which stresses direct economic action (e. g. strikes) with all means of production and

distribution under the control of loose federations of labor
unions.

Elliott, William Yandell.   The pragmatic revolt in politics;
    syndicalism, fascism, and the constitutional state.   New
    York, Macmillan, 1928.   540p.   (F184)

Rocker, Rudolf.   Anarcho-Syndicalism.   London, Secker and
    Warburg, 1938.   158p.   (Bibliography: p. 155-158) (F185)

Sorel, Georges.   Reflections on violence.   Tr. by T. E.
    Hulme and J. Roth.   Glencoe, Ill., Free Press, 1950.
    311p.   (F186)

Totalitarianism

        This is a form of authoritarianism that is of modern
derivation, in which nearly every aspect of the individual's
life is directed or controlled by the state.

American Academy of Arts and Sciences, Boston.   Totalitar-
    ianism; proceedings of a conference... Ed. by Carl J.
    Friedrich.   Cambridge, Harvard University Press, 1954.
    386p.   (F187)

Arendt, Hannah.   The origins of totalitarianism.   2d ed.
    New York, Meridian Books, 1958.   520p.   (F188)

Ebenstein, William.   Totalitarianism: new perspectives.
    New York, Holt, Rinehart & Winston, 1962.   80p. (F189)

Utilitarianism

        This is the political doctrine which indicates that the
useful is good and that right conduct is the usefulness of its
consequences.   Also inherent in utilitarian philosophy is the
belief that the aim of moral action is the largest possible
balance of pleasure over pain or, in other words, the greatest happiness for the greatest number of people.

MacKaye, James.   Politics of utility.   Boston, Little, Brown,
    1906.   179p.   (F190)

Plamenatz, John Petrov.   Mill's Utilitarianism, reprinted
    with a study of the English utilitarians.   Oxford, Black-
    well, 1949.   228p.   (F191)

Stephen, Leslie.   The English utilitarians.   New York, P.
   Smith, 1950.   3v. in 1.   (F192)

Concepts and Doctrines of Governmental Institutions

Many political concepts and doctrines are related to
the origin and development of governmental institutions.
Some are mostly concerned with the functions of different
governmental institutions; others concentrate on the relationship between the various types of governmental structures.

Constitutionalism

This is a political doctrine that embodies the belief
that governmental power should be limited by means of a
fundamental law in order that the basic constitutional rights
of individuals or groups will not be violated.

Friedrich, Carl Joachim.   Constitutional government and politics; nature and development.   New York, Harper, 1937.
   591p.   (Bibliography: p. 501-570)   (F193)

Strong, Charles Frederick.   Modern political constitutions;
   an introduction to the comparative study of their history
   and existing form.   New York, Putnam, 1930.   385p.
   (Books recommended: p. xiii-xviii)   (F194)

Federalism

Federalism is a political doctrine relative to a type
of governmental organization which allows independent states
to combine under a central government while retaining a portion of their former power and identity.

Bowie, Robert Richardson, ed.   Studies in federalism.   Ed.
   with Carl J. Friedrich.   Boston, Little, Brown, 1954.
   887p.   (Bibliography: p. 855-870)   (F195)

Macmahon, Arthur Whittier, ed.   Federalism mature and
   emergent.   Garden City, N.Y., Doubleday, 1955. 537p.
                                                               (F196)
Mogi, Sobel.   The problems of federalism; a study in the
   history of political theory.   London, Allen & Unwin, 1931.
   2v.   (Bibliography: p. 1117-1140)   (F197)

Separation of Powers

This is a concept concerning the allocation of law-making, enforcing and interpreting the functions of government to different groups in order to eliminate the tyranny that was supposed to result from joining legislative, executive and judicial powers in the same individual or group.

Bondy, William. Separation of governmental powers. New York, Sabiston, Murray, 1893. 129p.   (F198)

Vanderbilt, Arthur T. Doctrine of the separation of powers and its present-day significance. Lincoln, University of Nebraska Press, 1953. 144p.   (F199)

Special Topics or Movements

There is a rather nebulous area in the study of political concepts and doctrines that does not fit expressly in any of the previously listed categories. Consequently, they have been placed in a separate section.

Dictatorship

A dictatorship is a type of government where the absolute power of the state is vested in one person or a small clique.

Cobban, Alfred. Dictatorship: its history and theory. New York, Scribner, 1939. 352p.   (F200)

Gooch, George Peabody. Dictatorship in theory and practice. London, Watts, 1935. 50p.   (F201)

Kellett, Ernest Edward. The story of dictatorship from the earliest times till today. New York, E. P. Dutton, 1937. 231p.   (F202)

Sforza, Carlo. European dictatorship. New York, Brentano's, 1931. 257p.   (F203)

Political Ethics

Much has been written concerning the relationship of moral or ethical principles to politics. Since Plato and Aristotle, political and ethical principles have been closely interwoven into the fabric of political thought.

Carritt, Edgar Frederick.   Ethical and political thinking.
    Oxford, Eng. , Clarendon Press, 1947. 186p.   (F204)

Gordis, Robert.   Politics and ethics.   Santa Barbara, Calif. ,
    Center for the Study of Democratic Institutions, 1961.
    36p.   (F205)

Lieber, Francis.   Manual of political ethics, designed
    chiefly for the use of colleges and students at law. Phila-
    delphia, Lippincott, 1911.   2v.   (F206)

Ritchie, David George.   Studies in political and social ethics.
    New York, Macmillan, 1902.   283p.   (F207)

Robinson, Daniel Sommer.   Political ethics; an application
    of ethical principles to political relations.   New York,
    Crowell, c1935.   288p.   (F208)

Reform Movements

        Throughout the history of civilization, man has sought
to alter his situation to satisfy basic needs and desires. Reform movements have played a great part in the adjustment
of civilization to meet the political needs of man.

Davis, Jerome.   Contemporary social movements.   New
    York, Century, c1930.   901p.   (F209)

Schapiro, Jacob Salwyn.   Social reform and the reformation.
    New York, Columbia University, Longmans, Green, 1909.
    160p. (Bibliography: p. 154-160)   (F210)

---- ----.   The world in crisis; political and social move-
    ments in the twentieth century.   New York, McGraw-Hill,
    1950.   429p. (Bibliography: p. 411-419)   (F211)

Revolution

        As a part of political change, revolutions have been
the vehicles of gradual and many times violent change of political systems.

Carr, Edward Hallett.   Studies in revolution.   London, F.
    Cass, 1962.   i. e. 1963. 226p.   (F212)

Edwards, Lyford Paterson.   The natural history of revolu-
    tion.   Chicago, University of Chicago Press, 1927.

229p.   (F213)

Hildreth, Richard.   Theory of politics: an inquiry into the
    foundations of governments, and the causes and progress
    of political revolutions.   New York, Harper, 1854. 274p.
                                                                     (F214)

Sociology, Social Science and Political Theory

        Politics is only one aspect of social interaction, and
its relationship to society is an integral part of political
theory.

Barker, Ernest.   Principles of social & political theory.
    Oxford, Clarendon Press, 1951.   284p.   (F215)

Barnes, Harry Elmer.   Sociology and political theory, a
    consideration of the sociological basis of politics... New
    York, Knopf, 1924.   260p.   (Bibliography: p. 217-247)
                                                                     (F216)
Cole, George Douglas Howard.   Some relations between
    political and economic theory.   London, Macmillan, 1934.
    92p.   (F217)

Lacordaire, Jean Baptiste Henri Dominique de.   Political
    and social philosophy.   St. Louis, Herder, 1924.   247p.
                                                                     (F218)
Runciman, Walter Garrison.   Social science and political
    theory.   Cambridge, Eng., University Press, 1963. 200p.
                                                                     (F219)

Utopias

        Utopian thought in political theory has been closely
allied with moral and ethical considerations, especially with
respect to man's relation to the state and vice versa.   Concepts of this genre are concerned with prescriptive formulas
for political action.

Mannheim, Karl.   Ideology and utopia; an introduction to the
    sociology of knowledge.   New York, Harcourt, Brace,
    1936.   318p.   (F220)

Becker, Carl Lotus.   The heavenly city of the eighteenth-
    century philosophers.   New Haven, Yale University Press,
    1959.   168p.   (F221)

Shklar, Judith N.   After Utopia; the decline of political faith.

Princeton, N. J. , Princeton University Press, 1957. 309p.
(F222)

Major Works of Political Thought: A Chronology

A chronological listing of the major theoretical political philosophers and their works will be useful in placing their contributions to political theory in historical perspective.   Also included at the end of each major historical division is a number of works relating to the period, philosopher or concept.

Ancient

Greek

Plato (427-347 B.C.)

The Republic
The Laws
The Statesman

Aristotle (384-322 B. C.)

The Politics
The Constitution of Athens

Roman

Polybius (204-122 B. C.)

History of Rome

Cicero (106-43 B. C.)

The Republic
The Laws

Epictetus   (about 50-120 A. D.)

The Discourses
The Manual

Marcus Aurelius (121-180 A.D.)

Meditations

Works Related to the Ancient Period

Agard, Walter Raymond. What democracy meant to the
Greeks. Madison, University of Wisconsin Press, 1960,
c1942. 278p.   (F223)

Barker, Ernest. Greek political theory; Plato and his pred-
ecessors. New York, Barnes & Noble, 1960. 468p.
(F224)
---- ----. Political thought of Plato and Aristotle. New
York, Dover Publications, 1959. 559p.   (F225)

Fritz, Kurt von. Pythagorean politics in southern Italy; an
analysis of the sources. New York, Columbia University
Press, 1940. 113p.   (F226)

---- ----. The theory of the mixed constitution in antiquity:
a critical analysis of Polybius' political ideas. New York,
Columbia University Press, 1954. 490p.   (F227)

Gilmore, Myron Piper. Argument from Roman law in political thought, 1200-1600. Cambridge, Harvard University
Press, 1941. 148p. (Bibliography: p. 133-141)   (F228)

Hammond, Mason. City-State and world state in Greek and
Roman political theory until Augustus. Cambridge, Harvard University Press, 1951. 217p. (Bibliography: p.
205-211)   (F229)

Haskell, Henry Joseph. This was Cicero: modern politics
in a Roman toga. New York, Knopf, 1942. 406p. (Bibliography: p. 368-376)   (F230)

Homo, Leon Pol. Roman political institutions; from city to
state. Tr. by M.R. Dobie. New York, Barnes & Noble,
1962. 426p. (Bibliography: p. 375-383, 405-426) (F231)

Loos, Isaac Althaus. Studies in the Politics of Aristotle
and the Republic of Plato. Iowa City, Ia., University
Press, 1899. 296p.   (F232)

Myres, John Linton. Political ideas of the Greeks. New
York, Abingdon Press, c1927. 436p.   (F233)

Sinclair, Thomas Alan. A history of Greek political thought.
London, Routledge, 1961. 317p.   (F234)

Medieval

Saint Augustine (354-530 A. D.)

The City of God

John of Salisbury (about 1120-1180)

The Policraticus

Saint Thomas Aquinas (1225-1274)

The Rule of Princes
Summa Theologica
Commentaries on the Politics of Aristotle

Dante Aligheri (1265-1321)

De Monarchia

Marsiglio di Padova (1270-1342)

Defensor Pacis

Works Related to the Medieval Period

Baynes, Norman Hepburn. The political ideas of St. Augustine's De civitate Dei. London, Bell, 1936. 18p. (Bibliography: p. 18)   (F235)

Brookes, Edgar Harry. The city of God and the politics of crisis. New York, Oxford University Press, 1960. 111p.
(F236)
Carlyle, Robert Warrand. History of mediaeval political theory in the West. With A. J. Carlyle. London, Blackwook, 1928-36. 6v.   (F237)

Deane, Herbert Andrew. The political and social ideas of St. Augustine. New York, Columbia University Press, 1963. 356p.   (F238)

Figgis, John Neville. The political aspects of St. Augustine's 'City of God.' New York, Longmans, Green, 1921. 132p. (Bibliography: p. 118-122)   (F239)

Gierke, Otto Friedrich von. Political theories of the middle age. Cambridge, Eng. , Cambridge University Press, 1900.

197p.   (Authorities: p. ixiii-ixxxvii)   (F240)

Gilby, Thomas.   The political thought of Thomas Aquinas.
Chicago, University of Chicago Press, 1958. 357p. (F241)

Hearnshaw, Fossey John Cobb, ed.   The social and political
ideas of some great mediaeval thinkers.   New York,
Barnes & Noble, 1950.   223p.   (F242)

Lewis, Ewart (Kellogg) Medieval political ideas.   New York,
Knopf, 1954.   2v.   (F243)

Morral, John B.   Political thought in medieval times.   Lon-
don, Hutchinson, 1958.   151p.   (Bibliography: p. 137-146)
                                                        (F244)
Passerin d'Entreves, Alessandro.   Dante as a political
thinker.   Oxford, Eng., Clarendon Press, 1952. 119p.
                                                        (F245)
---- ----.   The medieval contribution to political thought,
Thomas Aquinas, Marsilius of Padua, Richard Hooker.
New York, Humanities Press, 1959, c1939.   148p. (F246)

The Modern Period

The Renaissance and Reformation

Nicolo Machiavelli (1469-1527)

The Prince
The Discourses

John Calvin (1509-1564)

Institutes of the Christian Religion

Jean Bodin (1530-1596)

The Six Books on the State
A Method for the Easy Understanding of History

The Puritan Movement

Richard Hooker (1554-1600)

Laws of Ecclesiastical Polity

James I (1566-1625)

The True Law of Free Monarchy

Roger Williams (1604?-1638)

The Bloody Tenet of Persecution

John Milton (1608-1674)

Tenure of Kings and Magistrates
Areopagitica

James Harrington (1611-1677)

Commonwealth of Oceania

Thomas Hobbes (1588-1679)

The Leviathan

From Hobbes to Locke

Benedictus de Spinoza (1632-1677)

Theologico-Political Treatise
Political Treatise

Samuel Pufendorf (1632-1694)

De Jure Naturae et Gentium.

Robert Filmer (?   -1653)

Patriarcha

Jacques B. Bossuet (1627-1704)

Politics as Derived from the Holy Scriptures

John Locke (1632-1704)

Two Treatises on Government
The Letter on Toleration

David Hume (1711-1776)

Political Discourses

French Liberalism and the Revolutionary Movement

Baron de la Brede et de Montesquieu (1689-1755)

Spirit of the Laws

Jean Jacques Rousseau (1712-1778)

Social Contract
Discourse on the Origin and Basis of Inequality
Among Men

Thomas Paine (1737-1809)

Common Sense
Rights of Man

The Reaction

Edmund Burke (1729-1797

Reflections on the Revolution in France
Appeal from the Old to the New Whigs

Joseph M. De Maistre (1753-1821)

Considerations Sur La France
Essai Sur le Principe Générateur de Constitutions
Politique Du Pape
Soirées de St. Peter

German Idealism

Johann G. Fichte (1762-1814)

Closed Commercial State
Addresses to the German People

Georg W.F. Hegel (1770-1831)

The Philosophy of Right
Philosophy of History

Utilitarianism

Jeremy Bentham (1748-1832)

A Fragment on Government
Principles of Morals and Legislation
Theory of Legislation

James Mill (1773-1836)

Elements of Political Economy
Essay on Government

John Austin (1790-1859)

Providence of Jurisprudence Determined

John Stuart Mill (1806-1873)

On Liberty
On Representative Government

American Political Theory

Federalist Papers - Hamilton, Madison & Jay

John C. Calhoun (1782-1850)

Disquisition on Government

Works Related to the Modern Period

Allen, John William.   A history of political thought in the
sixteenth century.   3d ed.   London, Methuen, 1951. 525p.
(F247)
Burke, Edmund.   The philosophy of Edmund Burke; a selec-
tion from his speeches and writings.   Ed. by Louis I.
Bredvold and Ralph G. Ross.   Ann Arbor, University of
Michigan Press, 1960.   276p.   (Bibliography: p. 271)
(F248)
Burnham, James.   The Machiavellians, defenders of free-
dom.   New York, John Day, 1943.   270p.   (F249)

Butterfield, Herbert.   The statecraft of Machiavelli.   New
York, Macmillan, 1956.   167p.   (F250)

Canavan, Francis P.   The political reason of Edmund Burke.

Durham, N. C. , Published by the Lilly Endowment Research Program in Christianity and Politics by the Duke
University Press, 1960.   222p.   (F251)

Cox, Richard Howard.   Locke on War and peace.   Oxford,
Clarendon Press, 1960.   220p.   (Bibliography: p. 196-
204)   (F252)

Daly, Lowrie John.   The political theory of John Wyclif.
Chicago, Loyola University Press, 1962. 168p. (Bibliography: p. 153-161)   (F253)

Dietze, Gottfried.   The Federalist, a classic on federalism
and free government.   Baltimore, Johns Hopkins Press,
1960, 1962. 378p. (Bibliography: p. 355-358)   (F254)

Durkheim, Emile.   Montesquieu and Rousseau: forerunners
of sociology.   Ann Arbor, University of Michigan Press,
1960.   115p.   (F255)

Figgis, John Neville.   Studies of political thought from Ger-
son to Grotius, 1414-1625.   Cambridge, University Press,
1907.   258p.   (F256)

Harrington, James.   Political writings: representative selections.   Ed. by Charles Blitzer.   New York, Liberal
Arts Press, 1955.   165p.   (F257)

Hart, Jeffrey, ed.   Political writers of eighteenth-century
England.   New York, Knopf, 1964.   374p. (Bibliography:
p. 370-374)   (F258)

Hearnshaw, Fossey John Cobb, ed.   The social and political
ideas of some great thinkers of the Renaissance and the
Reformation.   New York, Barnes & Noble, 1949. 215p.
                                                                 (F259)
---- ----.   The social & political ideas of some great
thinkers of the sixteenth and seventeenth centuries.   New
York, Barnes & Noble, 1949.   219p.   (F260)

---- ----.   The social & political ideas of some representative thinkers of the Revolutionary Era.   New York, Barnes
& Noble, 1950.   251p.   (F261)

---- ----.   The social & political ideas of some representative thinkers of the Victorian Age.   New York, Barnes &
Noble, 1950.   270p.   (F262)

Jensen, DeLamar, ed.   Machiavelli; cynic, patriot, or political scientist?   Boston, Heath, 1960. 111p.   (F263)

Kendall, Willmoore.   John Locke and the doctrine of majority rule.   Urbana, University of Illinois Press, 1959.
  141p. (Bibliography: p. 137-141)   (F264)

Lamprecht, Sterling Power.   The moral and political philos-
  ophy of John Locke.   Russell & Russell, 1962. 168p.
                                                        (F265)
MacCunn, John.   The political philosophy of Burke.   London,
  E. Arnold, 1913.   272p.   (F266)

Murray, Robert Henry.   The political consequences of the
  reformation; studies in sixteenth-century political thought.
  London, E. Benn, 1926.   301p.   (F267)

Ritchie, David George.   The principles of state interference;
  four essays on the political philosophy of Mr. Herbert
  Spencer, J.S. Mill and T.H. Green.   3d ed.   New York,
  Scribner, 1902.   172p.   (F268)

Rousseau, Jean Jacques.   Political writings.   Edited from
  the original mss. and authentic editions by C.E. Vaughn.
  New York, Wiley, 1962.   2v. (Books: p. xviii-xix) (F269)

Smith, Adam.   Adam Smith's moral and political philosophy.
  Ed. by Herbert W. Schneider.   New York, Hafner, 1948.
  484p. (Bibliographical guide: p. xxv-xxvii)   (F270)

Spinoza, Benedictus de.   The political works: the Tractatus
  theologico-politicus in part, and the Tractatus politicus in
  full.   Ed. by A.G. Wenham.   Oxford, Clarendon Press,
  1958.   463p. (Latin and English)   (F271)

Strauss, Leo.   The political philosophy of Hobbes, its basis
  and its genesis; translated from the German manuscript by
  Elsa M. Sinclair.   Chicago, University of Chicago Press,
  1952.   172p.   (F272)

---- ----.   Thoughts on Machiavelli.   Glencoe, Ill., Free
  Press, 1959, c1958.   348p.   (F273)

Street, Charles Larrabee.   Individualism and individuality in
  the philosophy of John Stuart Mill.   Milwaukee, Morehouse,
  c1926.   136p. (Bibliography: p. 117-120)   (F274)

Waring, Luther Hess.   Political theories of Martin Luther.
New York, Putnam, 1910.   293p.   (Bibliography: p. 283-
289)   (F275)

Contemporary Political Thought

Laissez Faire Individualism

Herbert Spencer (1820-1903)

Social Statistics
Man versus the State
Justice

W. G. Sumner (1840-1910)

The Challenge of Facts and Other Essays

Herbert Hoover (1874-1964)

American Individualism

Walter Lippmann (1889-   )

The Method of Freedom
Preface to Morals

Anarchism

Max Stirner (1806-1850?)

The Ego and His Own

Peter Kropitkin (1842-1921)

Mutual Aid
Conquest of Bread

Communism

Karl Marx (1818-1883)

Communist Manifesto
Das Kapital

Vladimer I. Lenin (1870-1924)

Imperialism

Syndicalism

Georges Sorel (1847-1902)

Reflections on Violence

Idealism

Thomas H. Green (1836-1882)

Principles of Political Obligation

Bernard Bosanquet (1848-1923)

Philosophical Theory of the State

Leonard T. Hobhouse (1864-1929)

Democracy and Reaction
Metaphysical Theory of the State

Nationalism and Fascism

Heinrich von Treitschke (1834-1896)

Politics

Oswald Spengler (1880-1936)

Decline of the West

Vilfredo Pareto (1848-1923)

Mind and Society

Giovanni Gentile (1875-1944)

Philosophic Basis of Fascism

Harold J. Laski (1893-   )

Problems of Sovereignty
Grammar of Politics

Harold J. Laski (1893-   ) (continued)

Authority and the Modern State
Foundations of Sovereignty
The Dangers of Obedience

John Dickenson (1894-   )

A Working Theory of Sovereignty

Leon Duguit (1859-1928)

Law in the Modern State

Works Related to the Contemporary Period

Barker, Ernest.   Political thought in England from Herbert
Spencer to the present day.   New York, Holt, 1915.
256p.   (Bibliography: p. 252-254)   (F276)

Birnbach, Martin.   Neo-Freudian social philosophy.   Stanford, Calif., Stanford University Press, 1961. 283p.
                                                            (F277)
Carritt, Edgar Frederick.   Morals and politics; theories of
their relation from Hobbes and Spinoza to Marx and Bosanquet.   Oxford, Clarendon Press, 1936.   216p.   (F278)

Cooperman, David.   Power and civilization: political thought
in the twentieth century.   With E.V. Walter.   New York,
Crowell, 1962.   587p.   (F279)

Davis, Henry William Carless.   Political thought of Heinrich
von Treitschke.   New York, Scribner, 1915. 295p. (F280)

Green, Thomas Hill.   The political theory of T.H. Green;
selected writings.   Edited by John P. Rodman.   New York,
Appleton-Century-Crofts, c1964.   179p.   (F281)

Havard, William C.   Henry Sidgwick & later utilitarian political philosophy.   Gainesville, University of Florida
Press, 1959.   197p.   (Bibliography: p. 181-187)   (F282)

Hearnshaw, Fossey John Cobb, ed.   The social & political
ideas of some representative thinkers of the age of reaction and reconstruction, 1815-1865.   New York, Barnes &
Noble, 1949.   219p.   (F283)

Kariel, Henry S., ed.   Sources in twentieth-century politi-
cal thought.   New York, Free Press, c1964.   308p.
(F284)
Lasswell, Harold Dwight.   Political writings.   Glencoe, Ill.,
Free Press, 1951.   525p.   (F285)

Morris, George Sylvester.   Hegel's philosophy of the state
and of history.   Chicago, S.C. Griggs, 1887.   306p.
(F286)
Neibuhr, Reinhold.   Reinhold Neibuhr on politics;   his political philosophy and its applications to our age as expressed
in his writings.   Ed. by Harry R. Davis and Robert C.
Good.   New York, Scribners, 1960.   364p.   (F287)

CHAPTER VIII

Law and Jurisprudence[1]

By the sheer enormity of its volume, the literature of law and jurisprudence would require several volumes to receive adequate treatment. A brief inclusion of the more important works is justified here because legal records and literature have for some time been one of the primary sources for political scientists. Law and legislation in recent years has had an increased relevance to the work of public administrators and political scientists which has led to the necessity for more familiarity with legal materials. Also, many educational institutions that do not have law schools incorporate pre-law courses as part of their political science curriculum.

The major portion of this chapter has been limited to American law and practice; however, the opportunity has been taken to include a number of bibliographies and guides whose scope is wide enough to provide direction to foreign practice.

Bibliographies, Guides, Reference Books

This section contains only the outstanding and comparatively recent works. Special attention has been given to foreign practice and particularly that of Great Britain. Lists of reference tools may be found in Winchell's Guide to reference books (A51) and in many of the bibliographies listed below.

---

[1]This section is based largely upon Lewis, Peter R., The Literature of the social sciences (A34) and Burchfield, Laverne, Student's guide to materials in political science (B91). Both works are extremely useful, particularly in providing bibliographical lists and reference tools.

General Bibliographies

Alexandrowicz, Charles Henry.   A bibliography of Indian law.
Madras, New York, Oxford University Press, 1958. 69p.
(G1)

Beardsley, Arthur Sydney.   Legal bibliography and the use
of law books.   With Oscar C. Orman.   2d ed.   Advance
pamphlet.   Brooklyn, Foundation Press, 1947. 172p. (G2)

Francisco, Vicente J.   Legal bibliography.   Manila, P.I.,
East Publishing, 1959.   354p.   (G3)

Harvard University.   Law School.   Library.   Annual legal
bibliography.   Cambridge, Mass., 1960/61+   v. 1+
(annual)   (G4)

International Association of Legal Science.   A register of
legal documentation in the world.   2d ed.   Prepared with
the International Committee for Social Science Documentation.   Paris, UNESCO, 1957.   423p.

    Lists current materials by countries: statutes, subsidiary
    legislation, law reports, etc.   (G5)

Jacobstein, J. Myron, ed.   Law books in print.   South
Hackensack, N.J., Glanville, 1959. 2v.   (G6)

---- ----.   Recommended non-legal reference books for law
libraries.   New York, 1958. 4p.   (G7)

Keitt, Lawrence.   An annotated bibliography of bibliographies
of statutory materials in the United States.   Cambridge,
Mass., Harvard University Press, 1934.   208p.   (G8)

Marke, Julius J., ed.   Deans' list of recommended reading
for pre-law and law students, selected by the deans and
faculties of American law schools.   New York, Oceana
Publications, 1958. 178p.   (G9)

Mid-European Law Project.   Legal sources and bibliography
of mid-European countries.   (Praeger)   To be completed in
6 vols.   First published were Hungary (1956), Bulgaria
(1957) and Czechoslovakia (1959)   (G10)

Oppenheim, Leonard.   Materials on legal bibliography.   New
Orleans, Tulane Book Store, c1948.   79p.   (G11)

Pimsleur, Meira G.   Check lists of basic American legal
  publications.   Published for American Association of Law
  Libraries.   South Hackensack, N.J., Fred B. Rothman,
  1962.   1v. (Loose-leaf)   (G12)

Plucknett, Theodore Frank Thomas.   Bibliography and legal
  history.   (In the papers of The Bibliographic Society of
  America.   Chicago, Ill., 1932.   v.26, pt. 1-2, 1932, p.
  128-142)   (G13)

Szladits, Charles.   Guide to foreign legal materials:
  French, German, Swiss.   New York, Published for the
  Parker School of Foreign and Comparative Law, Columbia
  University, by Oceana Publications, 1959. 599p.

  This is a valuable guide to non-Anglo-American legal systems.   Annual supplements are found in the American
  journal of comparative law.   (G14)

U.S. Library of Congress.   Law Library.   Guide to the law
  and legal literature of Latin American countries; some
  under an individual author.   Washington, Govt. Print. Off.,
  1943-48.   Volumes in the Library's Latin America series.
                                                             (G15)
U.S. Library of Congress.   Law Library.   Hispanic Law
  Division.   Index to Latin American legislation, 1950-1960.
  Boston, G.K. Hall, 1961.   2v.   (G16)

Anglo-American Law

Harvard University.   Law School.   Library.   Catalogue of
  the library of the Law School of Harvard University.
  Cambridge, The Law School, 1909.   2v.

  Contains only the books on the American and English common law.   (G17)

New York University.   School of Law.   Library.   A catalogue
  of the law collection at New York University, with selected
  annotations.   Compiled and edited by Julius J. Markle.
  New York, Law Center of New York University, 1953.
  1372p.

  Classified, with subject and author indexes.   To be kept
  up to date by pocket supplements.   This is an outstanding
  bibliography of Anglo-American and international law and
  also has valuable annotations.   (G18)

U.S. Library of Congress. Law Library. Anglo-American
legal bibliographies, an annotated guide. By William L.
Friend. Washington, U.S. Govt. Print. Off., 1944.
166p.   (G19)

Guides to Legal Research

Becker, Olga. Master research guide; a desk book corre-
lating all the law titles, and the subjects included therein,
of the major law digests, encyclopedias and like publications, together with other pertinent information presented
in a single alphabetical series. Indianapolis, Bobbs-Merrill, 1951. 531p.   (G20)

Hicks, Frederick Charles. Materials and methods of legal
research. 3d ed. Rochester, N.Y., The Lawyers Co-
operative Publishing Co., 1942. 659p.   (G21)

Notz, Rebecca Laurens (Love) Legal bibliography and legal
research. 3d ed. Chicago, Callaghan, 1952. 396p.

To be kept up to date by pocket supplements.   (G22)

Price, Miles Oscar. Effective legal research: a practical
manual of law books and their use. Englewood Cliffs,
N.J., Prentice-Hall, 1956. 633p.   (G23)

Putnam, Carlton B. How to find the law; a comprehensive
treatment of the problems of legal research with illustrations from various publications, together with a legal bibliography for each state and the Federal Government. A
legal reference handbook. 4th ed. St. Paul, West Pub.
Co., 1949. 740p.   (G24)

Weisiger, George Bates. Manual for the use of law books.
With Bernita Long Davies. 4th ed. Indianapolis, Bobbs-
Merrill, c1951. 142p.   (G25)

English Law

Beale, Joseph Henry, comp. A bibliography of early English law books. Cambridge, Harvard University Press,
1926. 304p.   (G26)

---- ----. A supplement to Beale's Bibliography of early
English law books. Compiled by Robert Bowie Anderson.
Cambridge, Harvard University Press, 1943. 50p. (G27)

A Bibliographical guide to the law of the United Kingdom,
the Channel Islands and the Isle of Man. London, University of London, Institute of Advanced Legal Studies, 1956.
219p.   (G28)

Coke, Sir Edward. A catalogue of the library of Sir Edward Coke. Ed. by W.O. Hassel. New Haven, Yale
University Press, 1950. 98p.   (G29)

Cowley, John Duncan. Bibliography of abridgements, digests, dictionaries and indexes of English law to 1800.
London, Quartich, 1932. 196p.   (G30)

Holdsworth, Sir William Searle. Sources and literature of
English law. Oxford, Clarendon Press, 1925. 247p.
                                                           (G31)
A Legal bibliography of the British Commonwealth of Na-
tions. London, Sweet & Maxwell, 1955+   (G32)

Plucknett, Theodore Frank Thomas. Early English legal
literature. Cambridge, University Press, 1958. 120p.
                                                           (G33)
Stevens, Ruben Hilary. Where to look for your law. 12th
ed. By C.W. Ringrose. London, Sweet, 1957. 190p.
                                                           (G34)
Thorne, S.E. Bibliography of English legal history. Cambridge, Harvard University Press, 1933.   (G35)

Winfield, Percy Henry. Chief sources of English legal history. Cambridge, Harvard University Press, 1925.
374p.   (G36)

Indexes, etc.

Index to foreign legal periodicals. London, Published by the
Institute of Advanced Legal Studies, University of London,
in cooperation with the American Association of Law Libraries, 1960+ (Issued quarterly, cumulating annually)
                                                           (G37)
An Index to legal periodical literature, 1791-1937. (Vols.
1-3, Boston Book Co., 1888-1919; v.4, Chipman, 1924;
v.5, Indianapolis, Bobbs-Merrill, 1933; v.6, Los Angeles, Parker & Baird, 1939)   (G38)

Index to legal periodicals. New York, H.W. Wilson, 1909+
v.1+ (Cumulates annually)   (G39)

An interim supplement to the Index to legal periodicals.
New York, Fred B. Rothman, 1950+   (Mimeographed)
(G40)
Legal periodical digest, 1928+   New York, Commerce
Clearing House, 1928+

Loose-leaf abstracting service, comprised of monthly issues of digests of the leading articles appearing in American, British and Canadian legal periodicals.   (G41)

Shepard, The Frank, Co.   A table of cases which have been
cited by popular name; federal and state, to January 1,
1951.   Colorado Springs, Colo., Shepard's Citations,
1950.   (G42)

Encyclopedias and Dictionaries

American jurisprudence.   A comprehensive text statement of
American case law, as developed in the cases and annotations in the annotated reports system; being a rewriting of
Ruling case law to reflect the modern developments of the
law.   Rochester, N.Y., Lawyers Co-op. Pub. Co.,
c1936+   (G43)

Ballentine, James Arthur.   Law dictionary with pronuncia-
tions, 1948 ed.   Rochester, N.Y., Lawyers Co-op. Pub.
Co., 1948.   1494p.

An excellent one-volume dictionary.   (G44)

Berger, Adolf.   Encyclopedic dictionary of Roman law.
Philadelphia, American Philosophical Society, 1953. 333-
808p.   (Bibliography: p. 786-808)   (G45)

Black, Henry Campbell.   Black's law dictionary; definitions
of the terms and phrases of American and English jurisprudence, ancient and modern.   4th ed.   St. Paul, West
Pub. Co., 1951.   1882p.   (G46)

Bouvier, John.   Bouvier's law dictionary.   Cleveland, Bonks-
Baldwin, c1934.   1245p.

A standard American law dictionary that has gone through
a number of printings.   (G47)

Cochran, William Cox.   Cochran's law lexicon, pronouncing
edition; a dictionary of legal words and phrases, includ-

ing Latin and French maxims translated, abbreviations
found in law books and reports and canons of professional
ethics.   4th ed.   Rev. by Robert A. Mace.   Cincinnati,
W. H. Anderson Co., 1956.   412p.   (G48)

Corpus juris; being a complete and systematic statement of
the whole body of the law as embodied in and developed by
all reported decisions.   Ed. by William Mack and W. B.
Hale.   New York, American Law Book Co., 1914-37. 72v.
                                                           (G49)
Corpus juris secundum; a complete restatement of the entire
American law by all reported cases, 1658 to date.   Brooklyn, American Law Book Co., 1936+   (Kept up to date by
cumulated pocket parts)

A new edition of the Corpus juris.   (G50)

Cyclopedia of law and procedure.   New York, American Law
Book Co., 1901-1912.   40v.   (G51)

Jowitt, William Allen Jowitt, ed.   The dictionary of English
law.   Ed., Clifford Walsh.   London, Sweet & Maxwell,
1959.   2v.   (G52)

Laws of England, being a complete statement of the whole
law of England, by the Rt. Hon. The Earl of Halsbury and
other lawyers.   2d ed.   Under the general editorship of
the Rt. Hon. The Viscount Hailsham.   London, Butterworth, 1931-42.   37v. (Kept up to date by annual supplements)   (G53)

Radin, Max.   Law dictionary.   Edited by Lawrence G.
Greene.   New York, Oceana, 1955. 408p.   (G54)

Robb, Louis Adams.   Dictionary of legal terms; Spanish-
English and English-Spanish.   New York, Wiley, 1955.
228p.   (G55)

Shumaker, Walter Adams.   The cyclopedic law dictionary.
3d ed.   By Frank D. Moore.   Chicago, Callaghan, 1940.
1188p.   (G56)

Stroud, Frederick.   Judicial dictionary of words and
phrases.   3d ed.   By Peter Allsop.   London, Sweet &
Maxwell, 1952+   (Kept up to date by supplements to be
issued periodically)   (G57)

Wharton, John Jane Smith. Wharton's law-lexicon; forming
an epitome of the laws of England under the statute and
case law, and containing explanations of technical terms
and phrases, ancient, modern and commercial, with selected titles relating to the civil, Scots and Indian law.
14th ed. By A. S. Oppe. London, Stevens, 1938. 1081p.
(G58)

Other Reference Tools

Biographical Materials & Directories

American Association of Law Libraries. Law libraries in
the United States and Canada, 1948. 5th ed. Chicago,
For the Association by Commerce Clearing House, June
1952. 79p.

Geographical arrangement of libraries, giving name, librarian and including the number of volumes, followed by
personnel index.   (G59)

The American Bar; the professional directory of the leading
lawyers of the United States and Canada, biographically
complete. Minneapolis, James C. Fifield Co., 1918+
(Annual)

Arrangement is by firm name under state and place. Includes brief statement of character of firm and type of
practice with short biographies of members of the firm.
It has no index.   (G60)

American Bar Association. Directory. Chicago, American
Bar Association, 19??+   (G61)

Association of American Law Schools. Directory of teachers
in member schools. St. Paul, West Pub. Co., 1923+
(Annual)

Contains an alphabetical list of teachers with biographies.
Was suspended from 1943 to 1945 and resumed 1946/47.
233p.   (G62)

Carswell's directory of Canadian lawyers, with a selected
list of United States attorneys. Toronto, Carswell Co.,
1958+   (G63)

Foss, Edward. Biographia juridica; a biographical dictionary of the judges of England...1066-1870. London, Mur-

ray, 1870. 792p.   (G64)

Kime's international law directory, 1962; a list of legal
practitioners in most of the principal towns throughout the
world; with telegraphic code and containing general
legal information, established by Philip Grabarn Kime; ed.
Watford, Hertfordshire, Eng., Kine's International Law
Directory, 1909+ (Vol. 70-1962; annual)   (G65)

Lawyers directory. Cincinnati, Ohio, Lawyers Directory,
1883+ (Annual)

A semiannual publication between 1888 and 1925, this work
includes digests of laws and a selection of leading lawyers
with biographical data. Less inclusive for lawyers directory but more inclusive for law digest than the Martindale-
Hubbell, listed below.   (G66)

Liebman, Charles, ed. Directory of American judges; with
a table of the Federal and state courts. Ed. and compiled with Merrie Anne Newman. Chicago, American Directories, 1955. 1v. unpaged.

Lists the federal and state courts with their judges, followed by brief biographical sketches. The first attempt to
compile a biographical dictionary of American judges.
                                                       (G67)
Martindale-Hubbell law directory... New York, Martindale-
Hubbell, c1931+ (Annual)

This work is a consolidation of Martindale's American law
directory, 1868-1930, and Hubbell's Legal directory, 1870-
1930; published annually in two volumes, continuing the edition numbering of Martindale's American law directory.
v.1, List of lawyers of the United States, Canada and
Newfoundland; Selected list of foreign lawyers; Roster of
registered patent attorneys; Biographical section. v.2,
Digests of the laws, of the United States, Canada and its
provinces, Newfoundland and foreign countries, also United
States patent, tax and trademark laws; Court calendars
and uniform acts.   (G68)

National Association of Legal Aid Organizations. 1949 legal
aid directory. Rochester, N.Y., The Association, 1949.
35p.   (G69)

Thomashower, Dorothy (Fisch), ed. Women lawyers in the

United States.   Compiled and edited by Dorothy Thomas,
pseud.   New York, Scarecrow Press, 1957. 747p.

Contains a listing of the names of over 6000 women ad-
mitted to the bar of any one of the United States or its
territories.   In some cases it gives biographical sketches
and in others just the addresses.   (G70)

Who's who in law; v.1, 1937, ed. by J. C. Schwarz.   New
York, Schwarz, c1937+

Gives a large number of biographies of lawyers, many of
whom are not included in Who's who in America.   (G71)

Handbooks

The American bar desk book; a manual for use with that
professional directory of leading lawyers throughout the
world.   Minneapolis, J. C. Fifield Co., 1958+   (G72)

Everyman's own lawyer; a handy book of the principles of
law and equity, comprising the rights and wrongs of individuals.   By a barrister.   68th ed.   To which is added a
concise dictionary of legal terms.   London, Technical
Press, 1955. 906p.   (G73)

Gray, Albert Woodruff.   Family legal adviser; a clear, reliable and up-to-date guide to your rights and remedies
under the law.   Ed. by Theodore R. Kupferman.   New rev.
ed.   New York, Hawthorne Books, 1957.   366p.   (G74)

Kling, Samuel G.   Popular legal encyclopedia for home and
business.   Garden City, N. Y., Hanover House, 1957.
473p.   (G75)

Mettler, Frederick Albert.   The medical sourcebook; a reference handbook for legal, legislative, and administrative
personnel.   Boston, Little, Brown, 1960. 1000p.   (G76)

Pullen, William Russell.   A checklist of legislative journals
issued since 1937 by the states of the United States of
America.   Chicago, American Library Association, 1955.
59p.   (G77)

Sources of Law

The sources of the law are comprised of legislative enactments (statute law) and judicial decisions (case law). The former category includes constitutions, government regulations, executive orders and rules of court. The latter category consists primarily of court judgements.

Statutes

American

In the United States laws may be classified as public or private. Public laws are those in which the interest of the public as a whole is affected, but private laws affect only an individual or group of individuals. There are also other classifications of law which include: declarative, affirmative or negative, prescriptive, prohibitive or permissive, prospective or retrospective, and remedial or penal.

At the end of every session of each legislative body, state and national, Session laws are gathered together. These appear in several forms. First, slip laws and statutes comprise all of the laws that are printed in chronological order as they are approved. Second, revised statutes are the result of revising and rearranging the statutory law and reenactment of the whole. Third, there are codifications of permanent and general laws already in force, and fourth, compilations are made that deal with specific subjects. Listed below are the various statutory compilations of particular importance.

Code of federal regulations, 1961 ed., containing a codification of documents of general applicability and future effect as of Jan. 1, 1961, with ancillaries and index. Pub. by the Division of the Federal Register, National Archives. Washington, Govt. Print. Off., 1961+

Is kept up to date by pocket supplements that are cumulated annually. Contains a "codification of the Federal Administrative rules and regulations, general and permanent." These form the basic volumes for the type of material published currently in the Federal register.   (G78)

United States. Federal register. Mar. 12, 1936+ Washington, Govt. Print. Off., 1936+ Daily, except Sun., Mon., and day following a legal holiday.

Includes all presidential proclamations and executive
orders, rules and regulations of the various bureaus and
departments of the government, and decisions of fact-find-
ing bodies. Has monthly, quarterly and annual indexes.

(G79)

U.S. Laws, Statutes, etc.   Federal code annotated; all federal laws of a general and permanent nature...fully annotated to the decisions of federal and state tribunals, together with annotations of uncodified laws and treaties...
Indianapolis, Bobbs-Merrill, 1937+

Volumes replaced at intervals by perpetual revision plan
and groups related material into volumes, e.g.; Federal
taxation, transportation and communication, bankruptcy,
etc. (Ten year cumulative supplement for v.1-13. Title
1-50, 1947+   )   (G80)

---- ----.   Index to the federal statutes 1789-1873, 1874-
1931, general and permanent law...Washington, Govt.
Print. Off., 1911-33.   2v.

Vol. 1, 1789-1873, indexes v.1-17 of the Statutes at
Large; vol. 2, 1874-1931 indexes v.18-46 of the Statutes
at Large and the Revised statutes of 1874.   (G81)

---- ----.   Revised statutes of the United States, passed at
the first session of the Forty-third Congress, 1873-74;
embracing the statutes of the United States, general and
permanent in their nature, in force Dec. 1, 1873.   2d ed.
Washington, Govt. Print. Off., 1878.   1394p.

A commission was appointed in 1867 to compile all the
general and permanent laws by subject.   The revisers
took certain liberties in the texts which the 2d ed. cor-
rected.   Supplements were made and published in 1891 and
1901, but these are largely superseded by the U. S. code.

(G82)

---- ----.   The statutes at large of the United States, con-
current resolutions, recent treaties, conventions and executive proclamations.   Boston, Little, Brown, 1845-1873;
Washington, Govt. Print. Off., 1875-1948.   v.1-61.

Each volume includes the acts and joint resolutions, public and private, permanent and temporary and the concur-
rent resolutions, treaties, conventions, and presidential
proclamations published during the congressional term.   It
is arranged chronologically by the date of the passage of

the act under the divisions: public laws, private laws,
treaties, etc.   Up to 1936 each volume covered the laws
of one Congress, i. e. two years.   Commencing with the
75th Congress, 1937, each volume covers one session.
The "Session" or "pamphlet" laws were preliminary compilations of "slip" laws, each volume covering one session of
Congress.   They were discontinued at the conclusion of the
74th Congress.   (G83)

---- ----.   United States code.   1958 ed.   Washington,
Govt. Print. Off., 1959+   13v.   (With annual supplements)

Supersedes previous editions published in 1926, 1934, 1940
and 1946.   Arrangement is under 50 titles with a general
index.   This code consolidates all general and permanent
laws of the United States in force on January 2, 1958.
                                                         (G84)
---- ----.   United States code annotated.   The code of laws
of the United States in force December 7, 1925, as en-
acted by Congress June 28 and approved June 30, 1926.
Annotated from all cases construing the laws.   St. Paul,
West Pub. Co., 1927-1949.   v. 1-76.

Each volume covers one title in the U.S. code (1926) and
the arrangement is identical with that code.   It is supplemented by pocket parts containing amendments and addi-
tions.   Later replacement volumes are issued in various
revised editions from time to time.   (G85)

---- ----.   United States Code Congressional Service.   Acts
of 76th Congress, Jan. 3, 1939+   St. Paul, West Pub.
Co., Brooklyn, N. Y., Edward Thompson Co., 1942+

A monthly publication (slightly irregular) with annual bound
cumulations.   Has a variable coverage with recent volumes containing all public laws (full text), congressional
comments, executive orders, Presidential proclamations,
administrative regulations, messages of the president, legislative history, popular names of laws, etc.   Current issues include index-digest of bills introduced.   (G86)

British

Chitty, Joseph.   Chitty's Statutes of practical utility.   Arranged in alphabetical and chronological order, with notes
and indexes.   6th ed. by W. H. Aggs.   London, Sweet &
Maxwell, 1911-13.   16v.

A compilation of selected statutes of general interest that
is annotated.   Kept up to date by annual supplements.
                                                              (G87)

Complete statutes of England, classified and annotated; in
continuation of Halsbury's Laws of England, and for ready
reference entitled "Halsbury's Statutes of England." London, Butterworth, 1923-31.

Kept up to date by annual continuation and supplementary
volumes.   (G88)

Gt. Brit.   Laws, Statutes, etc.   Acts and ordinances of the
interregnum, 1642-1660, ed. by C.H. Firth and R.S. Rait.
London, Stat. Off., 1911.   3v.

Covers the period of the Commonwealth.   (G89)

---- ----.   The statutes, from the twentieth year of King
Henry the Third to the tenth chapter of the twelfth, thir-
teenth, and fourteenth years of King George the Sixth, A.S.
1235-1948.   Prepared under the editorship of Sir Robert
Drayton.   3d ed.   London, Stat. Off., 1950.   32v.

"The text of this edition, down to the end of the reign of
Queen Anne is, like that of the First and Second revised
editions, based on the edition known as the 'Statutes of the
Realm' " (Pref.).   (G90)

Halsbury's Statutes of England.   2d ed.   London, Butterworth, 1949-61.   41v.   (G91)

Case Law

As was indicated above, case law as a source of the
law is derived from judicial judgments rendered by the
courts.

American

Law Reports

Decisions of the U.S. Supreme Court are published in
the United States Supreme Court reports.   The following is
a list of the series of these reports:

Dallas	(v. 1-4 U.S.)	1790-1800
Cranch	(v. 5-13 U.S.)	1801-1815
Wheaton	(v. 14-25 U.S.)	1816-1827
Peters	(v. 26-41 U.S.)	1828-1842
Howard	(v. 42-65 U.S.)	1843-1860
Black	(v. 66-67 U.S.)	1861-1862
Wallace	(v. 68-90 U.S.)	1863-1874
U. S.	(v. 91-to date)	1875-date

In citing any of the first 90 volumes, the name of the reporter (e.g., I Cranch) or the title (e.g., I U.S.) is used. Printing, publication and distribution have been handled by the Government printing office since 1922. The printing prior to that date was done through government contracts with private publishing houses.

Digest of the United States Supreme court reports, annotated with case annotations, dissenting and separate opinions since 1900+ Rochester, N.Y., Lawyers' Coop. Pub. Co., c1948+   (G92)

U.S. Supreme Court. United States Supreme Court reports, lawyers' edition. Rochester, N.Y., Lawyers' Coop. Pub. Co., 1790+

This set (commonly abbreviated L. ed.) reports every decision of the court in its entirety, with summaries of the arguments of counsel and extensive annotations. Each volume covers from three to five volumes of the United States Supreme Court reports, the paging of which is indicated in brackets. The set is kept up to date with bi-weekly advance sheets, and is indexed by the Digest of the United States Supreme Court reports (G92).   (G93)

Supreme court reports are also published in the National Reporter System, described on p. 197.

Decisions of Lower Federal Courts

Decisions of the United States Circuit Courts of Appeals (1891-date) are reported in the National Reporter System. These were also contained in the Circuit Courts of Appeals Reports up to 1920.

Since 1880, the National Reporter System (Federal Reporter series) have included the reports of the United States Circuit Courts (1789-1912) and the United States District

Courts (1789-date). Earlier reports have been printed in
Federal Cases (1789-1879) 31v. , a reprint of all available
cases decided by these courts during the period covered, a
collection which entirely supersedes the numerous unofficial
reports.

Official State Reports

Practically all of the early state reports were private.
The official state reports usually included selected cases decided by the highest or higher courts of the state, chosen
either by the judges or the reporters. Needless to say, they
vary greatly in completeness from state to state and from
period to period.

National Reporter System

Begun in 1874, the National Reporter System divides
the states into various groups with a separate series for the
decisions of the state courts of each group. The reporters
consist of all the decisions of all the state courts of last resort and later were added to reports of the intermediate
courts of appeal. This series of reporters is annotated and
omits summaries, arguments and briefs of counsel; however,
its digests and indexes to all cases are excellent. The advance sheets of the Reporters are issued weekly. These and
the bound volumes are keyed to the American Digest and the
Reporter Digest. Listed below is a summary of the National Reporter System:

Atlantic reporter; cases argued and determined in the courts
     of Connecticut, Delaware, Maine, Maryland, New Hamp-
     shire, New Jersey, Pennsylvania, Rhode Island, Vermont,
     with key number annotations. St. Paul, Minn. , West Pub.
     Co. , 1886-1938. 200v. (2d series, 1938+)   (G94)

The Federal reporter, with key number annotations. St.
     Paul, Minn. , West Pub. Co. , 1880-1925. 300v.

The Federal reporter, 2d ser. 1924+ with the first set
contains opinions of the United States Circuit Courts of Appeals, the United States Circuit Courts (abolished in 1912),
the United States District Courts (to October 31, 1932),
the Court of Appeals of the District of Columbia, the
Court of Customs and Patent Appeals (Patent cases), and
the Court of Claims (to October 31, 1932).   (G95)

Federal supplement, cases argued and determined in the
District courts of the United States and the Court of
Claims. St. Paul, Minn., West Pub. Co., 1833+   (G96)

New York Supplement; cases argued and determined in the
Court of Appeals, supreme and lower courts of record of
New York State, with key number annotations. St. Paul,
Minn., West Pub. Co., 1889-1938. 300v. (2d supplement,
1938+)   (G97)

North eastern reporter; cases argued and determined in the
courts of Illinois, Indiana, Massachusetts, New York,
Ohio, with key number annotations. St. Paul, Minn.,
West Pub. Co., 1885-1936. 200v. (2d series, 1936+)
                                                      (G98)
North western reporter; cases argued and determined in the
courts of Iowa, Michigan, Minnesota, Nebraska, North
Dakota, South Dakota, Wisconsin, with key number annotations. St. Paul, Minn., West Pub. Co., 1879-1942. 200v.
(2d series, 1942+)   (G99)

The Pacific reporter; containing all the decisions of the Su-
preme courts of California, Colorado, Kansas, Oregon,
Nevada, Arizona, Idaho, Montana, Washington, Wyoming,
Utah, New Mexico, Hawaii and Alaska. St. Paul, Minn.,
West Pub. Co., 1899-1931. 300v. (2d series, 1931+)
                                                     (G100)
South eastern reporter; cases argued and determined in the
courts of Georgia, North Carolina, South Carolina, Vir-
ginia, West Virginia, with key number annotations. St.
Paul, Minn., West Pub. Co., 1887+   (G101)

Southern reporter; cases argued and determined in the
courts of Alabama, Florida, Louisiana, Mississippi, with
key number annotations. St. Paul, Minn., West Pub. Co.,
1887-1941. 200v. (2d series, 1941+)   (G102)

South western reporter... Comprising all the current decisions of the Supreme courts of Arkansas, Missouri, Tennessee and Texas, with key number annotations. St. Paul,
Minn., 1887-1928. 300v. (2d series, 1928+)   (G103)

The Supreme Court Reporter, See (G93)

Annotated Reports System

In contrast to the Reporters, the series of Annotated

cases include only those that are considered generally useful. Local cases of importance as well as cases on points
well settled are not included. From 1888 to the present the
system also includes the most outstanding cases decided by
the federal courts. Two competing systems of annotated reports were published between 1888 and 1918, but they merged
to form the American Law Reports Annotated (ALR) in 1919.
The brief table below illustrates the Annotated Reports System:

(1) American Decisions
(2) American Reports
(3) Competing Systems:
    (a) American State Reports
       Lawyers' Reports Annotated (L. R.A.)
    (b) American and English Annotated Cases.
       Published also as American Annotated
       Cases in three series.
(4) American Law Reports Annotated (A. L. R.)

The American decisions, containing all the cases of general
    value and authority decided in the courts of the several
    states, from the earliest issue of state reports (1790) to
    the year 1869...San Francisco, Calif., A.L. Bancroft,
    1878-88. 100v.   (G104)

American law reports annotated. Rochester, N.Y., The
    Lawyers' Coop. Pub. Co., 1919+   (G105)

The American reports, containing all decisions of general
    interest decided in the courts of last resort of the several
    states, 1869-1887. Rochester, N.Y, The Lawyers' Coop.
    Pub. Co., 1912. 60v.   (G106)

The American state reports, containing the cases of general
    value and authority...decided in the courts of last resort
    of the several states. San Francisco, Calif., Bancroft-
    Whitney, 1888-1911. 140v.   (G107)

Lawyers' reports annotated...All current cases of general
    value and importance decided in the United States state and
    territorial courts with full annotations. Rochester, N.Y.,
    The Lawyers' Coop. Pub. Co., 1888-1906. 70v. (New
    series...1906-18. 76v.)   (G108)

American Digest System

A digest, in its simplest meaning, is an index of case law. The American Digest System is an elaborate and highly perfected subject index covering all reported cases from all of the courts of last resort in the United States. Also indexed are cases from a number of courts that are not primarily courts of last resort. The American Digest consists of eight parts. First there is the Century edition of fifty volumes covering the reports of all cases decided in the United States between 1658 and 1896. The next six parts are known as the 1st, 2d, 3d, 4th, 5th, and 6th Decennials, and each, as the name connotes, covers a period of ten years and all six from 1896-1956. Following 1956 there is the General Digest that is published monthly in pamphlet form and is cumulated into bound volumes approximately every three years. The General Digest is an interim or temporary set to be used until all the material that accumulates in a ten year period is cumulated and issued in a permanent unit.

Opinions of the Attorneys-General

Another important aspect of case law is the opinions of the attorneys general. These opinions are rendered on questions submitted. They perform the same function as judicial decisions in so far as they are accepted by the parties concerned. As precedents, opinions of the attorneys general are of value; therefore, the Federal Government and the states publish them at intervals. Only the Federal opinions are cited below:

United States Dept. of Justice. Digest of the Official opinions of the attorneys-general of the United States...1789-1921. Washington, Govt. Print. Off., 1885-1926. 3v.   (G109)

---- ----. Official opinions of the attorneys-general of the United States, advising the President and heads of departments in relation to their official duties. Washington, Govt. Print. Off., 1852-date.   (G110)

Ruling Case Law (R. C. L.)

This useful tool has the characteristics of a digest as well as an encyclopedia. The work is based on the various series of selected and annotated cases, and the material is arranged under 377 topics which are analyzed.

Complete R. C. L. index; master index of the matter in
R.C.L., vols. 1-28, R.C.L.   Permanent supplement 8
vols., and R.C.L.   Supplement 1930 and later.   Northport,
N.Y., Edward Thompson Co., 1931.   2v.   (G111)

Ruling case law as developed and established by the decisions and annotations contained in Lawyers' reports annotated, American decisions, American reports, American
state reports, American and English annotated cases,
American annotated cases, English ruling cases, British
ruling cases, United States Supreme Court reports, and
other series of selected cases.   Northport, N.Y., Edward
Thompson Co.; San Francisco, Bancroft-Whitney Co.,
1914-21.   28v. (Permanent supplement, 1929-30.   8v.)
                                                         (G112)

Citation Books

        These tools serve a number of useful purposes.   They
can be used in tracing the judicial history of a case or the
legislative and judicial history of a particular statute.   Citation books provide the student with the means of determining
where a specific court decision was cited, reviewed, examined, revised, overruled, criticized or commented upon.
Also it is possible to determine where a particular statute
has been renewed, amended, repealed or construed.

        Since citation books are very diverse in detail, they
are usually confined to a particular jurisdiction.   The most
commonly used citation books are published by the Frank
Shepard Company.   These include separate books for the
United States Supreme Court Reports, Federal Cases and
Federal Reporter combined, for each of nearly all the state
reports and for each of the Reporters of the National Reporter System.   These Citation books are kept up to date by
pamphlet supplements.

        For further and more detailed information on the
Shepard citation books see:

Shepard's citations; a detailed presentation of the scope and
uses of citation books, with illustrative examples of their
use and analysis of their relation to other methods of legal
research.   New York, Frank Shepard Co., 1931.   52p.
                                                         (G113)
        Also the following will be useful:

Rose's notes on the United States Supreme Court reports (2
   Dallas to 241 United States reports) showing the present
   value of authority of all cases therein reported as dis-
   closed by all subsequent citations in all the courts of last
   resort, both federal and state, and in the annotations in
   American decisions, American reports, American state reports, Annotated cases (American and English), Lawyers'
   reports annotated, English ruling cases, British ruling
   cases, Negligence and compensation cases annotated, with
   parallel references to the above mentioned annotated cases,
   the Lawyers' edition of the U.S. reports and the Reporter
   system.   Comp. rev. ed. , San Francisco, Bancroft-Whitney Co. , Rochester, N.Y. , Lawyers' Coop. Pub. Co. ,
   1917-20.   20v. (Supplement to 259 U.S.   San Francisco,
   Calif., Bancroft-Whitney Co. , 1925-26.   5v; Supplement,
   1930-35.   10v.)   (G114)

   British

      Law Reports

           A full account of all reports are contained in the
   Guide to law reports, statutes, etc.   The reports are indexed alphabetically and chronologically by courts and show
   where in English reports and Revised reports they are reprinted.

           The issuance of Law reports ended the publication of
   many existing reporters; however, there are at least three
   important collateral series of reports.   The Times law reports was latterly merged into Weekly law reports which
   evolved from Weekly notes and whose significant cases were
   later incorporated in the Law reports.   The Law times reports and Law journal reports were both absorbed by All
   England law reports which is currently the only other series
   of reports from all the courts.

           English reports is a reprint of the majority of re-
   ports prior to Law reports.   Revised reports is a reprint
   with revisions of the reports that were considered useful.

           Currently being published are a number of reports
   which include cases that may not appear in the general series.   These include Reports of tax cases, Reports of patents,
   designs and trade marks cases, Lloyd's list of law reports
   and Criminal appeal reports.   Many other reports of special
   cases are now merged, such as Commercial cases which is

incorporated into <u>Times law reports</u> and so into <u>Weekly law reports</u>.

The All England law reports... London, The Law Journal, 1936+   (G115)

The English reports.   London, Stevens, 1900-1930.   176v.
                                                         (G116)
English reports in law and equity.   Boston, Little, Brown, 1851-1858.   40v.   (G117)

Gt. Brit. Court of Criminal Appeal.   The criminal appeal reports.   With subject index, tables of cases and statutes cited... London, Sweet and Maxwell, 1908+   (G118)

Gt. Brit. Courts.   Reports of tax cases.   London, H.M. Stationery Office, 1875+   (G119)

Gt. Brit. Patent Office.   Patents, designs, and trade marks. Report of the comptroller-general of patents, designs, and trade marks, with appendices.   London, 1884+   (G120)

The Law journal reports.   London, The Law Journal Reports, 1822-1949.   115v.   (G121)

---- ----.   London, The Law Journal Reports, 1883+ (G122)

The Law reports.   Privy council appeals...London, W. Clowes, 1867-1875.   6v.   (G123)

The Law times reports... London, Butterworth, 1843-1948. 177v.   (G124)

Lloyd's list of law reports.   London, Lloyd's, 1919+ (G125)

The Revised reports... 1785-1866.   Boston, Little, Brown, 1891-1917.   149v.   (G126)

Sweet and Maxwell, ltd., London.   Guide to law reports, statutes and regnal years, with abbreviations used in citing law reports, etc.   2d ed.   London, 1948. 99p.   (G127)

The Times law reports...   London, G.E. Wright, 1885-1953. 71v.   (G128)

The Weekly law reports... London, Incorporated Council of Law Reporting, 1953+   (G129)

Weekly notes... London, W. Clowes, 1866-1952. 85v.

(G130)

Digests and Abridgments

Law reports digests of cases has twelve volumes for the period 1865-1950 and is followed by annual volumes. To trace back further it is necessary to consult sources such as Mews' digest of English case law and the English and empire digest, both of which are kept up to date by annual supplements. The All England law reports digest and the Law journal reports digests and analytical indexes cover more than one series of reports.

For research in earlier times, Crowley's Bibliography of abridgments, digests to 1800 is very helpful. For the modern era there is a service which professes to summarize all the law from every source. This service is known as Current Laws which is followed by the Current law yearbook and for which there has been a consolidation for the years 1947-1951.

The All England law reports annotated of cases decided... London, The Law Journal, 1936+   (G131)

Cowley, John Duncan. A bibliography of abridgements, digests, dictionaries and indexes of English law to the year 1800. London, Quartich, 1932. 196p.   (G132)

Current law consolidation. Being a complete statement of all the law from every source. London, Sweet and Maxwell, 1947+   (G133)

The English and empire digest... London, Butterworth, 1919-1930. 48v.   (G134)

Mews, John. Digest of English case law. 2d ed. London, Sweet and Maxwell, 1925-1928. 24v.   (G135)

Elements of Law and Jurisprudence

The following section is primarily a selected list of outstanding or important works on the elements that make up the history of the law and the philosophy of its nature and function in society.

Comparative Law

Eder, Phanor James. A comparative survey of Anglo-American and Latin American law. New York, New York University Press, 1950. 257p. (G136)

Gutteridge, Harold Cooke. Comparative law; an introduction to the comparative method of legal study and research. 2d ed. Cambridge, Eng., University Press, 1949. 214p. (G137)

Lloyd, Dennis. Public policy; a comparative study in English and French law. London, University of London, Athlone Press, 1953. 166p. (G138)

Schlesinger, Rudolf B. Comparative law; cases, text, materials. 2d ed. Brooklyn, Foundation Press, 1959. 635p. (G139)

Sherman, Charles Phineas. Roman law in the modern world. 3d ed. New York, Baker, Vorhis, 1937. 3v. (Bibliography: v.3, p. 255-273.) (G140)

Von Mehren, Arthur Taylor. Civil law system: cases and materials for the comparative study of law. Englewood Cliffs, N J., Prentice-Hall, 1957. 922p. (Bibliography: p. xv) (G141)

Von Rosenstiel, Werner H. Comparative law: selected case materials prepared for the use of law students of Rutgers Law School. Newark, N. J., Distributed by Rutgers University Bookstore, c1951. 242p. (G142)

Wigmore, John Henry. A panorama of the world's legal systems. Library ed. Washington, D. C., Washington Law Book Co., 1936. 1206p. (G143)

General Studies of Law and Legal History

Allen, Carleton Kemp. Law in the making. 5th ed. Oxford, Clarendon Press, 1951. 626p. (G144)

Burlamaqui, Jean Jacques. Principles of natural and politic law. Philadelphia, Lippincott, 1859. 283p. (G145)

Cairns, Huntington. Law and the social sciences. New York, Harcourt, Brace, 1935. 279p. (G146)

Cardozo, Benjamin Nathan. Law and literature and other

essays.   New York, Harcourt, Brace, c1931. 190p.
                                                    (G147)
Gray, John Chipman.   The nature and sources of the law.
2d ed. from the author's notes, by Ronald Gray.   New
York, Macmillan, 1948.   348p.   (G148)

Harvard Law Review.   An introduction to law; essays of general interest selected from the pages of the Harvard Law
Review.   Cambridge, Harvard Law Review Association,
1957.   436p.   (G149)

Laski, Harold Joseph.   Studies in law and politics.   New
Haven, Yale University Press, 1932.   299p.   (G150)

Pascual, Corsolito.   The nature and elements of the law, an
introductory study.   Manila, G. Rangel, 1954. 348p.
                                                    (G151)
Pekelis, Alexander Haim.   Law and social action; selected
essays.   Edited by Milton R. Konwitz.   Ithaca, Cornell
University Press, 1950.   272p.   (G152)

Rosenblum, Victor G.   Law as a political instrument.   New
York, Random House, 1961, c1955.   88p.   (G153)

Seagle, William.   The history of law.   New York, Tudor
Pub. Co. , 1946.   439p.   (G154)

Willoughby, Westel Woodbury.   The fundamental concepts of
public law. New York, Macmillan, 1924. 499p.   (G155)

Wormser, Rene Albert.   The story of the law and the men
who made it; from the earliest times to the present. Rev.
ed.   New York, Simon & Schuster, 1962. 606p.   (G156)

Zane, John Maxcy.   The story of law.   New York, I. Wash-
burn, 1927.   486p.   (G157)

African Legal History and Law

Allott, Antony N.   Essays in African law, with special reference to the law of Ghana.   London, Butterworth, 1960.
323p.   (G158)

Elias, Taslin Olawale.   The nature of African customary law.
Manchester, Manchester University Press, 1956. 318p.
                                                    (G159)

American Legal History and Law

Frankfurter, Felix.   Law and politics; occasional papers of
   Felix Frankfurter, 1913-1938.   Edited by Archibald Mac-
   Leash and E. F. Prichard.   New York, Harcourt, Brace,
   c1939.   352p.   (G160)

Howe, Mark De Wolfe, ed.   Readings in American legal history.   Cambridge, Harvard University Press, 1949.   528p.
                                                         (G161)
Hurst, James Willard.   The growth of American law: the
   law makers.   Boston, Little, Brown, 1950.   502p.   (G162)

---- ----.   Law and social process in United States history
   ... Ann Arbor, University of Michigan Law School, 1960.
   361p.   (G163)

Kunz, Josef Lauienz.   Latin-American philosophy of law in
   the twentieth century.   New York, Inter-American Law Institute, New York University School of Law, 1950.   120p.
                                                         (G164)
Pound, Roscoe.   The formative era of American law.   Boston, Little, Brown, 1938.   188p.   (G165)

The Supreme Court review.   Chicago, University of Chicago
   Press, 1960+   (Annual)

   Presents a number of scholarly articles critically analyzing the Supreme Court's opinions for the period covered.
                                                         (G166)

Anglo-American or Common Law History

Association of American Law Schools.   Select essays on
   Anglo-American legal history.   Comp. and Ed. by a committee of the Association.   Boston, Little, Brown, 1907-
   09.   3v.   (G167)

Kinnane, Charles Herman.   First book on Anglo-American
   law.   2d ed.   Indianapolis, Bobbs-Merrill, 1952.   810p.
                                                         (G168)
Pound, Roscoe.   The spirit of the common law.   Boston,
   Marshall Jones, c1921.   224p.   (G169)

Radin, Max.   Handbook of Anglo-American legal history.
   St. Paul, West Pub. Co., 1956.   612p. (Bibliography: p.
   535-538)   (G170)

Rodney, Thomas.   Anglo-American law of the frontier:
Thomas Rodney & his territorial cases.   Edited by William B. Hamilton.   Durham, N.C., Duke University Press,
1953.   498p.   (G171)

Walsh, William Francis.   A history of Anglo-American law.
2d ed.   Indianapolis, Bobbs-Merrill, 1932.   447p.   (Bibliography: p. xiii-xix)   (G172)

Asian Legal History and Law

Belli, Melvin M.   Belli looks at life and law in Japan.
With Danny R. Jones.   Indianapolis, Bobbs-Merrill, 1960.
320p.   (G173)

Bodde, Derk, comp.   Chinese law; a selected bibliography.
With a bibliography of the communist period by Anne B.
Clark.   Cambridge, Mass., East Asia Research Center,
1961.   8p.   (G174)

Ch'u, Tung-tsu.   Law and society in traditional China.   La
Haye, Mouton, 1961.   304p.   (G175)

Hogbin, Herbert Ian.   Law and order in Polynesia; a study
of primitive legal institutions.   Hamden, Conn., Shoe
String Press, 1961, c1934.   296p.   (Bibliography: p. 291-
293)   (G176)

Van Der Sprenkel, Sybille.   Legal institutions in Manchu
China; a sociological analysis.   London, University of London, Athlone Press, 1962.   178p.   (Bibliography: p. 154-
161)   (G177)

English Legal History and Law

Cameron, James Reese.   Frederick William Maitland and
the history of English law.   Norman, University of Oklahoma Press, 1961.   214p.   (Bibliography: p. 195-208)
                                                         (G178)
Friedmann, Wolfgang.   Law and social change in contemporary Britain.   London, Stevens, 1951.   322p.   (G179)

Ginsberg, Morris, ed.   Law and opinion in England in the
20th century.   Berkeley, University of California Press,
1959.   407p.   (G180)

Holdsworth, Sir William Searle.   A history of English law.

7th ed. Under the general editorship of A. L. Goodhart
and H. C. Hanburg. London, Methuen, 1956+   (G181)

---- ----. Some makers of English law. Cambridge, Eng.,
University Press, 1938. 308p.   (G182)

Lovell, Colin Rhys. English constitutional and legal history,
a survey. New York, Oxford University Press, 1962.
589p.   (G183)

Maitland, Frederic William. A sketch of English legal history. With Francis C. Mondague. New York, Putnam,
1915. 229p.   (G184)

European Legal History and Law

Bar, Karl Ludwig von. A history of continental criminal
law. Boston, Little, Brown, 1916. 561p.   (G185)

Brissaud, Jean Baptiste. A history of French private law.
Tr. by Rapelja Howell. Boston, Little, Brown, 1912.
922p.   (G186)

---- ----. A history of French public law. Tr. by James
W. Garner. Boston, Little, Brown, 1915. 581p.   (G187)

Calisse, Carlo. A history of Italian law. Tr. by Layton B.
Register. Boston, Little, Brown, 1928. 827p.   (G188)

Carpenter, William Seal, ed. Readings in early legal institutions. Ed. with Paul J. Staffor. New York, F. S.
Crofts, 1932. 357p.   (G189)

David, Rene. The French legal system; an introduction to
civil law system. With Henry P. deVries. New York,
Published by Oceana Publications for Parker School of
Foreign and Comparative Law, Columbia University, 1958.
152p.   (G190)

Englemann, Arthur. A history of continental civil procedure.
Tr. by Robert W. Millar. Boston, Little, Brown, 1927.
948p.   (G191)

Esmein, Adhemar. A history of continental criminal procedure, with special reference to France. Tr. by William
E. Mikell. Boston, Little, Brown, 1913. 640p. (G192)

A general survey of events, sources, persons and movements in continental legal history.   By various European
authors.   Boston, Little, Brown, 1912. 754p.   (G193)

Hazard, John Newbold.   Law and social change in the
  U.S.S.R.   London, Published under the auspices of the
  London Institute of World Affairs by Stevens, 1953. 310p.
  (Bibliography: p. 302-305)   (G194)

Hubner, Rudolf.   A history of Germanic private law.   Tr. by
  Francis S. Philbrick.   Boston, Little, Brown, 1918. 785p.
                                                       (G195)
Law in Eastern Europe.   Leyden, A.W. Sijthoff, 1958+ v.1+
  (A series of publications issued by the documentation office
  for East European Law, University of Leyden)   (G196)

Macdonell, Sir John, ed.   Great jurists of the world.   Edited
  with Edward Manson.   Boston, Little, Brown, 1914. 607p.
                                                       (G197)
The Progress of continental law in the nineteenth century.
  By various authors.   Boston, Little, Brown, 1918. 558p.
                                                       (G198)
Smith, Munroe.   The development of European law.   New
  York, Columbia University Press, 1928.   316p. (Refer-
  ences: p. 293-297)   (G199)

---- ----.   A general view of European legal history and
  other papers.   New York, Columbia University Press,
  1927. 446p.   (G200)

Legal Philosophy or Jurisprudence

Berolzheimer, Fritz.   World's legal philosophies.   Boston,
  Boston Book Co., 1912.   490p.   (G201)

Bodenheimer, Edgar.   Jurisprudence; the philosophy and
  method of the law.   Cambridge, Harvard University Press,
  1962. 402p.   (G202)

---- ----.   Readings in jurisprudence.   Salt Lake City,
  University of Utah, 1962.   170p.   (G203)

Bryce, James Bryce.   Studies in history and jurisprudence.
  New York, Oxford University Press, c1901. 2v.   (G204)

Cahn, Edmond Nathaniel.   The moral decision; right and
  wrong in the light of American law.   Bloomington, Indiana

University Press, 1955. 342p.   (G205)

Carpenter, William Seal. Foundations of modern jurisprudence. New York, Appleton-Century-Crofts, 1958. 230p.
                                                       (G206)
Cohen, Morris Raphael. Law and social order; essays in
legal philosophy. New York, Harcourt, Brace, c1933.
403p.   (G207)

Davitt, Thomas E. The nature of law. St. Louis, Herder,
1951. 274p.   (G208)

Dove, Patrick Edward. Theory of human progression and
natural probability of an origin of Justice. Ed. by Alexander Harven. New York, Humboldt, 1895. 412p. (G209)

Friedmann, Wolfgang. Legal theory. 3d ed. London,
Stevens, 1953, c1957. 520p.   (G210)

Friedrich, Carl Joachim. The philosophy of law in historical perspective. Chicago, University of Chicago Press,
1958. 252p.   (G211)

Fuller, Lon L. The problems of jurisprudence; a selection
of readings supplemented by comments prepared by the
editor. Temporary edition. Brooklyn, Foundation Press,
1949. 743p.   (G212)

Gareis, Karl von. Introduction to the science of law; systematic survey of the law and principles of legal study. Tr.
from the 3d rev. ed. by Albert Kocurck. Boston, Boston
Book Co., 1911. 375p.   (G213)

Godwin, William. Enquiry concerning political justice and
its influence on general virtue and happiness. New York,
Knopf, 1926. 2v. (Bibliography: v.2, p. 299)   (G214)

Hamburger, Max. The awakening of western legal thought.
Tr. by Bernard Miell. London, Allen & Unwin, 1942.
167p.   (G215)

Hart, Herbert Lionell Adolphus. The concept of law. Oxford, Clarendon Press, 1961. 263p.   (G216)

Hearn, William Edward. Aryan household: introduction to
comparative jurisprudence. London, Longmans, Green,
1879. 494p.   (G217)

Jhering, Rudolf von.   Law as a means to an end.   Tr. by
Isaac Husik.   Boston, Boston Book Co., 1913.   483p.
(G218)

Kelsen, Hans.   General theory of law and state.   Tr. by
Anders Wedbery.   New York, Russell & Russell, 1961,
c1945.   516p.   (Bibliography: p. 447-465)   (G219)

Kirchheimer, Otto.   Political justice; the use of legal procedure for political ends.   Princeton, N. J. , Princeton University Press, 1961.   452p.   (G220)

Kohler, Josef.   Philosophy of law.   Tr. by Adalbert Al-
brecht.   Boston, Boston Book Co. , 1914. 390p.   (G221)

Korkunov, Nikolai Mikhailovich.   General theory of law.   Tr.
by W. G. Hastings.   2d ed.   New York, Macmillan, 1922.
524p.   (G222)

Leoni, Bruno.   Freedom and the law.   Princeton, N. J. ,
Van Nostrand, 1961.   204p.   (G223)

Llewellyn, Karl Nickerson.   Jurisprudence: realism in
theory and practice.   Chicago, University of Chicago Press,
1962.   531p.   (G224)

Miraglia, Luigi.   Comparative legal philosophy applied to
legal institutions.   Tr. by John Lisle.   Boston, Boston
Book Co. , 1912. 793p.   (G225)

Modern French legal philosophy.   By A. Fouillee, et al.
Boston, Boston Book Co., 1916.   578p.   (G226)

Pollock, Sir Frederick.   Jurisprudence and legal essays.
Selected and introd. by A. L. Goodhart.   New York, Macmillan, 1961.   244p.   (G227)

Pound, Roscoe.   An introduction to the philosophy of law.
Rev. ed.   New Haven, Yale University Press, 1954. 201p.
(G228)

Sayre, Paul.   Philosophy of law.   Iowa City, State University of Iowa, 1954.   148p.   (G229)

Science of legal method; selected essays by various authors.
Translations by Ernest Bruncher and Layton B. Register.
Boston, Boston Book Co., 1917.   593p.   (G230)

Soviet legal philosophy.   Tr. by Hugh W. Babb.   Cambridge,

Harvard University Press, 1951.   465p.   (G231)

Stamnler, Rudolf.   The theory of justice.   Tr. by Isaac
   Husik.   New York, Macmillan, 1925.   591p.   (G232)

Tourtoulon, Pierre de.   Philosophy in the development of
   law.   Tr. by Martha M. Read.   New York, Macmillan,
   1922.   653p.   (G233)

Vecchio, Giorgio del.   The formal basis of law.   Tr. by
   John Lisle.   Boston, Boston Book Co., 1921. 412p.(G234)

Vinogradoff, Sir Paul.   Outlines of historical jurisprudence.
   London, Oxford University Press, 1920-22.   2v. (Bibliography: v.1, p. 373-398; v.2, p. 267-275)   (G235)

Wigmore, John Henry, ed.   Rational basis of legal institutions.   By various authors.   New York, Macmillan, 1923.
   603p.   (G236)

Constitutional Law

     As an integral part of case law, constitutional law in-
corporates a body of legal rules and principles that identifies the nature and limits of governmental power along with
the rights and duties of individuals in relation to the state
and its governmental institutions.   Normally these rules and
principles are formulated in a written constitution which is
interpreted and extended by courts of final jurisdiction
through the exercise of the power of judicial review.

Barrett, Edward L., ed.   Constitutional law: cases and materials.   With Paul W. Burton and John Honnold. 2d ed.
   Brooklyn, Foundation Press, 1963.   1339p.   (G237)

Cool, Forrest.   Constitutional law.   5th ed.   Rev. and ed.
   by Reginald Parker.   Woodland Hills, Calif., F. Cool Publications, 1950.   160p.   (G238)

Cooper, Khurshed Sorabji.   The elements of constitutional
   law.   With S.K. Desai.   3d ed.   Bombay, Lakhani Book
   Depot, 1960.   339p.   (G239)

Cracknell, Douglas George.   Constitutional law and the English legal system.   London, Butterworth, 1963.   179p.
                                                   (G240)

Forkosch, Morris D.   Constitutional law.   Brooklyn, Foundation Press, 1963.   541p.   (G241)

Freund, Paul Abraham, ed.   Constitutional law: cases and
other problems.   With others.   2d ed.   Boston, Little,
Brown, 1961.   2v.   (G242)

Groves, Harry E.   Comparative constitutional law: cases
and materials.   Dobbs Ferry, N.Y., Oceana Publications,
1963.   628p.   (G243)

McCloskey, Robert Green, ed.   Essays in constitutional law.
New York, Knopf, 1957.   429p.   (G244)

Schmidhauser, John Richard.   Constitutional law in the political process.   Chicago, Rand McNally, 1963.   544p.
                                                               (G245)
Wade, Emlyn Capel Stewart.   Constitutional law; an outline
of the law and practice of the Constitutions, including central and local government and the constitutional relations
of the British Commonwealth.   With G. Godfrey Phillips.
6th ed.   London, Longmans, 1960.   725p.   (G246)

CHAPTER IX

Public Administration

In its most general sense public administration is the process of managing public affairs, enforcing laws and carrying out public policy. Unlike the executive or legislative functions of government, public administration does not involve the power to determine and declare public policy. It is also not similar to the judicial function since decisions can be arrived at without strict adherence to formal procedural rules. However, these distinctions are rather vague due to the complexity of modern government in which independent commissions exercise quasi-judicial and legislative functions.

The primary source materials of public administration include laws and regulations, reports of executive and administrative officers, boards, and commissions, reports of special investigating commissions and committees, legislative hearings, budgets, etc. A large number of private or public agencies carry on research and other activities within this field. A selected list of these appear in Appendix C.

General Materials

Public Administration

General Works

Appleby, Paul Henson. Big democracy. New York, Knopf, 1945. 197p. (H1)

---- ----. Policy and administration. University, Ala., University of Alabama Press, 1949. 173p. (H2)

---- ----. Public administration for a welfare state. New York, Asia Pub. House, c1961. 105p. (H3)

Avasthi, Amreshwar. Public administration. With Shiram Maheshwari Agra, Lakshmi Narain Agarwal, 1962. 568p. (H4)

Barnard, Chester Irving.   The functions of the executive.
Cambridge, Mass., Harvard University Press, 1938. 334p.
                                                              (H5)

Barnett, Homer Garner.   Anthropology in administration.
Evanston, Ill., Row, Peterson, 1956. 196p.   (H6)

Bartholomew, Paul Charles.   Public administration.   Paterson, N.J., Littlefield, Adams, 1959. 150p.   (H7)

Brown, Edwin Taylor.   The sovereign people; analysis of
an illusion.   Melbourne, F.W. Cheshire, 1954. 271p. (H8)

Chapman, Brian.   The profession of government: the public
service in Europe.   New York, Macmillan, 1959. 352p.
(Bibliography: p. 323-344)   (H9)

Charlesworth, James Clyde.   Governmental administration.
New York, Harper, 1951.   713p.   (H10)

Childs, Richard Spencer.   Civic victories; the story of an
unfinished revolution.   New York, Harper, 1952. 350p.
                                                              (H11)
Claunch, John Miller, ed.   Political and social problems of
public administration in underdeveloped areas, a symposium.   Dallas, Southern Methodist University, Arnold Foundation, 1959.   80p.   (H12)

Dimock, Marshall Edward.   Public administration.   With
Gladys O. Dimock and Louis W. Koenig.   Rev. ed.   New
York, Rinehart, 1958. 573p.   (H13)

Finer, Samuel Edward.   A primer of public administration.
London, F. Muller, 1950.   160p.   (Bibliography: p. 159-
160)   (H14)

Gaus, John Merriman.   The frontiers of public administra-
tion.   With Leonard D. White and Marshall E. Dimock.
Chicago, University of Chicago Press, c1936.   146p.
                                                              (H15)
---- ----.   Reflections on public administration.   University,
Ala., University of Alabama Press, 1947. 153p.   (H16)

Gladden, Edgar Norman.   The essentials of public administration.   2d ed.   London, Staples Press, 1958. 253p.   (H17)

---- ----.   An introduction to public administration.   3d ed.
London, Staples Press, 1961.   260p.   (H18)

Graves, William Brooke. American intergovernmental relations: their origins, historical development, and current
status. New York, Scribner, 1964. 984p.   (H19)

Heady, Farrel, ed. Papers in comparative public administration. Ed. with Sybil L. Stokes. Ann Arbor, Institute
of Public Administration, University of Michigan, 1962.
243p.   (H20)

Inter-university Case Program. Essays on the case method.
By Edwin A. Bock, editor. n. p., International Institute of
Administrative Sciences, 1962. 119p.   (H21)

Leighton, Alexander Hamilton. The governing of men; general principles and recommendations based on experience
of a Japanese relocation camp. Princeton, N. J. , Princeton University Press, 1945. 404p.   (H22)

Lepawsky, Albert, ed. Administration; the art and science
of organization and management. New York, Knopf, 1949.
669p.   (H23)

Martin, Ronald Russell. Teach yourself public administration. London, English Universities Press, 1949. 168p.
                                                    (H24)
Millett, John David. Government and public administration;
the quest for responsible performance. New York, Mc-
Graw-Hill, 1959. 484p.   (H25)

Morstein- Marx, Fritz, ed. Elements of public administration. By James W. Fesler. 2d ed. Englewood Cliffs,
N.J. , Prentice-Hall, 1959. 572p.   (H26)

Nigro, Felix A., ed. Public administration readings and
documents. New York, Rinehart, 1951. 493p.   (H27)

Niles, Mary Cushing (Howard) The essence of management.
New York, Harper, 1959. 398p.   (H28)

Pfiffner, John McDonald. Public administration. With Robert V. Presthus. 4th ed. New York, Ronald Press Co. ,
1960. 570p.   (H29)

Riggs, Fred Warren. Convergences in the study of comparative public administration and local government.
Gainesville, Fla., 1962. 28p. (Bibliography: p. 24-28)
                                                    (H30)

---- ----. Models in the comparative study of public administration. n.p., 1959. 34 leaves. (mimeo)   (H31)

Rowat, Donald Cameron, ed. Basic issues in public administration. New York, Macmillan, 1961. 500p.   (H32)

Ruthanaswamy, Maridas. Principles and practice of public administration. 2d rev. Allahabad, Central Book Depot, 1956. 287p.   (H33)

Simon, Herbert Alexander. Public administration. With Donald W. Smithburg and Victor A. Thompson. New York, Knopf, 1950. 582p. (Bibliographical notes: p. 563-582)   (H34)

Stein, Harold, ed. Public administration and policy development, a case book. New York, Harcourt, Brace, 1952. 860p.   (H35)

Waldo, Dwight. The administrative state; a study of the political theory of American public administration. New York, Ronald Press Co., 1948. 227p.   (H36)

Study and Teaching

Bertrand, Andre. The techniques of governmental work in the modern state; a study in political science, public administration and comparative constitutional law. Brussels, International Institute of Administrative Services, 1959. 80p.   (H37)

Indiana. University. Dept. of Government. Toward the comparative study of public administration. Ed. by William J. Siffin. Bloomington, 1957. 331p.   (H38)

Molitor, Andre. The university teaching of social sciences: public administration; a report prepared for UNESCO at the request of the International Institute of Administrative Sciences. Paris, UNESCO, 1959. 192p.   (H39)

Oregon. University. School of Business Administration. The study of administration. By E. S. Wengert, and others. Eugene, 1961. 149p.   (H40)

Waldo, Dwight. The study of public administration. New York, Random House, 1961, c1955. 72p. (Bibliographical note: p. 71-72)   (H41)

Wilson, Woodrow.   The study of public administration.
Washington, Public Affairs Press, 1955. 23p.   (H42)

White, Leonard Dupee.   Introduction to the study of public
administration.   4th ed.   New York, Macmillan, 1955.
531p.   (H43)

Reference Materials

Bibliographies

Brooks, Alexander D.   Civil rights and liberties in the
United States, an annotated bibliography.   With a selected
list of fiction and audio visual materials.   Collected with
Virginia H. Ellison.   New York, Civil Liberties Educational Foundation, c1962.   151p.   (H44)

Cornell University.   School of Business and Public Administration.   Basic library in public administration.   Ithaca,
1956.   59p.   (H45)

Galloway, George Barnes.   American pamphlet literature of
public affairs (a descriptive list of current pamphlet series).   Washington, D. C. , National Economic and Social
Planning Association, 1937.   16p.   (H46)

Greer, Sarah.   A bibliography of civil service and personnel administration.   New York, McGraw-Hill, 1935. 143p.
                                                     (H47)
Institute of Public Administration, New York.   A bibliography of public administration.   By Sarah Greer, librarian
of National Institute of Public Administration and New York
Bureau of Municipal Research.   New York, National Institute of Public Administration, 1926.   238p.   (H48)

---- ----.   A bibliography of public administration... By
Sarah Greer.   New York, Institute of Public Administration, Columbia University, 1933+   (H49)

Kronenberg, Henry Harold.   Pamphlets on public affairs for
use in social studies classes.   With Rolla M. Tryon and
Hazen E. Nutter.   Cambridge, Mass. , Distributed by the
National Council for the Social Studies, 1937. 80p. (H50)

Mars, David, comp.   Suggested library in public administration.   Los Angeles, School of Public Administration, University of Southern California, 1962.   133p.   (H51)

Maybury, Catherine M.   Publications of the Institute of Gov-
ernment, 1930-1956.   Chapel Hill, N.C., 1957. 32 leaves.
                                                          (H52)
Michigan University.   Institute of Public Administration.
Comparative public administration: a selective annotated
bibliography.   2d ed.   By Ferrel Heady and Sybil L.
Stokes.   Ann Arbor, 1960.   98p.   (H53)

Pan American Union.   Columbus Memorial Library.   Bibliography on public administration in Latin America.   Washington, Dept. of Cultural Affairs, Pan American Union, 1954.
115p.   (H54)

Recent publications on governmental problems.   Chicago,
Governmental Research Association and Council of State
Governments, 1946?+   (Weekly)   (H55)

Seckler-Hudson, Catheryn.   Bibliography on public administration, annotated.   4th ed.   Washington, American University Press, 1953.   131p.   (H56)

Spitz, Alan A.   Development administration; an annotated bibliography.   Comp. with Edward W. Weidner.   Honolulu,
East-West Center Press, 1963.   116p.   (H57)

United Nations.   Technical Assistance Administration.   International bibliography of public administration.   New York,
1957.   101p.   (H58)

Research

California University.   Bureau of Public Administration.
Governmental research organizations in the western states;
a directory of agencies, and an index to their studies as of
January 1, 1939.   Comp. by Arthur Harris.   Berkeley,
Calif., Pub. for the Western Governmental Research Asso-
ciation, 1939.   123p.   (H59)

---- ----.   Western states research activity series.   Berkeley, Calif., 1935+   (Mimeographed)   (H60)

Goode, Cecil E.   Personnel research frontiers; a review of
personnel research activities and facilities, with special reference to their implication for government.   Chicago, Public Personnel Association, 1958.   176p.   (H61)

Pfiffner, John McDonald.   Research methods in public administration. New York, Ronald Press, c1940. 447p.

(H62)

Directories

A Directory of organizations in the field of public administration. Chicago, Public Administration Clearing House,
c1932+   (H63)

Governmental Research Association. A directory of organizations engaged in governmental research. Chicago, Governmental Research Association, 1935+   (H64)

Other Materials

Grainger, K.E. Administrative manuals. 2d ed. Brussels,
International Institute of Administrative Sciences, 1957.
38p.   (H65)

New York, State Library. Albany. Legislative Reference
Library. Source material for the study of public administration, Albany, 1958+   (H66)

Public policy; a yearbook of the Graduate School of Public
Administration, Harvard University, Cambridge, Mass.,
Harvard University Press, 1940+   (H67)

Special Libraries Association. Social Science Group. Source
materials in public administration, a selected bibliography
reprinted from Public administration libraries. Chicago,
Public Administration Service, 1948. 30p.   (H68)

Bureaucracy and Bureaucratic Systems

Bureaucracy is a term that is almost synonymous with
governmental administrative organization. Most modern governments employ the use of bureaus, more or less, within
the administrative structure to handle specific types of functions. Unfortunately, bureaucracies tend to reduce administration to the application of a set of rigid rules and formulas
that result in a slavish devotion to routine with the effect of
exasperating the public and slowing down official business.
They are inclined to be satisfied with existing methods and
are not disposed to experiment with new ones.

Historical Antecedents

Barker, Ernest. The development of public services in
western Europe, 1660-1930. New York, Oxford University
Press, 1944. 93p.   (H69)

---- ----, ed. & tr. Social and political thought in Byzan-
tium, from Justinian I to the last Palaeogogus; passages
from Byzantine writers and documents. Oxford, Clarendon Press, 1957. 239p.   (H70)

Baynes, Norman Hepburn. The Byzantine empire. New
York, Holt, c1926. 256p.   (H71)

Cohen, Emmeline W. The growth of the British civil service, 1780-1939. London, Allen & Unwin, 1941. 221p.
(Bibliography: p. 213-216)   (H72)

Craig, John Herbert McCutcheon. A history of red tape; an
account of the origin and development of the civil service.
London, Macdonald & Evans, 1955. 211p.   (H73)

Dorwart, Reinhold August. The administrative reforms of
Frederick William I of Prussia. Cambridge, Mass.,
Harvard University Press, 1953. 250p. (Bibliography:
p. 213-220)   (H74)

Eaton, Dorman Bridgman. Civil service in Great Britain;
a history of abuses and reforms, and their bearing upon
American politics. New York, Harper, 1880. 469p.
                                                         (H75)
Ghosal, Akshoy Kumar. Civil service in India under the
East India company, a study in administrative development.
Calcutta, University of Calcutta, 1944. 508p. (Bibliogra-
phy: p. 494-499)   (H76)

Gibb, Hamilton Alexander Rosskeen. Islamic society and the
west; a study of the impact of western civilization on Mos-
lem culture in the Near East. With Harold Bowen. New
York, Oxford University Press, 1950+   (H77)

Institute of Public Administration. Methods and techniques
of control of administrative action. By H.C. Dovey. Institute of Public Administration, London, Rio de Janero,
1952? 83 leaves. (Bibliography: Leaves 82-83) (H78)

Iwasaki, Uichi. The working forces in Japanese politics, a

brief account of political conflicts, 1867-1921. New York,
Columbia University Press, 1921. 141p. (Bibliography:
p. 136-141)   (H79)

Kracke, Edward A.   Civil service in early Sung China, 960-
1067; with particular emphasis on the development of controlled sponsorship to foster administrative responsibility.
Cambridge, Mass. , Harvard University Press, 1953. 262p.
(Bibliography: p. 237-249)   (H80)

Lyber, Albert Howe.   The government of the Ottoman empire in the time of Suleiman the Magnificent.   Cambridge,
Mass. , Harvard University Press, 1913.   349p. (Bibliographical notes: p. 305-330)   (H81)

Mattingly, Harold.   Roman imperial civilization.   Garden
City, N.Y. , Doubleday, 1959.   374p. (Bibliography: p.
357-359)   (H82)

Michael, Franz.   The origin of Manchu rule in China; frontier and bureaucracy as interacting forces in the Chinese
empire.   Baltimore, The Johns Hopkins Press, 1942.
127p. (Bibliography: p. 125-127)   (H83)

Rosenberg, Hans.   Bureaucracy, aristocracy and autocracy;
the Prussian experience, 1660-1815.   Cambridge, Mass.,
Harvard University Press, 1958. 247p.   (H84)

Stevenson, George Hope.   Roman provincial administration
till the age of Antomines.   New York, G.E. Stechert,
1939. 182p.   (H85)

Wittfogel, Karl August.   Oriental despotism; a comparative
study of total power.   New Haven, Yale University Press,
1957. 556p. (Bibliography: p. 491-529)   (H86)

Theory and General Characteristics

Blau, Peter Michael.   Bureaucracy in modern society. New
York, Random House, 1956. 127p.   (H87)

Burnham, James.   The managerial revolution; or, what is
happening in the world now. New York, Penguin Books,
1945. 238p.   (H88)

Dahl, Robert Alan.   Politics, economics, and welfare;
planning and politico-economic systems resolved into basic

social processes. With Charles E. Lindblom. New York,
Harper, 1953. 557p.   (H89)

Dubin, Robert, ed. Human relations in administration; the
sociology of organization, with readings and cases. New
York, Prentice-Hall, 1951. 573p.   (H90)

Francis, Roy G. Service and procedure in bureaucracy, a
case study. With Robert C. Stone. Minneapolis, University of Minnesota Press, 1956. 201p.   (H91)

McLean, Joseph Erigina, ed. The public service and university education. Princeton, N.J., Princeton University
Press, 1949. 246p.   (H92)

Merton, Robert King, ed. Reader in bureaucracy. Glencoe,
Ill., Free Press, 1952. 464p. (Bibliography: p. 451-
464)   (H93)

---- ----. Social theory and social structure; toward the
codification of theory and research. Glencoe, Ill., Free
Press, 1949. 423p. (Bibliography: p. 409-412)   (H94)

Morstein Marx, Fritz. The administrative state; an introduction to bureaucracy. Chicago, University of Chicago
Press, 1957. 202p.   (H95)

Mosca, Gaetano. The ruling class (Elementi di scienza politica) Tr. by H.D. Kohn. Ed. & rev. by Arthur Livingston. New York, McGraw-Hill, 1939. 514p.   (H96)

Riggs, Fred Warren. Comparative bureaucracy; the politics
of officialdom. Preliminary text. Bloomington, Ind.,
1962. 2v.   (H97)

Slesinger, Jonathan A. A model for the comparative study
of public bureaucracies. Ann Arbor, Bureau of Government, Institute of Public Administration, University of
Michigan, 1957. 26 leaves.   (H98)

White, Leonard Dupee, ed. The civil service in the modern
state; a collection of documents... Chicago, University of
Chicago Press, c1930. 563p.   (H99)

Major Bureaucratic Systems

United Kingdom

Bridges, Edward Ettingdene. Portrait of a profession; the
civil service tradition. Cambridge, Eng., University
Press, 1950. 32p.   (H100)

Critchley, Thomas Alan. The civil service today. London,
Gollancz, 1951. 150p.   (H101)

Dale, Harold Edward. The higher civil service of Great
Britain. London, Oxford University Press, 1942, c1941.
232p.   (H102)

DuSautoy, Peter. The civil service. New York, Oxford
University Press, 1957. 158p.   (H103)

Finer, Herman. The British civil service. London, The
Fabian Society, and Allen & Unwin, 1937. 254p. (Bibliography: p. 254)   (H104)

Gladden, Edgar Norman. Civil service or bureaucracy?
London, Staples Press, 1957. 224p. (Bibliography: p.
213-220)   (H105)

Greaves, Harold Goring. The civil service in a changing
state; a survey of civil service reform and the implications of a planned economy on public administration in
England. London, G. C. Harrap, 1947. 240p.   (H106)

Griffith, Llewelyn Wyn. The British Civil Service, 1854-
1954. London, H. M. Stationery Off., 1954. 31p.   (H107)

Kelsall, Roger Keith. Higher civil servants in Britain,
from 1870-to the present day. London, Routledge and
Paul, 1955. 233p.   (H108)

Kingsley, John Donald. Representative bureaucracy, an interpretation of the British civil service. Yellow Springs,
Ohio, The Antioch Press, 1944. 324p.   (H109)

Mackenzie, William James Millar. Central administration in
Britain. With J.W. Grove. New York, Longmans, Green,
1957. 487p.   (H110)

Monck, Bosworth. How the civil service works. London,
Phoenix House, 1952. 258p.   (H111)

Morrison, Herbert Stanley. Government and Parliament; a
survey from the inside. New York, Oxford University

Press, 1954.   363p.   (H112)

Robson, William Alexander, ed.   The civil service in Britain and France.   New York, Macmillan, 1956. 191p.
(H113)

Sisson, Charles Hubert.   The spirit of British administration and some European comparisons.   New York, Praeger, 1959.   162p.   (H114)

Wheare, Kenneth Clinton.   The civil service in the constitution. . . London, University of London, 1954. 34p.   (H115)

British Commonwealth

Appleby, Paul Henson.   Report on India's administrative system. . . New Delhi, Lok Sabha Secretariat, 1956. 55p.
(H116)

Apter, David Ernest.   The Gold Coast in transition.   Princeton, N. J., Princeton University Press, 1955. 355p. (Bibliography: p. 335-346)   (H117)

Bailey, Sydney Dawson.   Parliamentary government in southern Asia; a survey of developments in Burma, Ceylon, India, and Pakistan, 1947-1952.   New York, International Secretariat, Institute of Pacific Relations, 1953.
100p.   (H118)

Belshaw, Cyril S.   Island administration in the South West Pacific; government and reconstruction in New Caledonia, the New Hebrides, and the British Solomon Islands.   New York, Royal Institute of International Affairs, 1950. 158p.
(H119)

Collins, Charles Henry.   Public administration in Ceylon.
New York, Royal Institute of International Affairs, 1951.
162p.   (Bibliography: p. 155-158)   (H120)

Day, John Percival.   Public administration in the Highlands and islands of Scotland.   London, University of London Press, 1918.   407p.   (H121)

Dwarkadas, R.   Role of higher civil service in India.   Bombay, Popular Book Depot, 1958.   260p.   (H122)

Gorwala, Astad Dinshaw.   The role of the administrator: past, present and future.   Poona, Pub. by D. R. Gadgil, for the Gokhale Institute of Economics & Politics, 1952.
44p.   (H123)

Hailey, William Malcolm Hailey. Native administration in the British African territories. London, H. M. Stationery Off., 1950-51. 4v. (H124)

Hofmeyr, Jan Hendrik. South Africa. 2d ed. By J. P. Cope. New York, McGraw-Hill, 1952. 253p. (H125)

Jennings, William Ivor. The Commonwealth in Asia. Oxford, Clarendon Press, 1951. 124p. (H126)

Lipson, Leslie. The politics of equality; New Zealand's adventure in democracy. Chicago, University of Chicago Press, 1948. 520p. (Bibliography: p. 513-514) (H127)

Marquard, Leopold. The peoples and policies of South Africa. New York, Oxford University Press, 1952. 258p. (H128)

Morse, Alan Leslie. Internal control in the administration of local government. Sydney, Law Book Co., of Australasia, 1960. 152p. (H129)

Palande, Manohr Ramchandra. A textbook of Indian administration. 10th ed. New York, Indian Branch, Oxford University Press, 1947. 435p. (Bibliography: p. 429-430) (H130)

Phillipson, Sydney. The Nigerianization of the civil service, a review of policy machinery. With S.O. Adebo. Lagos, Govt. Printer, 1954. 124p. (H131)

Polaschek, R. J. Government administration in New Zealand. Wellington, New Zealand, Institute of Public Administration, 1958. 324p. (H132)

Scarrow, Howard A. The higher public service of the commonwealth of Australia. Durham, N. C., Pub. for the Duke University Commonwealth Studies Center by the Duke University Press, 1957. 180p. (H133)

Seminar of Leadership and Political Institutions in India, University of California, Berkeley, 1956. Leadership and political institutions in India. Ed. by Richard L. Park and Irene Tinker. Princeton, N. J., Princeton University Press, 1959. 486p. (H134)

Wiseman, H.V. The cabinet in the Commonwealth; postwar developments in Africa, the West Indies, and Southeast Asia. New York, Praeger, 1959, c1958. 364p. (H135)

Continental Europe

Blachly, Frederick Frank.   The government and administration of Germany.   With Merian E. Oatman.   Baltimore, Johns Hopkins Press, 1928.   770p.   (Bibliography: p. 680-749)   (H136)

Brecht, Arnold.   The art and technique of administration in German ministries.   With Comstock Glaser.   Cambridge, Mass., Harvard University Press, 1940.   191p.   (H137)

Friedrich, Carl Joachim.   Responsible bureaucracy; a study of the Swiss civil service.   With Taylor Cole.   Cambridge, Mass., Harvard University Press, 1932.   93p. (Bibliography: p. 90-93)   (H138)

Herlitz, Mils.   Sweden; a modern democracy on ancient foundations.   Minneapolis, University of Minnesota Press, c1939.   127p.   (H139)

Hesslen, Gunnar.   Public administration in Sweden.   Stockholm, The Swedish Institute, 1950.   64p.   (H140)

Liebesny, Herbert.   The government of French North Africa. Philadelphia, University of Pennsylvania Press, 1943. 130p.   (Guide to legal sources: p. 122-124)   (H141)

Litchfield, Edward Harold, ed.   Governing postwar Germany.   With associates Arnold Brecht and others. Ithaca, N.Y., Cornell University Press, 1953.   661p.   (H142)

Sharp, Walter Rice.   The French civil service, bureaucracy in transition.   New York, Macmillan, 1931.   588p. (H143)

United States

American Assembly.   The Federal Government service; its character, prestige and problems...New York, American Assembly, Graduate School of Business, Columbia University, 1954.   189p.   (H144)

Bendix, Reinhard.   Higher civil servants in American society; a study of the social origins, the careers and the power-position of higher Federal administration.   Boulder, University of Colorado Press, 1949.   129p.   (H145)

Bernstein, Marver H.   The job of the Federal executive.

Washington, Brookings Institution, 1958. 241p.   (H146)

Conac, Gerard.   La fonction publique aux Etats-Unis; essai
sur la régime du Civil Service fédéral.   Paris, A. Colin,
1958.   251p.   (Bibliography: p. 244-252)   (H147)

Corson, John Jay.   Executives for the Federal service; a
program for action in time of crisis.   New York, Columbia University Press, 1952.   91p.   (H148)

Kilpatrick, Franklin Peirce.   The image of the Federal
service.   With Milton C. Cummings, Jr., and M. Kent
Jenings.   Washington, D.C., Brookings Institution, c1964.
301p.   (H149)

McCamy, James Lucian.   The administration of American
foreign affairs.   New York, Knopf, 1950. 364p.   (H150)

Society for Personnel Administration, Washington, D. C.
The Federal career service: a look ahead...Washington,
1954.   110p.   (Its Pamphlet no. 8)   (H151)

Sweeney, Stephen Binnington, ed.   Achieving excellence in
public service...Ed. with James C. Charlesworth. Philadelphia, American Academy of Political and Social Science,
1963.   209p.   (Bibliography: p. 194-196)   (H152)

Van Riper, Paul P.   History of the United States civil service.   Evanston, Ill., Row, Peterson, 1958. 588p. (H153)

Communist States

Best, Harry.   The Soviet state and its inception.   New York,
Philosophical Library, 1950, c1951. 448p. (Bibliography:
p. 419-437)   (H154)

Fall, Bernard B.   The Viet-Minh regime; government and
administration in the Democratic Republic of Vietnam.
Rev. ed.   New York, Institute of Pacific Relations, 1956.
196p.   (Bibliography: p. 188-196)   (H155)

Harper, Samuel Northrup.   The government of the Soviet
Union.   With Roland Thompson.   2d ed.   New York, Van
Nostrand, 1949.   369p.   (H156)

Karpinskii, Viacheslav Alekseevich.   The social and state
structure of the U.S.S.R.   Moscow, Foreign Languages

Pub. House, 1950. 238p.   (H157)

Manning, Clarence Augustus. The forgotten republics. New
  York, Philosophical Library, 1952. 264p.   (H158)

Moore, Barrington. Soviet politics: the dilemma of power;
  the role of ideas in social change. Cambridge, Mass.,
  Harvard University Press, 1950. 503p. (Bibliography:
  p. 461-485)   (H159)

Rostow, Walt Whitman. The dynamics of Soviet Society. In
  collaboration with Alfred Levin, and with the assistance of
  others of the Center for International Studies, Mass. Institute of Technology. New York, Norton, 1953. 282p.
                                                           (H160)
Tang, Peter H.S. Communist China today; domestic and
  foreign policies. New York, Praeger, 1957. 536p. (Bibliography: p. 505-516)   (H161)

Thomas, S.B. Government and administration in Communist
  China. 2d ed. New York, International Secretariat, Institute of Pacific Relations, 1955. 196p.   (H162)

Nationalist China and Japan

Borton, Hugh, ed. Japan. Ithaca, N.Y., Cornell University Press, 1951, c1950. 320p.   (H163)

Fahs, Charles B. Government in Japan; recent trends in its
  scope and operation. New York, International Secretariat,
  Institute of Pacific Relations, 1940. 114p. (Bibliographical note: p. 90-99)   (H164)

Hou, Fu-wu. Central government of China 1912-1928, an
  institutional study. By Franklin W. Houn. Madison,
  University of Wisconsin Press, 1957. 246p. (Bibliography:
  p. 216-229)   (H165)

Menzel, Johanna Margarete, ed. The Chinese civil service;
  career open to talent? Boston, Heath, 1963. 110p. (H166)

Norman, E. Herbert. Japan's emergence as a modern state;
  political and economic problems of the Meiju period. New
  York, International Secretariat, Institute of Pacific Relations, 1940. 254p. (Bibliography: p. 211-234)   (H167)

Reischauer, Edwin Oldfather. Japan, past and present. 3d

ed. New York, Knopf, 1964. 292p.   (H168)

Yanaya, Chitoshi.   Japanese people and politics. New York,
Wiley, 1956. 408p.   (H169)

---- ----. Japan since Perry. New York, McGraw-Hill,
1949. 723p. (Bibliography: p. 661-693)   (H170)

Southeast Asia

Cole, Taylor, ed.   Post-war governments of the Far East.
Ed. with John H. Hallowell. Gainesville, Fla., Journal of
Politics, University of Florida, 1947. 271p.   (H171)

Collins, Charles Henry.   Public administration in Hong Kong.
New York, Royal Institute of International Affairs, 1952.
189p. (Bibliography: p. 182-184)   (H172)

Corpuz, Onofre D.   The bureaucracy in the Philippines.
Manila, Institute of Public Administration, University of
the Philippines, 1957. 268p.   (H173)

Donnison, F.S.V.   Public administration in Burma; a study
of development during the British connexion. New York,
Royal Institute of International Affairs, 1953. 119p. (H174)

Emerson, Rupert.   Representative government in southeast
Asia. Cambridge, Mass., Harvard University Press, 1955.
197p.   (H175)

Furnivall, John Sydenham.   Colonial policy and practice; a
comparative study of Burma and Netherlands, India. Cambridge, Eng., University Press, 1948. 568p.   (H176)

Hawley, Amos Henry.   Papers in demography and public
administration. Rev. Manila, Institute of Public Administration, University of the Philippines, 1954. 58p. (H177)

Hsueh, Shou-sheng, ed.   Public administration in south and
southeast Asia. Brussels, International Institute of Administrative Services, 1962. 256p.   (H178)

Jones, Stanley Wilson.   Public administration in Malaya.
New York, Royal Institute of International Affairs, 1953.
229p.   (H179)

Montgomery, John Dickey.   Cases in Vietnamese administra-

tion.   Saigon, Vietnam, Michigan State University, Vietnam
Advisory Group, 1959. 481p.   (H180)

Reeve, W. D.   Public administration in Siam.   New York,
Royal Institute of International Affairs, 1951. 93p.   (H181)

Riggs, Fred Warren.   Some problems of public administration in Southeast Asia.   New York, Public Administration
Clearing House, 1955.   140p.   (Mimeo)   (H182)

Stene, Edwin Otto, ed.   Public administration in the Philippines.   Manila, Bureau of Printing, 1955. 415p.   (H183)

Vella, Walter Francis.   The impact of the West on government in Thailand.   Berkeley, University of California
Press, 1955.   410p.   (Bibliography: p. 401-406)   (H184)

Middle East

Berger, Morroe.   Bureaucracy and society in modern Egypt;
a study of the higher civil service.   Princeton, N. J.,
Princeton University Press, 1957.   231p.   (H185)

Bernstein, Marver H.   The politics of Israel; the first
decade of statehood.   Princeton, N. J., Princeton University Press, 1957.   360p.   (H186)

Fisher, Sydney Nettleton, ed.   Social forces in the Middle
East.   Ithaca, N. Y., Cornell University Press, 1955.
282p.   (Bibliography: p. 263-274)   (H187)

Hourani, Albert Habib.   Syria and Lebanon; a political essay.   New York, Oxford University Press, 1946. 402p.
(Bibliographical note: p. 387-390)   (H188)

Khadduri, Majid.   Independent Iraq, a study on Iraque politics since 1932.   New York, Oxford University Press,
1951.   291p.   (H189)

Matthews, A.T. J.   Emergent Turkish administration; a study
of the vocational and social attitudes of junior and poten-
tial administrators.   Ankara, Turk Tarih Kurumu Bawimevi,
1955.   76p.   (H190)

Rustow, Dankwart A.   Politics and westernization in the
Near East.   Princeton, N. J., Center of International
Studies, Princeton University, 1956. 38p.   (H191)

Samuel, Edwin. Problems of government in the state of
Israel. Jerusalem, R. Mass, 1956. 107p.   (H192)

Thayer, Philip Warren, ed. Tensions in the Middle East.
Baltimore, Johns Hopkins Press, 1958. 350p.   (H193)

Latin America

Christensen, Asher Norman, ed. The evolution of Latin
American government; a book of readings. New York,
Holt, 1951. 747p.   (H194)

Proudfoot, Mary (Macdonald) Britain and the United States in
the Caribbean; a comparative study on methods of development. New York, Praeger, 1954. 434p. (Bibliography:
p. 363-369)   (H195)

Public Administration Clearing House, Chicago. Public Administration in Latin America: opportunities for progress
through technical cooperation...Washington, Inter-American
Economic and Social Council, Pan American Union, 1956.
74p.   (H196)

Tucker, William Pierce. The Mexican government today.
Minneapolis, University of Minnesota Press, 1957. 484p.
                                                   (H197)

Organization and Administrative Relationships

Administrative relationships in any organization, and
particularly in all levels of government, revolve around the
concept of authority, its organization, its extent, its decentralization, communication and coordination. In effect, these
form the principal subject matter of public administration.
The increasing importance of public administration is reflected in contemporary emphasis upon the proper articula-
tion of governmental agencies, improvement in the technique
of management, the substitution of trained for amateur personnel, and the growing attractiveness and prestige of public
service.

Theories of Administrative Organization

American Society for Public Administration. Guidelines for
administrative action. Ed. by Frederick C. Irion and
Eleanor Rosenthal. Albuquerque, Division of Governmental
Research, University of New Mexico, 1961. 120p. (H198)

Barnard, Chester Irving. Organization and management, selected papers. Cambridge, Mass., Harvard University
Press, 1948. 244p.   (H199)

Follett, Mary Parker. Dynamic administration; the collected
papers of Mary P. Follett. Ed. by Henry C. Metcalf and
L. Urwich. New York, Harper, 1942. 320p.   (H200)

Lasswell, Harold Dwight. The comparative study of symbols,
an introduction. With Daniel Lerner and Ithiel de Sola
Pool. Stanford, Calif., Stanford University Press, 1952.
87p.   (H201)

Learned, Edmund Philip. Executive action. With David N.
Ulrich and Donald R. Boaz. Boston, Division of Research,
Graduate School of Business Administration, Harvard Uni-
versity, 1951. 218p.   (H202)

Mailick, Sidney, ed. Concepts and issues in administrative
behavior. Ed. with Edward H. Van Ness. Englewood
Cliffs, N. J., Prentice-Hall, 1962. 201p.   (H203)

March, James G. Organizations. With Herbert A. Simon
and the collaboration of Harold Guetzkow. New York,
Wiley, 1958. 262p.   (H204)

Meyer, Paul. Administrative organization; a comparative
study of the organization of public administration. London,
Stevens, 1957. 322p.   (H205)

Simon, Herbert Alexander. Administrative behavior; a study
of decision-making processes in administrative organization. New York, Macmillan, 1947. 259p.   (H206)

Urwick, Lyndall. The elements of administration. New
York, Harper, 1944. 132p.   (H207)

Central Government Organization and Administrative Reform

Brookings Institution, Washington, D. C. International Studies Group. The administration of foreign affairs and overseas operation...Washington, 1951. 380p.   (H208)

Chanda, Asok Kumar. Indian administration. London, Allen
& Unwin, 1958. 274p.   (H209)

Cushman, Robert Eugene. The independent regulatory com-

missions. New York, Oxford University Press, 1941.
780p.   (H210)

Gorvine, Albert. Organization and functions of Turkish ministries. With Laurence L. Barber, Jr. Ankara, Ajaus-
Turk Matbaasi, 1957. 212p.   (H211)

Grassmuck, George L. A manual of Lebanese administration. With Kamal Salibi. Beirut, Lebanon, Public Administration Dept., American University of Beirut, 1955. 101p.
(Bibliography: p. 93-101)   (H212)

Gregoire, Roger. National administration and international
organizations...In collaboration with Mrs. R. Gregoire.
Paris, United Nations Educational, Scientific and Cultural
Organization, 195-. 84p. (Bibliography: p. 82-84)(H213)

Harvey, Heather J. Consultation and co-operation in the
Commonwealth; a handbook on methods and practices. New
York, Oxford University Press, 1952. 411p.   (H214)

Hensel, Herman Struve. Departmental management in Fed-
eral administration. With John D. Millett; staff. Walter
Dunham Jr. and others. Washington, U.S. Govt. Print.
Off., 1949. 60p.   (H215)

Hobbs, Edward Henry. Behind the President; a study of
Executive Office agencies. Washington, Public Affairs
Press, 1954. 248p.   (H216)

Howard, William Edward Harding. Public administration in
Ethiopia; a study in retrospect and prospect. Gronigen,
J.B. Walters, 1955. 204p. (Bibliography: p. 197-199)
                                                           (H217)
Indian Institute of Public Administration. The organization
of the Government of India. London, Asia Pub. House,
c1958. 416p.   (H218)

King, Frederick Charles, ed. Public administration in Ire-
land...Dublin, Parkside Press, 1944-1954. 3v.   (H219)

Leiserson, Avery. Administrative regulation, a study in
representation of interests. Chicago, University of Chicago Press, 1942. 292p.   (H220)

Parks, Wallace Judson. United States administration of its
international economic affairs. Baltimore, Johns Hopkins

Press, 1951. 315p.   (H221)

Roman, John Henry. The office of the Philippine President:
organization and function. Manila, Institute of Public Ad-
ministration, University of the Philippines, 1954. 31p.
                                                       (H222)
Royal Institute of Public Administration. The organization of
British central government, 1914-1956. Ed. by D.N.
Chester. Written by F.M.C. Willison. London, Allen &
Unwin, 1957. 457p. (Bibliographical note: p. 381-384)
                                                       (H223)
Seckler-Hudson, Catheryn. Organization and management:
theory and practice. Washington, American University
Press, 1955. 324p.   (H224)

Sharma, Sri Ram. Some aspects of the Indian administrative system. Sholapur, Institute of Public Administration,
1957. 160p.   (H225)

Stokes, William Sylvane. Honduras; an area study in government. Madison, University of Wisconsin Press, 1950.
351p. (Bibliography: p. 333-340)   (H226)

Wheare, Kenneth Clinton. Government by committee; an essay on the British constitution. Oxford Clarendon Press,
1955. 264p.   (H227)

Administration of Areas, Federalism, Field Administration, Decentralization.

Australian National University, Canberre. Federalism, an
Australian jubilee study. Ed. by Geoffrey Sawer. Melbourne, F.W. Cheshire, 1952. 284p.   (H228)

Bernstein, Marver H. Regulating business by independent
commission. Princeton, N.J., Princeton University Press,
1955. 306p.   (H229)

Brech, Arnold. Federalism and regionalism in Germany;
the division of Prussia. New York, Oxford University
Press, 1945. 202p.   (H230)

Chapman, Brian. Devolution of powers to autonomous institutions, including professional bodies and universities; general report...Brussels, International Institute of Administrative Sciences, 1959? 51p.   (H231)

---- ----. The prefects and provincial France.   London, Allen & Unwin, 1955. 246p.   (H232)

Fesler, James William.   Area and administration.   University, Ala., University of Alabama Press, 1949. 158p.
(H233)

Killingsworth, Charles C.   State labor relations acts, a study in public policy.   Chicago, University of Chicago Press, 1948.   327p.   (Select bibliography: p. 307-311)
(H234)

Krislov, Samuel, ed.   The politics of regulation; a reader. Ed. with Lloyd D. Musolf.   Boston, Houghton Mifflin, 1964.   261p.   (H235)

Schlesinger, Rudolf.   Federalism in central and eastern Europe.   London, K. Paul, Trench, Trubner, 1945. 533p.
(H236)

Taylor, George William.   Government regulation of industrial relations.   New York, Prentice-Hall, 1948. 383p.
(H237)

Public Enterprise and Planning

Appleby, Paul Henson.   Re-examination of India's administrative system with special reference to administration of government's industrial and commercial enterprises.   New Delhi, 1956.   59p.   (H238)

Ardant, Gabriel.   Technique de l'Etat; de la productivité du secteur public.   Paris, Presses Universitaires de France, 1953.   184p.   (H239)

Chester, Daniel Norman.   The nationalized industries; an analysis of the statutory provisions.   2d ed. London, Pub. for the Institute of Public Administration by Allen & Unwin, 1951.   93p.   (Bibliography: p. 90-93)   (H240)

Einaudi, Mario.   Nationalism in France and Italy.   With Maurice Bye and Ernesto Rossi.   Ithaca, N.Y., Cornell University Press, 1955.   260p.   (Bibliographical note: p. 247-256)   (H241)

Friedmann, Wolfgang, ed.   The public corporation, a comparative symposium.   Editorial board: Cecil A. Wright and others.   Toronto, Carswell, 1954.   612p.   (H242)

Hanson, Albert Henry.   Public enterprise and economic de-

velopment.   London, Routledge & K. Paul, 1959. 485p.
                                                        (H243)
---- ----, ed.   Public enterprise: a study of its organization and management in various countries.   Brussels, International Institute of Administrative service, 1955? 530p.
                                                        (H244)
Indian Institute of Public Administration.   Administrative
problems of state enterprise in India.   New Delhi, 1958.
188p.   (H245)

Lewis, Ben William.   British planning and nationalization.
New York, Twentieth Century Fund, 1952. 313p. (Bibliography: p. 286-301)   (H246)

Millett, John   David.   The process and organization of government planning.   New York, Columbia University Press,
1947. 187p.   (H247)

Musolf, Lloyd D.   Public ownership and accountability; the
Canadian experience.   Cambridge, Mass., Harvard University Press, 1959.   174p.   (H248)

Robson, William Alexander, ed.   Problems of nationalized industry.   New York, Oxford University Press, 1952. 390p.
(Select Bibliography: p. 369-380)   (H249)

United Nations.   Technical Assistance Administration. Some
problems in the organization and administration of public
enterprises in the industrial field...New York, 1954. 87p.
(Bibliography: p. 65-87)   (H250)

Administration of Technical Assistance and of International Organizations

Akzin, Benjamin.   New states and international organization;
a report prepared on behalf of the International Political
Science Association.   Paris, UNESCO, 1955. 200p. (H251)

Bock, Edwin A.   Fifty years of technical assistance; some
administrative experiences of U.S. voluntary agencies.
Chicago, Public Administration Clearing House, 1954. 65p.
(Bibliography: p. 65)   (H252)

Glick, Philip Milton.   The administration of technical assistance; growth in the Americas.   Chicago, University of
Chicago Press, 1957.   390p.   (H253)

Hoselitz, Bethold Frank, ed.   The progress of underdeveloped areas.   Chicago, University of Chicago Press, 1952. 296p.   (H254)

Laves, Walter Herman Carl.   Unesco: purpose, progress, prospects.   With Charles A. Thomson.   Bloomington, Indiana University Press, 1957.   469p.   (H255)

Loveday, Alexander.   Reflections on international administration.   Oxford. Clarendon Press, 1956.   334p.   (H256)

Sharp, Walter Rice.   International technical assistance: programs and organization.   Chicago, Public Administration Service, 1952.   146p.   (Bibliography: p. 129-131)
(H257)

Teaf, Howard Morris, ed.   Hands across frontiers; case studies in technical cooperation.   Ed. with Peter G. Franck.   Ithaca, N. Y.,   Dist. by Cornell University Press, 1955.   579p.   (H258)

United Nations.   Secretariat.   Technical Assistance Administration.   Special Committee on Public Administrative Problems.   Standards and techniques of public administration with special reference to technical assistance for underdeveloped countries; report.   New York, United Nations, Technical Assistance Administration, 1951.   65p.   (H259)

Von Goeckingk, Johanna.   United Nations Technical Assistance Board: a case study in international administration. New York, Woodrow Wilson Foundation, 1955. 40p. (H260)

Personnel Administration

The function of personnel management in public administration covers a broad area from the recruitment and training of personnel to the staff and supervisory relationships in the organizational structure.   For the most part personnel administration can be considered as the art of selecting new employees and making use of old ones in such a manner that the maximum quality and quantity of output and service are obtained from the working force.

General Works

Avery, Robert Sterling.   Experiment in management; personnel decentralization in the Tennessee Valley Authority.

Knoxville, University of Tennessee Press, 1954. 212p.
(H261)
Case, Harry Lawrence.   Personnel policy in a public agen-
cy; the TVA experience.   New York, Harper, 1955. 176p.
(H262)
Cole, Taylor.   The Canadian bureaucracy, a study of Can-
adian civil servants and other public employees, 1939-
1947.   Durham, N. C. , Duke University Press, 1949. 292p.
(H263)
Gordon, Oakley.   Personnel management in Utah State gov-
ernment.   With Reed Richardson and J. D. Williams.   Salt
Lake City, Institute of Government, University of Utah,
1962. 160p.   (H264)

National Civil Service League.   The law of civil service. By
H. Eliot Kaplan, general counsel. Albany, M. Bender,
1958. 440p.   (H265)

Nigro, Felix A.   Public personnel administration.   New York,
Holt, 1959. 499p.   (H266)

Stahl, Oscar Glenn.   Public personnel administration. 5th
ed.   New York, Harper & Row, 1962. 531p.   (H267)

Education, Recruitment and Training

Callard, Keith B.   Advanced administrative training in the
public service.   Toronto, Institute of Public Administration of Canada, 1958.   32p.   (H268)

David, Paul Theodore.   Executives for government; central
issues of federal personnel administration.   With Ross
Pollock. Washington, Brookings Institution, 1958, c1957.
196p.   (H269)

Royal Institute of Public Administration.   Training managers
in the public services: a symposium.   By F. Bray and
others.   London, Allen & Unwin, 1955. 84p. (Bibliography:
p. 84)   (H270)

Sayre, Wallace Stanley.   Training for specialized mission
personnel.   With Clarence E. Thurber.   Chicago, Public
Administration Service, 1952. 85p.   (H271)

Tickner, F. J.   Modern staff training; a survey of training
needs and methods today.   London, University of London
Press, 1952.   159p.   (H272)

Personnel Administration in International Agencies.

Scott, Francis Reginald.   The world's civil service.   New
    York, Carnegie Endowment for International Peace, 1954.
    64p.   (H273)

Young, Tien-cheng.   International civil service: principles
    and problems.   Brussels, International Institute of Admin-
    istrative Sciences, 1958.   268p.   (H274)

Staff Relations; Conditions of Work

Bursche, Herbert Adolf.   Increasing the efficiency of admin-
    istration by better motivation of the public servant.   Brus-
    sels, International Institute of Administrative Science,
    1959?   (H275)

Gladden, Edgar Norman.   Civil service staff relationships.
    London, Hodge, 1943.   184p.   (Bibliography: p. 161)
                                                            (H276)
Pfiffner, John McDonald.   The supervision of personnel; hu-
    man relations in the management of men.   2d ed.   Engle-
    wood Cliffs, N. J., Prentice-Hall, 1958.   500p.   (H277)

Spero, Sterling Denhard.   Government as employer.   New
    York, Remsen Press, 1948.   479p.   (H278)

---- ----.   Labor relations in British nationalized industry.
    New York, New York University Press, 1955.   83p. (H279)

Fiscal Administration

        The management of fiscal affairs in government per-
tains to finance, particularly to problems associated with public revenue, expenditure and debt.   Financial administration
is extremely important today because of the tremendous in-
crease in the amounts of money expended for governmental
services.   Because everything that government does requires
money, it is essential that sound principles and techniques
of financial administration be employed.   A great deal of the
literature in this area of public administration deals with the
development and perfection of these principles and techniques.

Anderson, Ronald Aberdeen.   Government and business.   2d
    ed.   Cincinnati, Southwestern Pub. Co., 1960.   681p.
                                                            (H280)

Anderson, William. Intergovernmental fiscal relations.
  With the assistance of Waite D. Durfee, Jr., and staff.
  Minneapolis, University of Minnesota Press, c1956. 131p.
                                                              (H281)
Baxter, Stephen B. The development of the Treasury, 1660-
  1702. Cambridge, Mass., Harvard University Press,
  1957. 301p.   (H282)

Beer, Samuel Hutchinson. Treasury control; the co-ordina-
  tion of financial and economic policy in Great Britain. Oxford, Clarendon Press, 1956. 138p.   (H283)

Birch, Anthony Harold. Federalism, finance, and social
  legislation in Canada, Australia, and the United States.
  Oxford, Clarendon Press, 1955. 314p.   (H284)

Buchanan, Norman Sharpe. Approaches to economic development. With Howard S. Ellis. New York, Twentieth
  Century Fund, 1955. 494p.   (H285)

Buck, Arthur Eugene. The budget in governments of today.
  New York, Macmillan, 1934. 349p. (Select bibliography:
  p. 313-332)   (H286)

---- ----. Financing Canadian government. Chicago, Public Administration Service, 1949. 367p. (Select bibliography: p. 349-357)   (H287)

---- ----. Public budgeting; a discussion of budgeting practice in the national, state and local governments of the
  United States. New York, Harper, 1929. 612p. (Bibliography: p. 539-597)   (H288)

Burkhead, Jesse. Government budgeting. New York, Wiley,
  1959, c1956. 498p.   (H289)

Chatters, Carl Hallack. An inventory of governmental ac-
  tivities in the United States. With Margorie L. Hoover.
  Chicago, Municipal Finance Officers Association of the
  United States and Canada, 1947. 15p.   (H290)

Dimock, Marshall Edward. Business and government, issues of public policy. 4th ed. New York, Holt, Rinehart
  and Winston, 1961. 505p.   (H291)

Due, John Fitzgerald. Government finance, an economic
  analysis. 3d ed. Homewood, Ill., R. D. Irwin,

1963. 618p.   (H292)

Groves, Harold Martin. Decentralization in decision-making
and finance. Urbana, Dept. of Political Science, University of Illinois, 1961. 16p.   (H293)

---- ----. Financing government. 5th ed. New York,
Holt, 1958. 630p.   (H294)

Hicks, Ursula Kathleen (Webb) British public finances, their
structure and development, 1886-1957. New York, Oxford
University Press, 1954. 225p.   (H295)

---- ----. Public finance. 2d ed. London, J. Nisbet,
1955. 358p.   (H296)

Holzman, Franklyn D. Soviet taxation; the fiscal and mone-
tary problems of a planned economy. Cambridge, Mass.,
Harvard University Press, 1955. 376p.   (H297)

Li, Chuan Shih. Central and local finance in China; a study
of the fiscal relations between the central, the provincial,
and the local governments. New York, Columbia University Press, 1922. 187p. (Bibliography: p. 182-187)
                                                         (H298)
Mason, Edward Sagendorph. Promoting economic development; the United States and southern Asia. Claremont,
Calif., Pub. by the Claremont College for the four associated colleges at Claremont, 1955. 83p.   (H299)

Misra, Babu Ram. Indian federal finance. Rev. ed. Bombay, Orient Longmans, 1954. 303p. (Bibliography: p.
298-299)   (H300)

Mosher, Frederick C. Program budgeting: theory and
practice, with particular reference to the United States
Department of the Army. Chicago, Public Administration
Service, 1954. 258p.   (H301)

Mund, Vernon Arthur. Government and business. 3d ed.
New York, Harper, 1960. 548p.   (H302)

Royal Institute of Public Administration. Budgeting in public
authorities... New York, Macmillan, 1959. 299p.   (H303)

Smithies, Arthur. The budgetary process in the United
States. New York, McGraw-Hill, 1955. 468p.   (H304)

Sundelson, Jacob Wilner.   Budgetary methods in national and
state governments.   Albany, J.B. Lyon, 1938.   640p.
(Bibliography: p. 620-626)   (H305)

Tax Institute.   Tax relations among governmental units.   By
Roy Blough, Philip H. Cornick, H. Laszle Ecker...and
others.   New York, Tax Policy League Inc., c1938. 226p.
(Bibliography: p. 219-226)   (H306)

Administration and the Public

One of the focal points of the field of public administration lies in the relationship of the functions of administration to the public need.   Within this area administrative law
regulates the conduct of public officials and determines the
rights of individuals in their dealings with these officers.
This also includes the body of law created by administrative
agencies in the form of rules and regulations, administrative
orders and administrative decisions.

Administrative Law and Procedure

Graham, George Adams, ed.   Regulatory administration, an
exploratory study.   Ed. with Henry Reining, Jr.   New
York, Wiley, 1943.   254p.   (H307)

Guins, George Constantine.   Soviet law and Soviet society...
The Hague, M. Nijhoff, 1954.   457p. (Bibliography: p.
379-442)   (H308)

Emerson, Thomas Irwin.   Political and civil rights in the
United States; a collection of legal and related materials.
With David Haber.   2d ed.   Buffalo, Dennis, 1958. 2v.
                                                        (H309)
Hamson, Charles John.   Executive discretion and judicial
control; an aspect of the French Conseil d'Etat.   London,
Stevens, 1954.   222p.   (H310)

Presthus, Robert Vance.   Statistical analysis in comparative
administration.   The Turkish Conseil d'Etat.   With Serda
Erem.   Ithaca, N.Y., Cornell University Press, 1958.
55p.   (H311)

Robson, William Alexander.   Justice and administrative law;
a study of the British Constitution.   3d ed.   London,
Stevens, 1951.   674p.   (H312)

Rosenblum, Victor G.   Public administration and public law;
mutual perspectives in regulatory agencies.   Evansville,
Ill. , 1959.   22 leaves.   (H313)

Schwartz, Bernard.   French administrative law and the com-
mon-law world.   New York, New York University Press,
1954.   367p.   (Bibliographical note: p. 339-341)   367p.
(H314)
---- ----.   Law and the executive in Britain, a comparative
study.   New York, New York University Press, 1949.
388p.   (H315)

Implementation of Programs

Furnivall, John Sydenham.   Educational progress in southeast Asia.   New York, International secretariat, Institute
of Pacific Relations, 1943.   186p.   (H316)

Hall, Mary Penelope.   The social services of modern England.   3d ed.   London, Routledge & Paul, 1955.   336p.
(Bibliography: p. 316-327)   (H317)

Moehlman, Arthur Henry, ed.   Comparative education.   Ed.
with Joseph S. Roucek.   New York, Dryden Press, 1952.
630p.   (H318)

Nelson, George R. , ed.   Freedom and welfare; social patterns in the northern countries of Europe.   Assisted by
Anne Makina-Ollinen and others.   Copenhagen?, 1953.
539p.   (Bibliography: p. 523-529)   (H319)

Administrative Ethics, Prestige of Public Employment

Appleby, Paul Henson.   Morality and administration in democratic government.   Baton Rouge, Louisiana State University Press, 1952. 261p.   (H320)

White, Leonard Dupee.   Further contributions to the prestige
value of public employment.   Chicago, University of Chicago Press, 1932.   88p.   (H321)

---- ----.   The prestige value of public employment in Chicago, an experimental study.   Chicago, University of Chicago Press, c1929.   183p.   (H322)

CHAPTER X

International Relations

Perhaps more than any other area in political science, the literature of international relations is the least self-contained and the most voluminous. Prior to World War I the content of international relations was traditionally considered to be diplomatic history and international law. Since then it has, as a field of scholarly inquiry, expanded immensely to take account of the increased significance of all kinds of socio-economic behavior that fall within national boundaries as factors in international relations. Source materials consist largely of official documents that include inter alia treaties, communiques, press releases and speeches. They also encompass cases and judicial opinions in international and municipal courts as well as the enactments of international bodies that affect national policy.

General Works

Ball, Mary Margaret. International relations. With Hugh B. Killough. New York, Ronald Press, 1956. 667p. (I1)

Buck, Philip Wallenstein, ed. Control of foreign relations in modern nations. New York, Norton, 1957. 865p. (I2)

The Changing environment of international relations. By Grayson Kirk and others. Washington, Brookings Institution, 1956. 158p. (I3)

DeGrazia, Alfred. World politics; a study in international relations. With Thomas H. Stevenson. New York, Barnes & Noble, 1962. 399p. (I4)

Ducheacek, Ivo. Conflict and cooperation among nations. With Kenneth W. Thompson. New York, Holt, Rinehart and Winston, 1960. 649p. (I5)

Frankel, Joseph. International relations. Oxford University Press, 1964. 227p. (I6)

Goldwin, Robert A. , ed. Readings in world politics. With
R. Lerner and G. Stourzh. New York, Oxford University
Press, 1959. 577p.   (I7)

Greene, Fred. Dynamics of international relations, power,
security, and order. New York, Holt, Rinehart and Winston, c1964. 733p.   (I8)

Gross, Feliks. Foreign policy and analysis. New York,
Philosophical Library, 1954. 179p.   (I9)

Haas, Ernst B. Dynamics of international relations. With
Allen S. Whiting. New York, McGraw-Hill, 1956. 557p.
                                                        (I10)

Hartman, Frederick H. The relations of nations. 2d ed.
New York, Macmillan, 1962. 710p.   (I11)

---- ----., ed. World in crisis; readings in international
relations. 2d ed. New York, Macmillan, 1962. 398p.
                                                        (I12)

Hill, Norman Llewellyn. International politics. New York,
Harper & Row, 1963. 458p.   (I13)

Lerche, Charles O. Principles of international politics.
New York, Oxford University Press, 1956. 430p.   (I14)

---- ----., ed. Readings in international politics; concepts
and issues. Ed. with Margaret E. Lerche. New York,
Oxford University Press, 1958. 358p.   (I15)

Liska, George. Nations in alliance; the limits of interde-
pendence. Baltimore, Johns Hopkins Press, 1962. 301p.
                                                        (I16)

McLellan, David S. , ed. The theory and practice of international relations. Ed. with W. C. Olson and Fred A. Son-
dermann. Englewood Cliffs, N. J. , Prentice-Hall, 1960.
542p.   (I17)

Macridis, Roy C. , ed. Foreign policy in world politics. 2d
ed. Englewood Cliffs, N. J. , Prentice-Hall, 1962. 374p.
                                                        (I18)

Massachusetts Institute of Technology. Dept. of Economics
and Social Science. International relations, a selection of
current readings, prepared by the International Relations
Division. Cambridge, Mass. , 1947+ v. 1+   (I19)

Mills, Lennox Algernon. World politics in transition. With
C.H. McLaughlin. New York, Holt, 1956. 751p.   (I20)

Morgenthau, Hans Joachim. Politics among nations; the
struggle for power and peace. 3d ed. New York, 1961,
c1960. 631p.   (I21)

---- ----., ed. Principles and problems of international
politics; selected readings. Ed. with Kenneth W. Thompson. New York, Knopf, 1956. 463p.   (I22)

Ogburn, William Fielding, ed. Technology and international
relations. By Bernard Brodie and others. Chicago, University of Chicago Press, 1949. 201p.   (I23)

Organski, A.F.K. World politics. New York, Knopf,
1958. 461p.   (I24)

Padelford, Norman Judson. The dynamics of international
politics. With George A. Londoln. New York, Macmillan,
1962. 634p.   (I25)

Palmer, Norman Dunbar. International relations; the world
community in transition. With Howard C. Perkins. 2d ed.
Boston, Houghton Mifflin, 1957. 870p.   (I26)

Rienow, Robert. Contemporary international politics. New
York, Crowell, 1961. 431p.   (I27)

Schleicher, Charles P. International relations: cooperation
and conflict. Englewood Cliffs, N.J., Prentice-Hall, 1962.
651p.   (I28)

Schuman, Frederick Lewis. International politics; the western state system and the world community. 6th ed. New
York, McGraw-Hill, 1958. 745p.   (I29)

Schwarzenberger, Georg. Power politics; a study of international society. 2d ed. London, Stevens, 1951. 898p.
(Bibliography: p. 817-873)   (I30)

Simonds, Frank Herbert. The great powers in world poli-
tics; international relations and economic nationalism.
With Brooks Emeny. New ed. New York, American Book
Co., c1939. 731p. (Bibliography: p. ixxxv-cxxv)   (I31)

Strausz-Hupé, Robert. International relations in the age of

conflict between democracy and dictatorship.   With Stefan
T. Possony.   2d ed.   New York, McGraw-Hill, 1954.
826p.   (I32)

Van Dyke, Vernon.   International politics.   New York, Appleton-Century-Crofts, 1957.   483p.   (I33)

Study and Teaching

Since the end of World War II there has been a trend
developing in the methodology and manner in which international relations is viewed.   This trend involves the attempt
to conceptualize the relations of nations and to put in a sub-
ordinate role the historical-descriptive approach so long in
vogue within the field.   Evidence of this movement is contained in various approaches such as decision-making, simulation and game theory that pervade the literature.   The
items cited below illustrate this trend.

General Works

Cohen, Bernard Cecil.   Citizen education in world affairs.
Princeton, N.J., Center of International Studies, Princeton University, 1953.   145p.   (I34)

Cole, Fred.   International relations in institutions of higher
education in the South.   Washington, American Council on
Education, 1958.   169p.   (I35)

Fuller, C. Dale.   Training of specialists in international relations.   Washington, American Council on Education, 1957.
136p.   (I36)

Graham, Gladys (Murphy).   We earn the future; a handbook
for international relations chairmen and others...Washing-
ton, American Association of University Women, 1946.
41p.   (I37)

International Studies Conference, 11th Prague, 1958.   University teaching of international relations...Ed. by Alfred
Zimmern.   Paris, International Institute of Intellectual Cooperation, League of Nations, 1939.   353p.   (I38)

Kirk, Grayson Louis.   The study of international relations in
American colleges and universities.   New York, Council on
Foreign Relations, 1947.   113p.   (I39)

Manning, Charles Anthony Woodward. The university teaching of the social sciences: international relations...Paris,
UNESCO, 1954. 100p.   (I40)

Preston, Ralph Clausius, ed. Teaching world understanding.
New York, Prentice-Hall, 1955. 207p.   (I41)

Swift, Richard N. World affairs and the college curriculum.
Washington, American Council on Education, 1959. 194p.
                                                            (I42)
Symons, Farrell, ed. Courses on international affairs in
American colleges, 1930-31. Boston, World Peace Foun-
dation, 1931. 353p.   (I43)

Vlekke, Bernard Hubertus Maria. On the study of international political science...London, David Davies Memorial
Institute of International Studies, 1956. 16p.   (I44)

Ware, Edith Ellen, ed. The study of international relations
in the United States, survey for 1934. New York, Columbia University Press, 1934. 508p.   (I45)

Wilson, Howard Eugene. American higher education and
world affairs. With Florence H. Wilson. Washington,
American Council on Education, 1963. 158p.   (I46)

---- ----. Universities and world affairs. New York, Carnegie Endowment for International Peace, 1951. 88p. (I47)

Wright, Quincy. The study of international relations. New
York, Appleton-Century-Crofts, 1955. 642p.   (I48)

Approaches to the Study of International Relations

Bernard, Luther Lee. Sociology and the study of international relations. With Jessie Bernard. St. Louis, Washington University. 1934. 115p.   (I49)

Boasson, Charles. Approaches to the study of international
relations. New York, Humanities Press, 1964. 100p.
                                                            (I50)
Boulding, Kenneth Ewart. Conflict and defense: a general
theory. New York, Harper, 1962. 349p.   (I51)

Carr, Edward Hallett. The twenty years' crisis, 1919-1939;
an introduction to the study of international relations. 2d
ed. London, Macmillan, 1954. 243p.   (I52)

Christiansen, Bj/orn.   Attitudes towards foreign affairs as a
function of personality. New York, Humanities Press, 1959.
283p.   (I53)

Deutsch, Karl Wolfgang.   Political community at the international level: problems of definition and measurement.
Garden City, N.Y., Doubleday, 1954. 70p. (Bibliography:
p. 68-69)   (I54)

Fox, William Thornton Rickert, ed.   Theoretical aspects of
international relations.   Notre Dame, Ind., University of
Notre Dame Press, 1959. 118p.   (I55)

Harrison, Horace V., ed.   The role of theory in international relations.   Princeton, N.J., Van Nostrand, 1964.
118p.   (I56)

Hoffmann, Stanley, ed.   Contemporary theory in international relations.   Englewood Cliffs, N.J., Prentice-Hall,
1960. 293p.   (I57)

Hyvarinen, Risto.   Monistic and pluralistic interpretations in
the study of international politics; a methodological examination.   Helsinki, 1958. 157p. (Bibliography: p. 138-
153)   (I58)

International Congress of Applied Psychology.   14th, Copenhagen, 1961.   Psychology and international affairs. Can
we contribute? Copenhagen, Munksgaard, 1962. 132p.
                                                             (I59)
Kaplan, Morton A.   Some problems in the strategic analysis
of international politics.   Princeton, N.J., Center of International Studies, Woodrow Wilson School of Public and International Affairs, Princeton University, 1959. 37p. (I60)

---- ----.   System and process in international politics.
New York, Wiley, 1957. 283p.   (I61)

Kisker, George W., ed.   World tension; the psychopathology
of international relations. New York, Prentice-Hall, 1951.
324p.   (I62)

Knorr, Klaus Eugen, ed.   The international system, theoretical essays.   Ed. with Sidney Verba. Princeton, N.J.,
Princeton University Press, 1961. 237p.   (I63)

Lasswell, Harold Dwight.   World politics and personal insecurity. New York, McGraw-Hill, c1935. 307p.   (I64)

Lerche, Charles O. Concepts of international politics. With
Abdul A. Said. Englewood Cliffs, N.J., Prentice-Hall,
1963. 314p.   (I65)

Liska, George. International equilibrium; a theoretical essay on the politics and organization of security. Cambridge,
Mass., Harvard University Press, 1957. 223p.   (I66)

Madariaga, Salvador de. Theory and practice in international relations. Philadelphia, University of Pennsylvania
Press, 1937. 105p.   (I67)

Manning, Charles Anthony Woodward. The nature of international society. New York, Wiley, 1962. 220p.   (I68)

Modelski, George A. A theory of foreign policy. New York,
Praeger, 1962. 152p.   (I69)

Rosenau, James N., ed. International politics and foreign
policy; a reader in research and theory. New York, Free
Press of Glencoe, 1961. 511p.   (I70)

Russell, Frank Marion. Theories of international relations.
New York, D. Appleton-Century, c1936. 651p.   (I71)

Snyder, Richard Carlton. Decision-making as an approach to
the study of international politics. With H.W. Bruck, and
Burton Sapin. Princeton, N.J., Organizational Behavior
Section, Princeton University, 1954. 120p.   (I72)

Sprout Harold Hance. Man-milieu relationship hypotheses in
the context of international politics. With Margaret Sprout.
Princeton, N.J., Center of International Studies, Princeton University, 1956. 101p.   (I73)

Stratton, George Malcolm. Social psychology of international
conduct. New York, D. Appleton, 1929. 387p.   (I74)

Van Dyke, Vernon. Some approaches and concepts used in
the teaching of international politics...Iowa City, State University of Iowa, c1957. 69p.   (I75)

Methodology and Research

Beardsley, Seymour Willis. Human relations in international affairs, a guide to significant interpretation and research. With Alvin G. Edgell. Washington, Public Affairs Press, 1956. 40p.   (I76)

Carnegie Endowment for International Peace. Current research in international affairs; a selected bibliography of work in progress by private research agencies in Australia, Canada, India, Pakistan, Union of South Africa, United Kingdom and the United States. New York, 1948+   (I77)

Gange, John. University research on international affairs. Washington, D. C. , American Council on Education, 1958. 147p. (Bibliography: p. 134-141)   (I78)

Mathisen, Trygve. Methodology in the study of international relations. New York, Macmillan, 1959. 265p. (Bibliography: p. 253-256)   (I79)

Rosenau, James N. Calculated control as a unifying concept in the study of international politics and foreign policy. Princeton, N.J. , Center of International Studies Woodrow Wilson School of Public and International Affairs, Princeton University, 1963. 58p.   (I80)

Reference Materials

There are many useful reference works available in the field of international relations. Bibliographically this area of political science is well covered. Other works are somewhat out of date such as Theimers encyclopedia and need revision.

Bibliographies

American Universities Field Staff. A select bibliography: Asia, Africa, Eastern Europe, Latin America. New York, 1960. 543p. (Supplement, 1961)   (I81)

Bradley, Phillips. A bibliography of the Monroe Doctrine, 1919-1929. London, London School of Economics, 1929. 39p.   (I82)

Carnell, Francis. The politics of the new states; a select annotated bibliography with special reference to the commonwealth. London, Oxford University Press, 1961. 171p.
(I83)

Deutsch, Karl Wolfgang. Interdisciplinary bibliography on

nationalism.   Cambridge, Mass., Technology Press of
M.I.T., 1956.   165p.   (I84)

Foreign affairs bibliography: a selected and annotated list
of books on international relations.   New York, Russell &
Russell, 1960+   (Now issued in 4 vols. 1919-1962, most
current volume pub. by R.R. Bowker)   (I85)

Mickey, Margaret Portia.   A bibliography of South and South-
west China.   Ann Arbor, University Microfilms, 1961?
161p.   (I86)

Miller, William Robert.   Bibliography of books on war,
pacifism, non-violence, and related studies.   Rev. ed.,
with addenda and author index.   Nyack, N.Y., Fellowship
of Reconciliation, 1961.   37p.   (I87)

Pinson, Koppel Shub.   A bibliographical introduction to nationalism.   New York, Columbia University Press, 1935.
70p.   (Classified and annotated with author index)   (I88)

Plischke, Elmer.   American diplomacy; a bibliography of
bibliographies, autobiographies and commentaries.   College
Park, Bureau of Governmental Research, College of Business and Public Administration, University of Maryland,
1957.   27p.   (I89)

---- ----.   American foreign relations, a bibliography of
official sources.   College Park, Bureau of Governmental
Research, College of Business and Public Administration,
University of Maryland, 1956, c1955.   71p.   (I90)

Savord, Ruth.   World affairs; a foreign service reading list.
With Donald Wasson.   Washington, Foreign Service Journal, 1954.   23p.   (I91)

The United States and Europe; a bibliographical examination
of thought expressed in American publications.   Washington, Library of Congress, Reference Dept., European Affairs Division, 1948+   (I92)

United World Federalists.   Panorama of recent books, films,
and journals on world federation, the United Nations and
world peace.   Washington, 1960.   26 leaves.   (I93)

World Affairs Book Fair, 3d, 1956.   Third world affairs
book fair, political and cultural, 1956.   Catalogue of the

combined book exhibit. New York, Carnegie Endowment
International Center, 1956.   31p.   (I94)

Dictionaries and Encyclopedias

DeKoster, Lester.   Vocabulary of communism, definitions of
key terms, summaries of central ideas, short biographies
of leading figures, descriptions of significant things and
events.   Grand Rapids, Eerdmans, 1964. 224p.   (I95)

Hyamson, Albert Montefiore.   A dictionary of international
affairs.   Washington, Public Affairs Press, 1947. 353p.

A dictionary arrangement of events in international relations up to 1947.   (I96)

Rappoport, Angelo Solomon.   Dictionary of socialism.   London, T. F. Unwin, 1924.   271p.   (I97)

Roback, Abraham Aaron.   A dictionary of international slurs
(ethnophanlisms) With a supplementary essay on aspects of
ethnic prejudice.   Cambridge, Mass., Sci-art Publishers,
1944.   394p.   (Bibliography: p. 345-370)   (I98)

Tandan, N. C. , comp.   Political dictionary, digest of world
affairs with special reference to the present war.   Lahore,
Indian Print Works, 1943.   206p.   (I99)

Theimer, Walter.   An encyclopedia of modern world politics.
New York, Rinehart, 1950.   696p.

A survey of political terms, problems, treaties, and
catchwords of the contemporary world in an alphabetical
arrangement.   Also includes short political sketches of
many countries with a few biographical notes on important
political figures.   (I100)

Worldmark encyclopedia of the nations.   Ed. and pub. :
Moshe Y. Suchs. New York, Worldmark Press, 1963. 5v.

A compendium of information on many countries and some
international organizations.   Now issued in five volumes
as follows: v. 1, United Nations; v. 2, Africa; v. 3, Americas; v. 4, Asia and Australasia; and v.5, United States and
Europe.   (I101)

Directories

American agencies interested in international affairs. Comp.
  by Ruth Savord and Donald Wasson.   4th ed. New York,
  Council on Foreign Relations, 1955,   289p.

  Primarily a directory of research and groups in the United
  States active, directly or indirectly, in the various fields
  related to international relations.   A new edition is in
  preparation.   (I102)

Asia Society.   American institutions and organizations interested in Asia, a reference directory.   2d ed. New
  York, Taplinger, 1961. 581p.

  Includes descriptive listing of over 1,000 programs relating to Asia by American organizations. Entries contain
  name, address, name and title of ranking officials, organizational data, publications and activities that concern Asia.
                                                            (I103)
Carnegie Endowment for International Peace.   Institutes of
  international affairs.   New York, 1953. 131p.

  Introductory chapters give background data on the history
  of institutes, and are followed by an alphabetical list of
  institutes; information given includes addresses, officers,
  aims, activities and historical outline.   (I104)

The International yearbook and statesmen's Who's who.
  London, Burke's Peerage, 1953+

  Combines information concerning political and economic
  conditions of the world with an international biographical
  directory which gives short sketches of about 10,000 persons of international importance such as statesmen, diplomats, military leaders, etc.   (I105)

The World diplomatic directory and world diplomatic biography.   London, World Diplomatic Directory Service, 1950+

  First edition was divided into two parts each arranged
  alphabetically by country.   Part 1 gives the principal missions and consular offices abroad of each country including
  the U.N.   Part 2 includes brief biographical data for officers listed in the part.   Supplements are issued at irregular intervals.   (I106)

Atlases

Boyd, Andrew Kirk Henry. An atlas of African affairs.
With Patrick von Rensburg. New York, Praeger, 1962.
133p.

All of the atlases in this section follow essentially the
same format. They include maps on the important aspects
of contemporary world affairs. A brief concise text ac-
companies each map, giving background information and
summarizing the situation.   (I107)

---- ----. An atlas of world affairs. 4th ed. New York,
Praeger, 1963, c1962. 160p.   (I108)

Hudson, Geoffrey Francis. An atlas of Far Eastern politics.
With Marthe Rajchman. New York, John Day, 1942.
207p.   (I109)

Pounds, Norman John Grenville. An atlas of European affairs. New York, Praeger, 1964. 135p.   (I110)

---- ----. An atlas of Middle Eastern affairs. New York,
Praeger, 1963. 117p.   (I111)

Guides

Bemis, Samuel Flagg. Guide to the diplomatic history of
the United States, 1775-1921. With Grace G. Griffin.
Washington, U.S. Govt. Print. Off., 1935. 979p.

An extremely important bibliography and guide to printed
materials and manuscript sources. It is divided into two
main parts: pt. 1, Bibliography, p. 3-779, listing 5,318
items, with comments; pt. 2, Remarks on the sources, p.
781-942, including manuscript sources. Indexes of collections of personal papers, p. 943-945 and authors, p.
946-979.   (I112)

Legum, Colin, ed. Africa; a handbook to the continent.
New York, Praeger, 1962. 553p.

An excellent guide to the continent of Africa with a variety
of information on each country.   (I113)

Moon, Parker Thomas. Syllabus on international relations.
New York, Macmillan, 1925. 280p. (Bibliography:

p. 239-276)

An outline guide to the field.   Good for historical purposes but is out of date.   (I114)

Thomas, Daniel H., ed.   Guide to the diplomatic archives of
Western Europe.   Ed. with Lynn M. Case.   Philadelphia,
University of Pennsylvania Press, 1959.   389p.

Invaluable source for the diplomatic resources of Western
Europe.   Includes a great many bibliographical references.
                                                             (I115)
U.S. Library of Congress.   General Reference and Bibliography Division.   A guide to bibliographic tools for research
in foreign affairs.   Comp. by Helen F. Conover.   2d ed.,
with supplement.   Washington, 1958. 145p.

Items are listed in two sections, including bibliographies,
manuals, indexes, and other publications, selected primarily for use in connection with current foreign affairs.
                                                             (I116)
Other Reference Materials

Almanac of current world leaders.   Los Angeles, Calif.,
1958+

Issued quarterly.   A current listing of major government
officers in 124 countries and 15 organizations and alli-
ances.   (I117)

Background on world politics; an interdisciplinary digest.
Waco, Texas, 1957+

Digests articles dealing with international affairs from publications not generally associated with the field.   (I118)

Current thought on peace and war.   Durham, N.C., 1960+

Primarily a digest of literature and research in progress
on the problems of world conflict and order.   Issued semi-
annually.   (I119)

Deadline data on foreign affairs.   New York, Deadline Data,
Inc., 1956+

5 x 8 cards in catalog trays.   Kept up to date by supplementary cards issued weekly.   Factual information listed

in chronological order.   (I120)

Foreign Policy Association World Affairs Center.   Careers
in world affairs; at home and abroad.   Garden City,
N.Y., Doubleday, 1961.   140p.

A brief work indicating the opportunities for working in
contemporary international affairs.   (I121)

Die Internationale politik.   München, Oldenbourg, 1955+

Issued annually.   Surveys international affairs and includes
references to many items of importance.   Considered a
scholarly and reliable source of information that is prepared by specialists.   (I122)

Survey of international affairs, 1920-23+   London, Oxford
University Press, 1925+

Each year the most prominent events occuring in world
politics are reviewed.   Profusely documented, this series
is a most useful tool for reliable information.   (I123)

The Yearbook of world affairs.   London, Stevens, 1947+

Published under the auspices of the London Institute of
World Affairs, this annual volume contains survey articles,
book reviews, and factual information on international affairs.   (I124)

Source Materials

      Documents form the primary source matter for inter-
national relations.   Many governments and some independent
agencies publish their documents dealing with foreign affairs
at regular intervals.   Some works are selected compilations
from the basic sources.

Documents on international affairs.   New York, Oxford University Press, 1929+   (I125)

Goebel, Dorothy (Burne) ed.   American foreign policy, a
documentary survey, 1776-1960.   New York, Holt, Rinehart and Winston, 1961.   458p.   (I126)

Harley, John Eugene.   Documentary textbook in international
relations; a text and reference study emphasizing official

documents and materials relating to world peace and international cooperation.   Los Angeles, Calif., Sutton House,
1934.   848p.   (I127)

Hill, Norman Llewellyn.   International relations; documents
and readings.   New York, Oxford University Press, 1950.
536p.   (I128)

Plischke, Elmer, ed.   International relations; basic documents.   2d ed.   Princeton, N.J., Van Nostrand, 1962.
194p.   (I129)

International Politics

International politics is only one aspect of international relations.   In a general sense this aspect is concerned
with those relations among nation states that have as their
most distinguishable quality, the employment of power or influence to achieve specific goals or objectives.   Power, when
viewed within the context of international politics, is the ability to control the actions of others.   Thus the resources of
nations may be employed in competition and cooperation as
well as in conflict.

Rise of the Nation-State System

The nation-states in our present world are the product
of an historical evolutionary process from preliterary times.
Dating from the early families, tribes and clans, national
cultural ties, strengthened by natural boundaries, proved a
foundation for combining feudal territories into larger political divisions.   Actually, the nation-state system has changed
little since the seventeenth century; however, advances in
communication, transportation and technology have far out-
stripped progress in international social adjustment.

Brinton, Clarence Crane.   From many, one; the process of
political integration, the problem of world government.
Cambridge, Mass., Harvard University Press, 1948. 126p.
                                                           (I130)
Burns, Edward McNall.   Western civilizations, their history
and their culture.   6th ed.   New York, Norton, 1963.
1083p.   (I131)

Herz, John H.   International politics in the atomic age.
New York, Columbia University Press, 1959. 360p. (I132)

Toynbee, Arnold Joseph. The world and the west. New
York, Oxford University Press, 1953. 99p. (I133)

Welles, Sumner. Seven decisions that shaped history. New
York, Harper, 1951. 236p. (I134)

Wright, Quincy. Problems of stability and progress in international relations. Berkeley, University of California
Press, 1954. 378p. (I135)

Factors of International Politics

Many complex factors are the prime ingredients of
international politics. Only a few of the more important are
included here to illustrate their diverse nature as well as
their significance to the international political process.

Political Nationalism

One of the most pervasive and powerful forces that
exists in the world is political nationalism. Nationalism is
an attitude held by a group of people who think of themselves
as a nation and owe supreme allegiance to the state of which
they are a part. Nationalism is not the product of any single
factor but a combination of such things as culture, history,
language, religion, race and government.

Chadwick, Hecter Munro. The nationalities of Europe and
the growth of national ideologies. Cambridge, Eng., the
University Press, 1945. 209p. (I136)

Deutsch, Karl Wolfgang. Nationalism and social communication; an inquiry into the foundations of nationality. Cambridge, Mass., New York, Wiley, 1953. 292p. (Bibliography: p. 251-266) (I137)

Hayes, Carlton Joseph Huntley. The historical evolution of
modern nationalism. New York, Macmillan, 1948. 327p.
(I138)
---- ----. Nationalism, a religion. New York, Macmillan,
1960. 187p. (I139)

Kohn, Hans. Nationalism, its meaning and history. Princeton, N.J., Van Nostrand, 1955. 192p. (I140)

Shafer, Boyd C. Nationalism: myth and reality. New York,
Harcourt, Brace, 1955. 319p. (I141)

Snyder, Louis Leo, ed. The dynamics of nationalism;
   readings in its meaning and development. Princeton, N.J.,
   Van Nostrand, 1964. 382p. (Bibliography: p. 377-378)
                                                        (I142)

National Character and Ideology

It is important in international relations to be able to
assess correctly any peculiarities in the cultural pattern of
a people which help to explain its international attitudes. In
effect, there are national differences which go beyond speech
and dress and affect outlook, ideals, and patterns. National
character is a combination of those uniform character traits
located within a national society that result from the shared
experience within the nation-state and the characteristic institutions it produces, (e.g. linguistic, educational, political,
legal and economic). Ideologies are primarily organized
systems of ideas, beliefs, and values that can be artificially
disseminated through propaganda or education.

Barker, Ernest. National character and the factors in its
   formation. 4th ed. London, Methuen, 1948. 268p. (I143)

Benedict, Ruth (Fulton) The chrysanthemum and the sword;
   patterns of Japanese culture. Boston, Houghton Mifflin,
   1946. 324p.   (I144)

Buchanan, William. How nations see each other, a study in
   public opinion. With Hadley Cantril and others. Urbana,
   University of Illinois Press, 1953. 220p.   (I145)

Cartwright, Dorwin, ed. Group dynamics, research and
   theory. Ed. with Alvin Zander. Evanston, Ill., Row,
   Peterson, 1953. 642p.   (I146)

Commager, Henry Steele, ed. America in perspective; the
   United States through foreign eyes. New York, Random
   House, 1947. 389p. (Bibliography: p. 387-389) (I147)

Fearey, Robert A. The U.S. versus the U.S.S.R.; ideologies in conflict. Washington, Public Affairs Press, 1959.
   48p.   (I148)

Gorer, Geoffrey. The American people; a study in national
   character. Rev. ed. New York, Norton, 1964. 267p.
                                                        (I149)
---- ----. The people of Great Russia; a psychological
   study. With John Rickman. New York, Chanticleer Press,

1950.   235p.   (I150)

Joseph, Franz M. , ed.   As others see us; the United States
through foreign eyes.   With contributions by Raymond Aron
and others.   Princeton, N. J. , Princeton University Press,
1959.   360p.   (I151)

Klineberg, Otto.   Tensions affecting international understanding.   New York, Social Science Research Council, 1950.
227p.   (I152)

Leites, Nathan Constantin.   A study of Bolshevism.   Glencoe, Ill., Free Press, 1953.   639p.   (Bibliography: p.
630-634)   (I153)

Lloyd, Christopher.   Democracy and its rivals; an introduction to modern political theories.   New York, Longmans,
Green, 1946.   199p.   (I154)

Madariaga, Salvador de.   Englishmen, Frenchmen, Spaniards;
an essay in comparative psychology.   London, Oxford University Press, 1931.   256p.   (I155)

Mannheim, Karl.   Ideology and utopia; an introduction to the
sociology of knowledge.   New York, Harcourt, Brace,
1936.   318p.   (I156)

Mead, Margaret.   And keep your powder dry; an anthro-
pologist looks at America.   New York, W. Morrow, 1942.
274p.   (Bibliography: p. 265-274)   (I157)

---- ----.   Soviet attitudes toward authority; an inter-disciplinary approach to problems of Soviet character.   New
York, McGraw-Hill, 1951.   148p.   (I158)

Northrop, Filmer Stuart Cuckow, ed.   Ideological differences
and world order; studies in the philosophy and science of
the world's cultures.   New Haven, Yale University Press,
1949.   486p.   (I159)

Stoetzel, Jean.   Without the chrysanthemum and the sword;
a study of the attitudes of youth in post-war Japan.   New
York, Columbia University Press, 1955. 334p.   (I160)

Force and Power Politics

The use of force to achieve aims or ambitions is as

old as man himself.   Power of one kind or another is the
inescapable means by which the state carries out its policies,
and this is as true in the domestic as in the foreign field.

American Historical Association.   War as a social institution; the historian's perspective.   Ed. by J.D. Clarkson
and T. C. Cochran.   New York, Columbia University Press,
1941.   333p.   (I61)

Appadorai, Angadipuran.   The use of force in international
relations.   Bombay, Asia Pub. House, 1958. 124p. (I162)

Earle, Edward Mead, ed.   Makers of modern strategy; military thought from Machiavelli to Hitler.   Princeton, N. J.,
Princeton University Press, 1943.   553p.   (I163)

Ogburn, William Fielding, ed.   Technology and international
relations.   Chicago, University of Chicago Press, 1949.
201p.   (I164)

Puleston, William Dilworth.   The influence of force in foreign relations.   New York, Van Nostrand, c1955. 254p.
(Bibliography: p. 239-240)   (I165)

Reynolds, Philip Alan.   War in the twentieth century. Car-
diff, University of Wales Press, 1951. 29p.   (I166)

Vagts, Alfred.   A history of militarism; romance and realities of a profession.   New York, Norton, c1937. 510p.
                                                           (I167)
Waltz, Kenneth Neal.   Man, the state, and war; a theoretical analysis.   New York, Columbia University Press, 1959.
263p.   (I168)

Wight, Martin.   Power politics.   New York, Royal Institute
of International Affairs, 1949.   66p.   (I169)

Wright, Quincy.   A study of war.   Chicago, University of
Chicago Press, 1942.   2v.   (I170)

Techniques of Political Propaganda

Propaganda may be defined as a systematic attempt
through the means of mass communication to influence the
thinking, and thereby the behavior, of people in the interest
of some particular person or group.   Some of these techniques include the offering of materialistic rewards or threats

of physical harm for non-compliance.   Others include subtle
manipulation of bias detectable in certain groups of people.

Barrett, Edward W.   Truth is our weapon.   New York,
    Funk & Wagnalls, 1953.   355p.   (Bibliography: p. 345-
    346)   (I171)

Carroll, Wallace.   Persuade or perish.   Boston, Houghton
    Mifflin, 1948.   392p.   (I172)

Chase, Allan.   Falange; the axis secret army in the Ameri-
    cas.   New York, Putnam, 1943.   278p.   (I173)

Fraser, Lindley Macnaghten.   Germany between two wars,
    a study of propaganda and war-guilt.   New York, Oxford
    University Press, 1945.   184p.   (I174)

Inkeles, Alex.   Public opinion in Soviet Russia, a study in
    mass persuasion.   Cambridge, Mass. , Harvard University
    Press, 1950.   379p.   (Bibliography: p. 355-364)   (I175)

Kris, Ernst.   German radio propaganda.   New York, Oxford
    University Press, 1944.   529p.   (I176)

Lerner, Daniel, ed.   Propaganda in war and crisis, materi-
    als for American policy.   New York, Stewart, 1951. 500p.
                                                          (I177)
---- ----.   Sykewar; psychological warfare against Germany,
    D-Day to VE-Day.   New York, Stewart, 1949.   463p.
    (Bibliography: p. 347-399)   (I178)

Markel, Lister.   Public opinion and foreign policy.   New
    York, Harper, 1949.   227p.   (I179)

Miksche, Ferdinand Otto.   Secret forces; the technique of
    underground movements.   London, Faber and Faber, 1950.
    181p.   (I180)

Possony, Stefan Thomas.   A century of conflict; communist
    techniques of world revolution.   Chicago, H. Regnery,
    1953.   439p.   (I181)

Rosenau, James N.   National leadership and foreign policy;
    a case study in the mobilization of public support.   Prince-
    ton, N. J. , Princeton University Press, 1963.   409p.
                                                          (I182)
---- ----.   Public opinion and foreign policy; an operational

formulation. New York, Random House, c1961. 118p.
(I183)
Rowan, Richard Wilmer. The story of the secret service.
Garden City, N.Y., Doubleday Doran, 1937. 732p. (Bib-
liography: p. 671-732)
(I184)

Economic Nationalism

The counterpart of political nationalism is located in
the field of economics. Since 1918 economic nationalism has
dominated the world and is largely concerned with the further-
ance of national aims through regulation of international economic relations.

Basch, Antonin. The new economic warfare. New York,
Columbia University Press, 1941. 190p.
(I185)

Cundliffe, John Bell. International trade and economic nationalism. New York, Carnegie Endowment for International Peace, 1951. (International conciliation, no. 476,
pp. 547-581)
(I186)

Einzig, Paul. Economic warfare, 1939-1940. London, Macmillan, 1941. 150p.
(I187)

---- ----. World finance, 1914-1935. New York, Macmillan, 1935. 382p.
(I188)

Ellsworth, Paul Theodore. The international economy; its
structure and operation. New York, Macmillan, 1950.
922p. (Bibliography: p. 887-907)
(I189)

Gordon, David Livingston. The hidden weapon; the story of
economic warfare. With Royden Dangerfield. New York,
Harper, 1947. 238p.
(I190)

Hexner, Ervin. International cartels. Chapel Hill, The University of North Carolina Press, 1945. 555p. (I191)

Hodgson, James Goodwin, comp. Economic nationalism.
New York, H.W. Wilson, 1933. 208p. (Bibliography: p.
25-44)
(I192)

Meyer, F.V. Britain's colonies in world trade. New York,
Oxford University Press, 1948. 281p. (Bibliography: p.
269-273)
(I193)

Staley, Eugene.   World economy in transition; technology vs.
politics, laissez faire vs. planning, power vs. welfare.
New York, Council on Foreign Relations, c1939. 340p.
                                                      (I194)

Imperialism

        In modern international relations the outstanding mode
of behavior for states is imperialism.   It has existed in
many times and places.   Imperialism consists of the influence or control, or efforts to procure them, of one state
over another, or over a dependent area, usually by force.

Hobson, John Atkinson.   Imperialism, a study.   London,
    Allen and Unwin, 1938.   386p.   (I195)

Moon, Parker Thomas.   Imperialism and world politics.
    New York, Macmillan, 1926.   583p.   (I196)

Schumpeter, Joseph Alois.   Imperialism and social classes;
    two essays.   Tr. by Heinz Norden.   New York, Meridian
    Books, 1955, c1951.   182p.   (I197)

Seton-Watson, Hugh.   The new imperialism.   Chester Springs,
    Pa. , Dufor Editions, 1962, c1961.   136p.   (I198)

Winslow, Earl Micajah.   The pattern of imperialism, a
    study of theories of power.   New York, Columbia Univer-
    sity Press, 1950, c1948.   278p.   (I199)

Population and Food

        One of the most serious factors evidenced in interna-
tional politics at the present time concerns the tremendous
rise in world population and the shortage of food to feed
everyone.   In spite of the great amount of food produced
there are still many areas of starving people in the world.
This problem, needless to say, is far from being solved.

American Assembly.   The population dilemma.   Englewood
    Cliffs, N. J. , Prentice-Hall, 1963.   188p.   (I200)

Carr Saunders, Alexander Morris.   World population; past
    growth and present trends.   Oxford, Clarendon Press,
    1936.   336p.   (Bibliography: p. xiv-xv)   (I201)

Clark, Frederick LeGros, ed.   Four thousand million
    mouths; scientific humanism and the shadow of world hun-

ger.   Ed. with N.W. Price.   New York, Oxford University Press, 1951.   222p.   (I202)

Davis, Kingsley.   The population of India and Pakistan.
Princeton, N.J. , Princeton, University Press, 1951. 263p.
(Bibliography: p. 252-258)   (I203)

Northwestern University, Evanston, Ill.   World population
and future resources.   Ed. by Paul K. Hatt.   New York,
American Book Co., 1952.   262p.   (I204)

Stamp, Laurence Dudley.   Our underdeveloped world. London, Faber and Faber, 1953.   186p.   (I205)

Thompson, Warren Simpson.   Plenty of people; the world's
population pressures, problems and policies and how they
concern us.   Rev. ed. New York, Ronald Press, 1948.
281p.   (I206)

Vogt, William.   Road to survival. New York, Sloane, 1948.
335p.   (Bibliography: p. 298-301)   (I207)

Diplomacy

         In its very broadest sense, diplomacy is the art or
practice of international negotiation and the administrative
management of such negotiations.   Diplomacy is wrapped in
a complex etiquette, almost impossible to describe, since it
depends largely upon tact.   It is administered by a considerable personnel, whose functions everywhere are for the most
part similar.

Corbett, Percy Ellwood.   Law and diplomacy.   Princeton,
N.J. , Princeton University Press, 1959. 290p.   (I208)

Craig, Gordon Alexander, ed.   The diplomats: 1919-1939.
Ed. with Felix Gilbert.   Princeton, N.J. , Princeton University Press, 1953.   700p.   (I209)

Heatley, David Playfair. Diplomacy and the study of international relations.   Oxford, Clarendon Press, 1919. 292p.
                                                            (I210)
Kertesz, Stephen Denis, ed.   Diplomacy in the changing
world.   Ed. with M.A. Fitzsimons.   Notre Dame, Ind. ,
University of Notre Dame Press, 1959. 407p.   (I211)

Nicolson, Harold George.   Diplomacy.   3d ed.   New York,

Oxford University Press, 1963.   286p.   (Bibliography: p.
263)   (I212)

---- ----. The evolution of diplomatic method.   London,
Constable, 1954.   93p.   (I213)

Panikkar, Kavalan Madhava.   The principles and practice of
diplomacy.   Bombay, Asia Pub. House, 1957. 99p. (I214)

Satow, Ernest Mason.   A guide to diplomatic practice. 4th
ed.   Ed. by Nevile Bland.   New York, Longmans, Green,
1958.   510p.   (I215)

Wriston, Henry Merritt.   Diplomacy in a democracy.   New
York, Harper, 1956.   115p.   (I216)

Military Policy

Military policy is important in international politics
because armed forces are useful as instruments of foreign
policy whether or not they are actually employed in physical
combat.   Even within domestic societies, military power can
be used to preserve order in countries lacking in consensus
and stable political institutions.

Furniss, Edgar Stephenson.   American military policy;
strategy and aspects of world political geography.   New
York, Rinehart, 1957.   494p.   (I217)

Howard, Michael, ed.   Soldiers and governments; nine studies in civil-military relations.   Bloomington, Indiana University Press, 1959.   192p.   (I218)

Janowitz, Morris.   The military in the political development
of new nations; an essay in comparative analysis.   Chicago, University of Chicago Press, c1964. 134p.   (I219)

Sapin, Burton M.   The role of the military in American foreign policy.   With Richard C. Snyder.   Garden City, N.Y.,
Doubleday, 1954.   84p.   (Bibliography: p. 83-84)   (I220)

Vagts, Alfred.   Defense and diplomacy; the soldier and the
conduct of foreign relations.   New York, King's Crown
Press, 1956.   547p.   (Bibliography: p. 533-547)   (I221)

Foreign Aid

As an instrument of foreign policy, foreign aid is of relatively recent derivation. States employ this tactic to induce friendship or to spread an ideology. The United States spends millions of dollars each year on various types of projects in foreign countries in an effort to relieve hardship and to help create stable governments.

Feis, Herbert. Foreign aid and foreign policy. New York, St. Martin's Press, 1964. 246p. (I222)

Liska, George. The new statecraft; foreign aid in American foreign policy. Chicago, University of Chicago Press, 1960. 246p. (I223)

Wolf, Charles. Foreign aid: theory and practice in southern Asia. Princeton, N.J., Princeton University Press, 1960. 442p. (I224)

Formulation and Control of Foreign Policy

There are a great many factors that go into the formulation and control of foreign policy. In general, foreign policy is a course of action followed by a nation-state to achieve certain aims or goals. Many of these courses of action depend on a nation's resources, skill in using the resources and the climate or conditions of international interaction.

Almond, Gabriel Abraham. The American people and foreign policy. New York, Praeger, 1960. 296p. (I225)

Brookings Institution, Washington, D.C. United States foreign policy: the formulation and administration of United States foreign policy. Washington, U.S. Govt. Print. Off., 1960. 191p. (I226)

Cheever, Daniel S. American foreign policy and the separation of powers. With H.F. Haviland, Jr. Cambridge, Mass., Harvard University Press, 1952. 244p. (I227)

Corwin, Edward Samuel. The President's control of foreign relations. Princeton, N.J., Princeton University Press, 1917. 216p. (I228)

Dahl, Robert Alan. Congress and foreign policy. New York,

Harcourt, Brace, 1950.   305p.   (I229)

Dangerfield, Royden James.   In defense of the Senate; a
    study in treaty making.   Norman, University of Oklahoma
    Press, 1933.   365p. (Bibliography: p. 353-357)   (I230)

Elder, Robert Ellsworth.   The policy machine; the Depart-
    ment of State and American foreign policy.   Syracuse,
    N.Y., Syracuse University Press, 1960. 238p.   (I231)

Friedrich, Carl Joachim.   Foreign policy in the making; the
    search for a new balance of power.   New York, Norton,
    c1938.   296p.   (I232)

London, Kurt.   How foreign policy is made. 2d ed.   New
    York, Van Nostrand, 1950.   277p. (Bibliography: p. 260-
    265)   (I233)

Macridis, Roy C., ed.   Foreign policy in world politics.
    2d ed.   Englewood Cliffs, N.J., Prentice-Hall, 1962.
    374p.   (I234)

Mangone, Gerard J.   A guide to United States foreign policy.
    Syracuse, N.Y., Syracuse University Press, 1959. 48p.
                                                       (I235)
Robinson, James Arthur.   Congress and foreign policy-
    making; a study in legislative influence and initiative.
    Homewood, Ill., Dorsey Press, 1962. 262p. (Bibliogra-
    phy: p. 235-253)   (I236)

Snyder, Richard Carlton.   American foreign policy; formula-
    tion, principles and programs. With Edgar S. Furniss,
    Jr.   New York, Rinehart, 1954.   846p.   (I237)

Woodrow Wilson Foundation.   United States foreign policy:
    its organization and control.   New York, Columbia Univer-
    sity Press, 1952.   288p.   (I238)

Foreign Affairs Administration

        The administration of foreign affairs differs from
country to country.   Many nations employ the use of a career
civil service; others choose members from a political party.
There is no firm, set pattern for the administration of foreign affairs in the world today.

Ashton-Gwatkin, Frank Trelaway Arthur.   The British For-

eign Service; a discussion of the development and function
of the British Foreign Service. Syracuse, N.Y., Syracuse
University Press, 1950. 94p.   (I239)

Brookings Institution, Washington, D.C. The administration
of foreign affairs and overseas operation. Washington,
1961. 380p.   (I240)

Childs, James Rives. American foreign service. New York,
Holt, 1948. 261p.   (I241)

Gosses, Frans. The management of British foreign policy
before the First World War... Leiden, A.W. Sijthoff, 1948.
172p. (Bibliography: p. 10-18)   (I242)

McCamy, James Lucian. The administration of American
foreign affairs. New York, Knopf, 1950. 304p.   (I243)

Macmahon, Arthur Whittier. Administration of foreign affairs. University, Ala., University of Alabama Press,
1953. 275p.   (I244)

Strang, William Strang. The Foreign Office. New York,
Oxford University Press, 1955. 266p.   (I245)

Stuart, Graham Henry. American diplomatic and consular
practice. 2d ed. New York, Appleton-Century-Crofts,
1952. 477p. (Bibliography: p. 453-460)   (I246)

---- ----. The Department of State; a history of its organization, procedure, and personnel. New York, Macmillan,
1949. 517p.   (I247)

The Practice of International Politics

        To a large extent international relations are shaped
by the policies of the leading powers, in alliance or at times
in antagonism toward one another. The policies of the great
powers are manifestations of nationalism, since each one is
primarily concerned with the advancement of its own interests.
The following section cites a number of works that illustrate
the policies of the leading world powers. Included also, however, are a number of works dealing with power vacuums or
underdeveloped nations. This latter area constitutes one of
the most frustrating problems extant in international relations today.

American Region

Berle, Adolf Augustus. Tides of crisis; a primer of foreign relations. New York, Reynal, 1957. 328p.   (I248)

Bloomfield, Lincoln Palmer. The United Nations and U.S. foreign policy; a new look at the national interest. Boston, Little, Brown, 1960. 276p.   (I249)

Brookings Institution, Washington, D.C. Major problems of United States foreign policy. A study guide. Washington, 1947-1954. 5v. (No longer published)   (I250)

Carleton, William Graves. The revolution in American foreign policy: its global range. New York, Random House, 1963. 530p. (Bibliography: p. 481-516)   (I251)

Documents on American foreign relations. Boston, World Peace Foundation, 1939+   (I252)

Finletter, Thomas Knight.   Foreign policy; the next phase, the 1960's. 2d ed. New York, Harper, 1960. 235p.
                                                    (I253)
Furniss, Edgar Stephenson. An introduction to American foreign policy. With Richard C. Snyder. New York, Rinehart, 1957. 252p.   (I254)

Gange, John. American foreign relations: permanent problems and changing policies. New York, Ronald Press, 1959. 593p.   (I255)

Goldwin, Robert A., ed. Readings in American foreign policy. With R. Lerner, and G. Stourzh. New York, Oxford University Press, 1956. 709p.   (I256)

Holt, Robert T. Strategic psychological operations and American foreign policy. With R.W van de Velde. Chicago, University of Chicago Press, 1960. 243p.   (I257)

Kennan, George Frost. American diplomacy, 1900-1950. Chicago, University of Chicago Press, 1951. 154p. (I258)

Northrop, Filmer Stuart Cuckow. European union and United States foreign policy; a study in sociological jurisprudence. New York, Macmillan, 1954. 230p.   (I259)

Pratt, Julius William. A history of United States foreign

policy.   Englewood Cliffs, N.J., Prentice-Hall, 1958.
808p.   (I260)

Riddell, Walter Alexander, ed.   Documents on Canadian foreign policy, 1917-1939.   Toronto, Oxford University Press,
1962. 806p. (Bibliography: p. 781-785)   (I261)

Rockefeller Brothers Fund.   The mid-century challenge to
U.S. foreign policy. Garden City, N.Y., Doubleday, 1959.
74p.   (I262)

Rostow, Walt Whitman.   The United States in the world
arena; an essay in recent history. New York, Harper,
1960. 586p.   (I263)

Smith, Daniel Malloy, ed.   Major problems in American
diplomatic history: documents and readings. Boston,
Heath, 1964. 677p.   (I264)

Steiner, Zara S.   The State Department and the Foreign
Service; the Wriston report-four years later. Princeton,
N.J., Center of International Studies, Princeton Univer-
sity, 1958. 57p.   (I265)

Stillman, Edmund O.   The politics of hysteria; the sources
of twentieth century conflict. With W. Pfaff. New York,
Harper and Row, c1964. 273p.   (I266)

Strausz-Hupé, Robert.   A forward strategy for America.
With W.R. Kintner and S.T. Possony. New York, Harper,
1961. 451p.   (I267)

Thompson, Kenneth W.   Political realism and the crisis of
world politics; an American approach to foreign policy.
Princeton, N.J., Princeton University Press, 1960. 261p.
                                                                       (I268)
The United States in world affairs; an account of American
relations.   New York, Harper, 1932+   (I269)

European Region

Bathurst, Maurice Edward.   Germany and the North Atlantic
community; a legal survey. With J.L. Simpson. New
York, Praeger, 1956. 217p.   (I270)

Bolles, Blair.   The big change in Europe. New York, Norton, 1958. 527p.   (I271)

Butz, Otto. Germany: dilemma for American foreign policy. Garden City, N.Y., Doubleday, 1954. 69p.   (I272)

Catlin, George Edward Gordon. The Atlantic community.
London, Coram, 1959. 146p.   (I273)

Dehio, Ludwig. Germany and world politics in the twentieth
century. New York, Knopf, 1959. 141p.   (I274)

Deutsch, Karl Wolfgang. Germany rejoins the powers; mass
opinion, interest groups, and elites in contemporary German foreign policy. With L.J. Edinger. Stanford, Calif.,
Stanford University Press, 1959. 320p. (Bibliography: p.
293-298)   (I275)

Epstein, Leon D. Britain-uneasy ally. Chicago, University
of Chicago Press, 1954. 279p.   (I276)

Furniss, Edgar Stephenson. France, troubled ally; De-
Gaulle's heritage and prospects. New York, Harper,
1960. 512p.   (I277)

Gelber, Lionel Morris. America in Britain's place; the
leadership of the West and Anglo-American unity. New
York, Praeger, 1961. 356p.   (I278)

Grindrod, Muriel. The rebuilding of Italy, politics and economics, 1945-1955. New York, Royal Institute of International Affairs, 1955. 269p. (Bibliography: p. 254-258)
                                                  (I279)
Howard, Michael. Disengagement in Europe. Baltimore,
Penguin Books, 1958. 92p.   (I280)

Lerner, Daniel, ed. France defeats EDC. Ed. with R.
Aron. New York, Praeger, 1957. 225p.   (I281)

Macridis, Roy C. The DeGaulle republic: quest for unity.
With B.E. Brown. Homewood, Ill., Dorsey Press, 1960.
400p.   (I282)

Schlamm, William Siegmund. Germany and the East-West
crisis; the decisive challenge to American policy. New
York, D. McKay Co., 1959. 237p.   (I283)

Speier, Hans, ed. West Germany leadership and foreign
policy. Ed. with W.P. Davison. Evanston, Ill., Row,
Peterson, 1957. 323p.   (I284)

Williams, Philip Maynard. DeGaulle's Republic. With M.
Harrison. 2d ed. London, Longmans, 1961. 279p. (I285)

Wolfers, Arnold, ed. The Anglo-American tradition in foreign affairs; readings from Thomas More to Woodrow Wilson. Ed. with L.W. Martin. New Haven, Yale University Press, 1956. 286p.   (I286)

Wright, Richard. Pagan Spain. New York, Harper, 1957.
241p.   (I287)

Soviet Union

Allen, Robert Loring. Soviet economic warfare. Washington, Public Affairs Press, 1960. 293p.   (I288)

Armstrong, John Alexander. The Soviet bureaucratic elite;
a case study of the Ukrainian apparatus. New York,
Praeger, 1959. 174p. (Bibliography: p. 152-162) (I289)

Aubrey, Henry G. Coexistence: economic challenge and
response. Washington, National Planning Association,
1961. 323p.   (I290)

Barghoorn, Frederick Charles. The Soviet cultural offen-
sive; the role of cultural diplomacy in Soviet foreign policy. Princeton, N.J., Princeton University Press, 1961.
353p.   (I291)

Berliner, Joseph S. Soviet economic aid; the new aid and
trade policy in underdeveloped countries. New York,
Praeger, 1958. 232p. (Bibliography: p. 224-228) (I292)

Brzezinski, Zbibniew K. The Soviet bloc, unity and conflict.
Rev. ed. New York, Praeger, 1961. 543p.   (I293)

Campbell, Robert Wellington. Soviet economic power; its
organization, growth, and challenge. Ed. by Carl Kaysen.
Boston, Houghton Mifflin, 1960. 209p.   (I294)

Conference on a Century of Russian Foreign Policy, Yale
University, 1961. Russian foreign policy, essays in his-
torical perspective. Ed. by Ivo J. Lederer. New Haven,
Yale University Press, 1962. 620p.   (I295)

Dallin, Alexander, comp. Soviet conduct in world affairs; a
selection of readings. New York, Columbia University

Press, 1960.   318p.   (I296)

---- ----.   The Soviet Union at the United Nations; an inquiry into Soviet motives and objectives.   New York,
Praeger, 1962.   244p.   (I297)

Dallin, David J.   Soviet foreign policy after Stalin.   Philadelphia, Lippincott, 1961.   543p.   (I298)

Dinerstein, Herbert Samuel.   War and the Soviet Union;
nuclear weapons and the revolution in Soviet military and
political thinking.   New York, Praeger, 1959.   268p.
                                                        (I299)
Fischer, Louis.   Russia, America, and the world.   New
York, Harper, 1961.   244p.   (I300)

---- ----.   The soviets in world affairs; a history of the
Soviet Union and the rest of the world, 1917-1929.   New
York, Vintage, 1960.   616p.   (I301)

Fitzsimmons, Thomas.   USSR: its people, its society, its
culture.   With others.   New Haven, Human Relations Area
Files, 1960.   590p. (Bibliography: p. 521-548)   (I302)

Goldwin, Robert A., ed.   Readings in Russian foreign policy.
Ed. with G. Stourzh and M. Zetterbaum.   New York, Oxford University Press, 1959.   775p.   (I303)

Khrushchev, Nikita Sergeevich.   For victory in peaceful
competition with capitalism.   New York, Dutton, 1960.
783p.   (I304)

Kovner, Milton.   The challenge of coexistence; a study of
Soviet economic diplomacy.   Washington, Public Affairs
Press, c1961.   130p. (Bibliography: p. 113-128) (I305)

Kulski, Wladyslaw Wszbor.   Peaceful co-existence; an analysis of Soviet foreign policy.   Chicago, H. Regnery, 1959.
662p. (Bibliography: p. 623-636)   (I306)

McClosky, Herbert.   The Soviet dictatorship.   With J. E.
Turner.   New York, McGraw-Hill, 1960. 657p.   (I307)

Marcuse, Herbert.   Soviet Marxism, a critical analysis.
New York, Vintage Books, 1961.   252p.   (I308)

Pistrak, Lazar.   The grand tactician; Khrushchev's rise to

power.   New York, Praeger, 1961.   296p.   (I309)

Problems of Communism.   Russia under Khrushchev: an
anthology from problems.   Ed. by Abraham Brumberg.
New York, Praeger, 1962.   660p.   (I310)

Rauch, Geary von.   A history of Soviet Russia.   3d ed.
New York, Praeger, 1962.   524p.   (I311)

Reshetar, John Stephen.   Problems of analyzing and predicting Soviet behavior.   Garden City, N.Y., Doubleday, 1955.
69p.   (Bibliography: p. 63-69)   (I312)

Roberts, Henry L.   Russia and America, dangers and prospects.   New York, Harper, 1956.   251p.   (I313)

Rubenstein, Alvin Z., ed.   The foreign policy of the Soviet
Union.   New York, Random House, 1960.   457p.   (I314)

Salisbury, Harrison Evans.   To Moscow-and beyond; a re-
porter's narrative.   New York, Harper, 1960. 301p.
                                                  (I315)
Seton-Watson, Hugh.   From Lenin to Khrushchev, the history
of world communism.   New York, Praeger, 1960. 432p.
                                                  (I316)
Treadgold, Donald W.   Twentieth century Russia.   Chicago,
Rand McNally, 1959.   550p.   (I317)

Warth, Robert D.   Soviet Russia in world politics.   New
York, Twayne, 1963.   544p.   (I318)

Latin American Region

American Assembly.   The United States and Latin America.
New York, 1959.   221p.   (I319)

Council on Foreign Relations.   Social change in Latin America today; its implications for United States policy.   By
Richard N. Adams and others.   New York, Harper, c1960.
353p.   (I320)

Dozer, Donald Marquand.   Are we good neighbors?   Three
decades of inter-American relations, 1930-1960.   Gainesville, Fla., University of Florida Press, 1959. 456p.
                                                  (I321)
Perkins, Dexter.   The United States and Latin America.
Baton Rouge, La., Louisiana State University Press,

1961. 124p.   (I322)

Rippy, James Fred.   Globe and hemisphere; Latin America's
place in the post-war foreign relations of the United States.
Chicago, H. Regnery Co., 1958. 276p.   (I323)

Stokes, William Sylvane.   Latin American politics.   New
York, Crowell, 1959. 538p.   (I324)

Stuart, Graham Henry.   Latin America and the United States.
5th ed. New York, Appleton-Century-Crofts, c1955. 493p.
                                                   (I325)

East Asian Region

Barnett, A. Doak.   Communist China and Asia; challenge to
American policy. New York, Harper, 1960. 575p. (I326)

Brandt, Conrad.   Stalin's failure in China, 1924-1927.   Cambridge, Mass., Harvard University Press, 1958. 226p.
(Bibliography: p. 181-188)   (I327)

Dening, Maberly Esler.   Japan. New York, Praeger, 1961,
c1960. 263p.   (I328)

East, William Gordon, ed.   The changing map of Asia, a
political geography. Ed. with O.H.K. Spate. 4th ed. New
York, Dutton, 1961. 436p.   (I329)

Fairbank, John King.   The United States and China. New
York, Viking Press, 1962. 369p.   (I330)

Holland, William Lancelot, ed.   Asian nationalism and the
West... New York, Macmillan, 1953. 449p.   (I331)

Hudson, Geoffrey Francis.   The Chinese communes, a documentary review and analysis of the "great leap forward."
New York, Institute of Pacific Relations, 1960. 79p.
                                                   (I332)
Kawai, Kazuo.   Japan's American interlude. Chicago, University of Chicago Press, 1960. 257p.   (I333)

North, Robert Carver.   Moscow and the Chinese communists. Stanford, Calif., Stanford University Press, 1953.
306p. (Bibliography: p. 287-295)   (I334)

Reischauer, Edwin Oldfather.   Japan, past and present. 3d
ed. New York, Knopf, 1964. 353p.   (I335)

---- ----. The United States and Japan. Rev. ed. New
York, Viking Press, 1962, c1957. 394p. (Bibliography:
p. 380-384)   (I336)

---- ----. Wanted: an Asian policy. New York, Knopf,
1955. 276p.   (I337)

Zinkin, Maurice. Asia and the West. Rev. ed. New
York, International Secretariat, Institute of Pacific Relations, 1953. 304p.   (I338)

South Asian Region

Grunder, Gorel A. The Philippines and the United States.
With E. Livezey. Norman, University of Oklahoma Press,
1951. 315p. (Bibliography: p. 286-305)   (I339)

Smith, Robert Aura. Philippine freedom, 1946-1958. New
York, Columbia University Press, 1958. 375p.   (I340)

Southeast Asian Region

Blanchard, Wendell. Thailand: its people, its society, its
culture. New Haven, Human Relations Area Files Press,
1958. 528p. (Bibliography: p. 497-516)   (I341)

Buttinger, Joseph. The smaller dragon; a political history
of Vietnam. New York, Praeger, 1958. 535p. (Bibliography: p. 470-520)   (I342)

Cady, John Frank. A history of modern Burma. Ithaca,
N.Y., Cornell University Press, 1958. 682p.   (I343)

Farley, Miriam Southwell. United States relations with Southeast Asia. Rev. ed. New York, American Institute of
Pacific Relations, 1955. 81p.   (I344)

Fifield, Russell Hunt. The diplomacy of Southeast Asia:
1945-1958. New York, Harper, 1958. 584p. (Bibliography: p. 520-566)   (I345)

---- ----. Southeast Asia in United States policy. New
York, Praeger, 1963. 488p.   (I346)

Ginsburg, Norton Sydney. Malaya. With C.F. Roberts, Jr.
Seattle, University of Washington Press, 1958. 533p. (Bibliography: p. 509-524)   (I347)

Hammer, Ellen Joy.   The struggle for Indochina.   Stanford,
Calif., Stanford University Press, 1954. 342p. (Bibliography: p. 325-332)   (I348)

Kahin, George McTurnan.   Nationalism and revolution in
Indonesia.   Ithaca, N. Y., Cornell University Press, 1959.
490p.   (I349)

King, John Kerry.   Southeast Asia in perspective.   New
York, Macmillan, 1956.   309p.   (I350)

Mills, Lennox Algernon.   Malaya: a political and economic
appraisal.   Minneapolis, University of Minnesota Press,
1958.   234p.   (I351)

Pye, Lucian W.   Guerrilla communism in Malaya, its social
and political meaning.   Princeton, N. J., Princeton University Press, 1956.   369p.   (I352)

---- ----.   Politics, personality, and nation building;
Burma's search for identity.   New Haven, Yale University
Press, 1962.   307p.   (I353)

Tinker, Hugh.   The Union of Burma; a study of the first
years of independence.   3d ed.   New York, Oxford University Press, 1961.   424p.   (I354)

African Region

American Assembly.   The United States and Africa.   Ed. by
Walter Goldschmidt.   Rev. ed.   New York, Praeger, 1963.
298p.   (I355)

Kimble, George Herbert Tinley.   Tropical Africa.   New
York, Twentieth Century Fund, 1960.   2v.   (I356)

London, Kurt, ed.   New nations in a divided world; the international relations of the Afro-Asian states.   New York,
Praeger, 1964.   c1963.   336p.   (I357)

Merriam, Alan P.   Congo, background of conflict.   Evans-
ton, Ill., Northwestern University Press, 1961. 368p.
                                                         (I358)
Scott, John.   Africa: world's last frontier.   New York,
Foreign Policy Association, 1959. 62p.   (I359)

Middle Eastern Region

Adams, Michael. Suez and after; year of crisis. Boston, Beacon Press, 1958. 225p.   (I360)

Ahmad, Mushtaq. The United Nations and Pakistan. Karachi, Pakistan Institute of International Affairs, 1955. 162p. (Bibliography: p. 157-160)   (I361)

American Assembly. The United States and the Middle East. Englewood Cliffs, N.J., Prentice-Hall, 1964. 182p. (I362)

Berkes, Ross N. The diplomacy of India; Indian foreign policy in the United Nations. With M.S. Bedi. Stanford, Calif., Stanford University Press, 1958. 221p.   (I363)

Bowles, Chester. Ambassador's report. New York, Harper, 1954. 415p.   (I364)

Campbell, John Coert. Defense of the Middle East; problems of American policy. 2d ed. New York, Harper, 1960. 400p.   (I365)

Conference on India and the United States, Washington, D.C., 1959. India and the United States. Ed. by Selig S. Hamson. New York, Macmillan, 1961. 244p.   (I366)

Hurewitz, Jacob Coleman, ed. Diplomacy in the Near and Middle East; a documentary record. Princeton, N.J., Van Nostrand, 1956. 2v.   (I367)

---- ----. Middle East dilemmas; the background of United States policy. New York, Harper, 1953. 272p.   (I368)

Karunakaran, Kotta P. India in world affairs; a review of India's foreign relations. New York, Oxford University Press, 1952-58. 2v. (Bibliography: v.1, p. 369-400; v.2, p. 255-259)   (I369)

Korbel, Josef. Danger in Kashmir. Princeton, N.J., Princeton University Press, 1954. 351p.   (I370)

Lenczowski, George. The Middle East in world affairs. 3d ed. Ithaca, N.Y., Cornell University Press, 1962. 723p.   (I371)

Ramachandra Rao, P.R. India and Ceylon; a study. Bombay, Orient Longmans, 1954.   111p.   (I372)

Talbot, Phillips.   India and America; a study of their rela-
tions.   With S. L. Pupla.   New York, Harper, 1958. 200p.
                                                       (I373)
Thayer, Philip Warren, ed.   Tensions in the Middle East.
Baltimore, Johns Hopkins Press, 1958. 350p.   (I374)

Wriggins, William Howard.   Ceylon: dilemmas of a new nation.   Princeton, N. J., Princeton University Press, 1961.
505p.   (Bibliography: p.   471-483)   (I375)

Underdeveloped Countries

Almond, Gabriel Abraham, ed.   The politics of developing
areas.   Ed. with James S. Coleman.   Princeton, N.J.,
Princeton University Press, 1960.   591p.   (I376)

American Academy of Political and Social Science, Philadelphia.   Aiding underdeveloped areas abroad.   Ed. by Hal-
ford L. Hoskins.   Philadelphia, 1950.   259p.   (I377)

Arnold, Harry John Philip.   Aid for developing countries, a
comparative study.   London, Bodley Head, 1963, c1962.
159p.   (I378)

Broekmeijer, M.W. J.M.   Developing countries and N.A. T. O.
... Leyden, A.W. Sijthoff, 1963.   208p.   (I379)

Brookings Institution, Washington, D. C.   Development of
emerging countries; an agenda for research.   By Robert E.
Asher and others.   Washington, 1962.   239p.   (I380)

Johnson, John J. , ed.   The role of the military in underdeveloped countries.   Princeton, N. J., Princeton University Press, 1962.   427p.   (I381)

Kautsky, John H. , ed.   Political change in underdeveloped
countries; nationalism and communism.   New York, Wiley,
1962.   347p.   (I382)

Nurkse, Ragnar.   Problems of capital formation in underdeveloped countries.   5th ed.   New York, Oxford University Press, 1957.   163p.   (I383)

International Organization

The past century has witnessed the development of many international associations. These have appeared in the form of international administrative unions and world tribunals and, later, in the more ambitious forms of the League of Nations and the United Nations. Most of these organizations have had in common the universal longing for peace and orderliness in world affairs. The term "international organization" is often considered as embracing only governmental, presumably universal bodies such as the United Nations. International organizations are not necessarily political; they are often not even intended to be universal. They are created with varying degrees of control of the central authorities over the several members.

General Works

Bloomfield, Lincoln Palmer. The future course of international organization during 1965-1970. Santa Barbara, General Electric Co., Technical Military Planning Operation, 1958. 15 leaves.   (I384)

Cheever, Daniel S. Organizing for peace; international organization in world affairs. With H. F. Haviland, Jr. Boston, Houghton Mifflin, 1954. 917p.   (I385)

Claude, Inis L. Swords into plowshares, the problems and progress of international organization. 3d ed. New York, Random House, 1964. 458p.   (I386)

Eagleton, Clyde. International government. 3d ed. New York, Ronald Press Co., 1957. 665p.   (I387)

Goodspeed, Stephen S. The nature and function of international organization. New York, Oxford University Press, 1959. 676p.   (I388)

Hill, David Jayne. World organization as affected by the nature of the modern state. New York, Columbia University Press, 1911. 214p.   (I389)

Hill, Norman Llewellyn. International organization. New York, Harper, 1952. 627p.   (I390)

Leonard, Leonard Larry. International organization. New York, McGraw-Hill, 1951. 630p.   (I391)

Levi, Werner. Fundamentals of world organization. Minneapolis, University of Minnesota Press, 1950. 233p. (I392)

Mangone, Gerard J. A short history of international organization. New York, McGraw-Hill, 1954. 326p.   (I393)

Union of International Associations. International congress
organizational theory and practice. Brussels, 1961. 128p.
(Bibliography: p. 126-127)   (I394)

Reference Materials

Retrospective Bibliographies

Aufricht, Hans. World organization, an annotated bibliography. 7th ed. New York, Woodrow Wilson Memorial Library, 1946. 28p.   (I395)

International Labor Office. Library. Bibliography of international periodicals. Geneva, 1952. 107p.   (I396)

Rogers, William Cecil, comp. International administration;
a bibliography. Chicago, Public Administration Service,
1945. 32p.   (I397)

Speeckaert, Georges Patrick. International institutions and
international organization; a select bibliography. Brussels,
Published with assistance from UNESCO and in collaboration with the International Federation for Documentation,
1956. 116p.   (I398)

Current Bibliography

Bibliographical services throughout the world, 1950-1959.
By Robert L. Collison. Paris, UNESCO, c1961. 228p.
                                                   (I399)

Handbooks and Directories

League of Nations. Handbook of international organizations.
Geneva, 1938. 491p.

Arrangement is by subject with alphabetical and geographical indexes. Gives detailed information when possible in
English and French, date of founding, object, members,
etc.   (I400)

Union of International Associations. Associations internationales.   International Associations.   Brussels, 1949+

A listing of current international organizations with recent
data on organization, membership, etc.   (I401)

---- ----.   Directory of periodicals published by international organizations.   2d ed.   Brussels, 1959.   241p.

Includes founding date, frequency, publisher, size, and
comments for all titles; has an agency and title index.
(I402)
United Nations Educational, Scientific and Cultural Organiza-
tion.   An international directory of education associations.
Paris, UNESCO, 1959.   91p.

A list of educational associations throughout the world.   A
useful guide.   (I403)

Document Collections

Peaslee, Amos Jenkins, ed.   International governmental organizations: constitutional documents.   2d ed.   The Hague,
M. Nijhoff, c1961.   2v.   (I404)

Union of International Associations.   Documents.   Brussels,
1956+   (I405)

Watkins, James Thomas, ed.   General international organization, a source book.   With J.W. Robinson.   Princeton,
N.J., Van Nostrand, c1956.   248p.   (I406)

The League of Nations

Formed largely by the efforts of a number of ideal-
ists, the League of Nations came into being at Versailles in
1919.   It eventually failed because of the lack of membership of the United States and the expansionist policies of a
number of the other great powers.

General Works

Burton, Margaret Ernestine.   The Assembly of the League of
Nations.   Chicago, University of Chicago Press, 1941.   441p.
(Bibliography: p. 419-421)   (I407)

Davis, Harriet Ide (Eager) ed.   Pioneers in world order; an
American appraisal of the League of Nations.   New York,

International Relations

287

Columbia University Press, 1944. 272p.   (I408)

Hill, Martin. The economic and financial organization of the
League of Nations...Washington, Carnegie Endowment for
International Peace, 1946. 168p.   (I409)

Walters, Francis Paul. A history of the League of Nations.
New York, Oxford University Press, 1960. 832p.   (I410)

Zimmern, Alfred Eckhard.   The League of Nations and the
rule of law, 1918-1935.   2d ed.   London, Macmillan,
1939. 542p.   (I411)

Reference Materials

Aufricht, Hans.   Guide to League of Nations publications; a
bibliographical survey of the work of the League, 1920-
1947. New York, Columbia University Press, 1951. 682p.

A selective guide that includes some items that were confidential and a number that were never on public sale. It is
arranged under broad subject headings and includes an index.   (I412)

Breycha-Vanthier, Arthur Carl von.   Sources of information;
a handbook on the publications of the League of Nations.
New York, Columbia University Press, 1939. 118p. (Bibliography: p. 102-105)

Includes descriptions of a selected number of publications
of the League of Nations. It is intended to be an introduction to all of its publications.   (I413)

World Peace Foundation, Boston. Key to League of Nations
documents placed on sale, 1920-1929. By Marie J. Carroll...Boston, World Peace Foundation, 1930. 340p.

Has 4 supplements to 1936.   (I414)

---- ----. Subject index to the economic and financial documents of the League of Nations, 1927-1930. By Eric C.
Wendelin.   Boston, World Peace Foundation, 1932. 190p.
                                                          (I415)

The United Nations

    Profiting from lessons learned in the League, the na-
tions which engaged against the Axis powers in World War II

determined to establish a new and stronger international organization. The United Nations was organized in San Francisco in 1945, and it has been functioning since that time.

General Works

Boyd, Andrew Kirk Henry.   United Nations: piety, myth, and truth.   Baltimore, Penguin Books, 1963, c1962. 185p.
                                                                                 (I416)

Coyle, David Cushman.   The United Nations and how it works. Rev. ed.   New York, New American Library, 1962. 222p.
                                                                                 (I417)

Goodrich, Leland Matthew.   Charter of the United Nations; commentary and documents.   With E. Hambro. 2d ed. Boston, World Peace Foundation, 1949. 710p. (Bibliography: p. 659-681)   (I418)

---- ----.   Development of the General Assembly.   New York, Carnegie Endowment for International Peace, 1951. 281p.   (I419)

---- ----.   The United Nations.   New York, Crowell, 1959. 419p.   (I420)

Hyde, Louis K.   The United States and the United Nations ... New York, Manhattan Pub. Co., 1961. 249p.   (I421)

Lawson, Ruth Catherine.   International regional organizations: Constitutional foundations.   New York, Praeger, 1962. 387p.   (I422)

Riggs, Robert Edwon.   Politics in the United Nations; a study of United States influence in the General Assembly.   Urbana, University of Illinois Press, 1958. 208p.   (I423)

Theobald, Robert, ed.   The U.N. and its future.   New York, H.W. Wilson Co., 1963.   190p.   (I424)

Van den bosch, Amry.   Toward world order.   With W.N. Hogan.   New York, McGraw-Hill, c1963. 389p.   (I425)

Wortley, Ben Atkinson, ed.   The United Nations; the first ten years.   New York, Oceana Publications, c1957. 206p.
                                                                                 (I426)

Study and Teaching

Kenworthy, Leonard Stout.   Telling the U.N. story; new approaches to teaching about the United Nations and its related agencies.   Paris, UNESCO, 1963.   166p.   (I427)

Reference Materials

Bibliographies

American Association for the United Nations.   Read your way to world understanding; a selected annotated reading guide of books about the United Nations...New York, Scarecrow Press, 1963.   307p.   (I428)

Thompson, Elizabeth M.   Resources for teaching about the United Nations, with annotated bibliographies...Washington, National Education Association of the United States, 1962. 90p.   (I429)

U.S. Office of Education.   The United Nations and related organizations: a bibliography.   Washington, 1960. 17p.
                                                                    (I430)

Guides and Handbooks

Chamberlin, Waldo.   A chronology and fact book of the United Nations, 1941-1961.   With T. Hovet.   New York, Oceana Publications, 1961.   64p.

A good, clear, and concise picture of the operations of the United Nations from 1941-61.   (I431)

Everyman's United Nations, a ready reference to the structure, functions and work of the United Nations and its related agencies.   New York, United Nations, Dept. of Public Information, 1948+

The basic handbook on the United Nations.   Explains its structure, functions and work of various agencies.   New 7th ed. published in 1964.   This ed. brings up-to-date the total picture including changes in responsibility and organization.   (I432)

New Zealand.   Dept. of External Affairs.   The United Nations and specialized agencies handbook, 1962. 115p.

A brief handbook explaining the functions of United Nations

specialized agencies.   (I433)

Yearbooks

Annual review of United Nations affairs. New York, New
York University Press, 1949+ (Annual, now published by
Oceana Publications by arrangement with New York Univer-
sity Press)

Intended to serve as a critical companion to the U.N. Yearbook, (I436) it includes a series of articles by leading
scholars reviewing U.N. activities and problems. (I434)

The Diplomatic yearbook. New York, Funk & Wagnalls,
1950+

Compiled by the editors of the United Nations World. Includes sections on diplomatic practices and procedures and
lists for the various persons in the diplomatic service
throughout the world.   (I435)

United Nations. Yearbook. New York, Columbia University
Press in cooperation with the United Nations, 1946/47+

A very useful annual summarizing the activities and
achievements of the United Nations. Includes texts of documents, a selected bibliography and a "Who's Who."
                                                   (I436)
Yearbook on human rights. New York, United Nations,
1946+

Includes a survey of the constitutional and legal provisions
of the various nations of the world with regard to human
rights. Consists of extracts from national laws, constitutions, etc. Each supplementary volume has a distinctive
title.   (I437)

Publications and Documents

Documents of international organizations; a selected bibliography. Boston, World Peace Foundation, 1947-1950. 3v.
(No longer published)

Lists a selection of many important publications of the various major international organizations.   (I438)

United Nations. Economic and Social Council. Committee on

Non-Governmental Organization. List of non-governmental
organizations in consultative relationship with the Economic and Social Council. New York, United Nations, 1953+
                                                        (I439)
United Nations. Library. Index to proceedings of the General Assembly. New York, 1950/51+   (I440)

---- ----. List of selected articles. New York, 1949+
                                                        (I441)
United Nations. Office of Public Information. United Nations publications. New York, 1945/48+

Basically a sales catalog, this work lists publications with
prices.   (I442)

Other International Organizations

    This section deals with those international organiza-
tions of a regional or collective security nature.

General Works

International congresses and conferences, 1840-1937; a union
list of their publications available in libraries of the United
States and Canada. Ed. by Winifred Gregory under the
auspices of the Bibliographical Society of America... New
York, H.W. Wilson, 1938. 229p.   (I443)

Yearbook of international organizations. Brussels, Union of
International Associations, 1948+   (I444)

Intergovernmental Organizations

Annuaire européen. European year book. La Haye, Nijhoff,
1955+   (I445)

Council of Europe Directorate of Information. Handbook of
European organization. Strasbourg, Secretariat General of
the Council of Europe, 1956+   (I446)

Haas, Ernst B. The uniting of Europe: political, social,
and economic forces, 1950-57. Stanford, Calif., Stanford
University Press, 1958. 552p. (Bibliography: p. 529-
536)   (I447)

Roussier, Michel. Les publications officielles des institutions européennes... Paris, Dotation Carnegie pour la paix

internationale, Centre européen, 1954.   73p.   (I448)

Council of Europe

Robertson, Arthur Henry. The Council of Europe: its
structure, functions and achievements. 2d ed. New York,
Praeger, 1961. 288p. (Bibliography: p. 271-275) (I449)

---- ----. European institutions: co-operation, integration,
unification. New York, Praeger, 1959. 372p.   (I450)

European Coal and Steel Community

European Coal and Steel Community. Common Assembly.
Bibliographie analytique de plan Schuman et de la C.E.C.A.
Lusembourg, Communauté européene du charbon et de
l'acier, Assemblée commune, service d'études et de documentation, 1955+   (I451)

---- ----. Jahrbuch-Handbuch... Lusemberg, 1956+ (I452)

North Atlantic Treaty Organization

Knorr, Klaus Eugen, ed. NATO and American security.
Princeton, N.J., Princeton University Press, 1959. 342p.
                                                      (I453)
North Atlantic Treaty Organization. The North Atlantic
Treaty Organization. Paris, 1952+   (I454)

---- ----. NATO bibliography... Paris, 1955? 44p. (I455)

North Atlantic Treaty Organization. Information Service.
Facts about NATO. 2d ed. Paris, 1959+ (Loose-leaf)
                                                      (I456)
Osgood, Robert Endicott. NATO, the entangling alliance.
Chicago, University of Chicago Press, 1962. 416p. (I457)

Organization for European Economic Cooperation

Organization for European Economic Cooperation. General
catalogue of books published from 1948-1958. Paris,
1958. 109p.   (I458)

---- ----. History and structure. 7th ed. Paris, Chateau
de la Muette, 1958. 59p.   (I459)

Royal Institute of International Affairs. Information Dept.

The organization for European Economic Co-operation
(OEEC). New York, Oxford University Press, 1958. 16p.
(I460)

Organization of American States

Organization of American States. Annals. Washington, Dept.
of International Law and Organizations, Pan American
Union, 1949+   (I461)

Pan American Union. Columbus Memorial Library. Bibliografia de las conferencias interamericanas. Washington,
Departamento de Asuntes culturales, Unios Pan-americana,
1954. 277p.   (I462)

Pan American Union. Department of Legal Affairs. The
Organization of American States and the United Nations.
Washington, 1949+   (I463)

Pan American Union. Status of Inter-American treaties and
conventions. Washington, D.C., 1961. 35p.   (I464)

International Law

International law may be defined as that body of rules
which regulates relations among states and other entities
which possess international legal personality such as international organizations and perhaps, to a very limited degree,
private persons. Unlike national or municipal law, international law is not supported by any sovereign enforcing body.
However, national law does not repose upon force alone; it
has a great amount of custom and reliance upon public opinion. Likewise, international law is partially the product of
custom and some notions of international morality.

General Works

Brierly, James Leslie. The law of nations; an introduction
to the international law of peace. 6th ed. Ed. by Humph-
rey Waldock. Oxford, Clarendon Press, 1963. 442p.
(I465)
Carlston, Kenneth Smith. Law and organization in world so-
ciety. Urbana, University of Illinois Press, 1962. 356p.
(I466)
Corbett, Percy Ellwood. The study of international law.
Garden City, N.Y., Doubleday, 1955. 55p.   (I467)

Falk, Richard A.   Law, morality, and war in the contemporary world.   New York, Praeger, 1963.   120p.   (I468)

Gould, Wesley L.   An introduction to international law.   New
York, Harper, 1957.   809p.   (I469)

Higgins, Roselyn.   The development of international law
through the political organs of the United Nations.   New
York, Oxford University Press, 1963.   402p.   (Bibliography: p. 284-395)   (I470)

International law in a changing world.   Dobbs Ferry, N.Y.,
Oceana Publications, 1963.   125p.   (I471)

Jacobini, H.B.   International law; a text.   Homewood, Ill.,
Dorsey Press, 1962.   324p.   (I472)

Jessup, Philip Caryl.   A modern law of nations, an introduction.   New York, Macmillan, 1948.   236p.   (I473)

Kaplan, Morton A.   The political foundations of international
law.   With N.B.   Katzenbach.   New York, Wiley, 1961.
372p.   (I474)

Kelsen, Hans.   Principles of international law.   New York,
Rinehart, 1952.   461p.   (I475)

Lauterpacht, Hersh.   The development of international law
by the International Court.   New York, Praeger, 1958.
408p.   (I476)

Nussbaum, Arthur.   A concise history of the law of nations.
Rev. ed.   New York, Macmillan, 1954.   376p.   (I477)

Oppenheim, Lassa Francis Lawrence.   International law; a
treatise.   5th ed.   Ed. by H. Lauterpacht.   London,
Longmans, 1960+   (I478)

Ronning, C. Neale.   Law and politics in inter-American diplomacy.   New York, Wiley, 1963.   167p.   (I479)

Schwarzenberger, Georg.   International law.   3d ed.   London,
Stevens, 1957+   (I480)

Starke, Joseph Gabriel.   An introduction to international law.
4th ed.   London, Butterworth, 1958.   467p.   (I481)

Wright, Quincy. Contemporary international law; a balance
sheet. Garden City, N.Y., Doubleday, 1955. 65p. (I482)

---- ----. International law and the United Nations. New
York, Asia Pub. House, 1960. 134p.   (I483)

Study and Teaching

American Society of International Law. A survey of the
teaching of international law in political science departments. Conducted under the joint auspices of the American Society of International Law and American Political
Science Association. Washington?, 1963. 113p. (I484)

Reference Materials

Bibliographies

Grotius Society, London. Library. Catalog of the books in
the library of the society. London, Sweet and Maxwell,
1923. 65p.   (I485)

Hague. Palace of Peace. Catalog. Par P.C. Malhuysen et
E.R. Oppenheim. Lyde, A.W. Sijthoff, 1916+ (Supplemented to present)   (I486)

U.S. Library of Congress. Law Library. The bibliography
of international law. By Edwin M. Borchad. Washington,
U.S. Govt. Print. Off., 1913. 93p.   (I487)

Guides and Manuals

Mendlovitz, Saul H., ed. Readings and discussion guide for
a seminar on legal and political problems of world order.
New York, Fund for Education Concerning World Peace
Through World Law, 1962. 858p.   (I488)

Schwarzenberger, Georg. A manual of international law.
4th ed. New York, Praeger, 1960. 2v.   (I489)

Sources of Law

International law is largely customary in nature and,
therefore, contains little statutory material. The principal
sources may be summarized as follows: (1) established
practices of nations; (2) writings of jurists; (3) declarations
of international congresses; (4) multilateral treaties regu-

lating certain phases of international conduct; (5) bilateral
treaties which sometimes contain provisions declaring existing law; (6) proclamations of heads of state, opinions of
their foreign offices, and orders to their military com-
manders--all of which are frequently cited; (7) decisions of
arbitration tribunals, of commissions of inquiry, and of
courts dealing with international questions or with prize
cases--all of which may constitute precedents for later decisions; and (8) failure of a state to protest against principles to which other states have expressly consented, for
such a failure may be taken as evidence of tacit consent.

Treaties

United Nations.   Treaty series; treaties and international
    agreements, registered or filed and recorded with the
    Secretariat of the United Nations.   New York, 1946/47+
                                                          (I490)
United Nations.   Office of Legal Affairs.   Status of multi-
    lateral conventions in respect of which the Secretary Gen-
    eral acts as depository.   Rev. ed.   New York, United Na-
    tions, 1959+   (Loose-leaf)   (I491)

U.S. Dept. of State.   Office of Legal Advisor.   Treaties in
    force; a list of treaties and other international agreements
    of the United States.   Comp. by the Treaty Affairs Staff
    ...Washington, U.S. Govt. Print. Off., 1955+   (I492)

U.S. Treaties, etc.   Treaties and other international acts of
    the United States of America.   Ed. by Hunter Miller...
    Washington, U.S. Govt. Print. Off., 1931+   (I493)

---- ----.   Treaties, conventions, international acts, proto-
    cols, and agreements between the United States of America
    and other powers.   Washington, U.S. Govt. Print. Off.,
    1910+   (I494)

---- ----.   United States treaties and other international
    agreements.   Washington, Dept. of State, 1950+   (annual)
                                                          (I495)

Law Reports and Cases

Bishop, William Warner, ed.   International law: cases and
    materials.   2d ed.   Boston, Little, Brown, 1962. 964p.
                                                          (I496)
Dickinson, Edwin DeWitt.   Cases and materials on interna-
    tional law.   Brooklyn, Foundation Press, 1950. 740p.(I497)

Hague. International Court of Justice. Reports of judg-
ments, advisory opinions and orders. The Hague, 1947+
(I498)
Hague. International Court of Justice. Registry. Reports
of international arbitral awards. Lake Success, United
Nations, 1948+ (I499)

Hague. Permanent Court of International Justice. The case
law of the International Court. Leyden, A.W. Sijthoff,
1952+ (I500)

Hudson, Manley Ottmer, ed. Cases and other materials on
international law. 3d ed. St. Paul, West Pub. Co., 1951.
770p. (I501)

McNair, Arnold Duncan, ed. International law opinions, selected and annotated. Cambridge, Eng., University Press,
1956. 3v. (I502)

Mangone, Gerard J. The elements of international law; a
casebook. Homewood, Ill., Dorsey Press, 1963. 387p.
(I503)
Sohn, Louis B., ed. Cases on United Nations law. Brooklyn, Foundation Press, 1956. 1048p. (I504)

U.S. Naval War College. International law documents.
Washington, U.S. Govt. Print. Off., 1894-1900+ (I505)

Digests

Hackworth, Green Haywood. Digest of international law.
Washington, U.S. Govt. Print. Off., 1940-44. 8v. (I506)

Moore, John Bassett. A digest of international law. Washington, U.S. Govt. Print. Off., 1906. 8v. (I507)

Whiteman, Marjorie Millace. Digest of international law.
Washington, U.S. Dept. of State; for sale by the Superin-
tendent of Documents, U.S. Govt. Print. Off., 1963+
(Successor to Hackworth) (I508)

Yearbooks

Anuario juridico interamericane. Inter-American juridical
yearbook. Washington, Pan American Union, 1948+ (I509)

The British yearbook of international law. London, Oxford

University Press, 1920+   (I510)

The Canadian yearbook of international law. Vancouver,
   Publishing Centre, University of British Columbia, 1963+
                                                          (I511)

Grotius; annuaire international. La Haye, M. Nijhoff,
   1913+   (I512)

The Jewish yearbook of international law. Jerusalem, R.
   Mass, 1948+   (I513)

United Nations. International Law Commission. Yearbook.
   New York, 1957+   (I514)

World Polity; a yearbook of studies in international law and
   organization.   Washington, Institute of World Polity,
   Georgetown University, 1957+   (I515)

Appendix A

Periodicals

The number of periodicals dealing with political science or one of its specialized sub-disciplines is rising. Since 1950 the volume of periodical material has almost doubled. This appendix will consist of only a selected number of the periodicals available. Bibliographic form is based on Ulrich's Periodicals directory (A72) including abbreviations.

Abbreviations Used

Abstracting and Indexing Services

Abr. R. G. = Abridged Reader's Guide to Periodical Literature
Br. Hum. Ind. = British Humanities Index
Cath. Ind. = Catholic Index
Fin. Ind. = Financial Index
Int. Ind. = International Index
Leg. Per. = Legal Periodicals Index
Psych. Abstr. = Psychological Abstracts
P. A. I. S. = Public Affairs Information Service
R. G. = Reader's Guide to Periodical Literature
Soc. Abstr. = Sociology Abstracts

General

abstr. = abstracts
adv. = advertisements
bibl. = bibliography
bi-m. = bi-monthly
bk. rev. = book reviews
cum. = cumulative
fortn. = fortnightly
illus. = illustrations
irreg. = irregular
m. = monthly
q. = quarterly
s-a. = semi-annual

ACADEMY of Political Science. Proceedings. 1910. irreg.
Academy of Political Science, Columbia University, New
York, N.Y. Index. Indexed: Int. Ind. P.A.I.S.

ADMINISTRATION. 1953. 4 times a year. Institute of Public Administration, Dublin, Eire. adv. bk.rev. index.
cum. index every 5 years (approx.)

AFRICA Report. (Including section of reviews of books and
periodicals) (Formerly: African Special Report) 1956. m.
(Oct.-Aug.) African-American Institute, Washington, D.C.
adv. bk.rev. illus. maps. Indexed: P.A.I.S.

AMERICAN Academy of Political and Social Science. Annals.
1890. bi-m. Philadelphia, Pennsylvania. adv. bibl. bk.
rev. cum. index every 5 years; Jan. 1890-July 1926 (in 3
vols.); v. 127-212 (1926-1940) (in 3 vols.); 1946-1950;
1951-1955; 1956-1960. Indexed: P.A.I.S. R.G.

ABS. American Behavioral Scientist. (Formerly: P.R.O.D.)
1957. m. Metron, Inc., Princeton, N.J. adv. bibl. bk.
rev. illus. index. cum. index every 5 years. Indexed:
P.A.I.S.

AMERICAN Political Science Review. 1906. q. American
Political Science Association, Washington, D.C. adv. bibl.
bk. rev. index. cum. index irregularly (1906-1963 issued
in 1964) Indexed: Int. Ind. P.A.I.S.

ARBITRATION Journal. 1937. q. American Arbitration Association, Inc., New York, N.Y. bibl. index. Indexed:
Leg. Per. P.A.I.S.

ASIAN Survey. (Supersedes, Far Eastern Survey) 1961. m.
Institute of International Studies, University of California,
Berkeley, Calif. Indexed: Int. Ind. P.A.I.S.

AUSSENPOLITIK; Zeitschrift für internationale Fragen.
1950. m. Deutsche Verlags-Anstalt Gmbh, Stuttgart, Germany. adv. bk.rev. index.

AUSTRALIAN Journal of Politics and History. 1955. s-a.
University of Queensland Press, Brisbane, Australia. adv.
bk. rev. index. biennially. Indexed: P.A.I.S. Soc.
Abstr.

BACKGROUND on World Politics; a digest of military, scientific, economic and social developments bearing on world politics. 1957. q. Center for Foreign Service Studies, Baylor University, Waco, Texas. abstr. adv. index.

CHINA Quarterly. 1960. q. Congress for Cultural Freedom, Paris, France. adv. bk. rev. charts. index. Indexed: P.A. I. S.

COLUMBIA University Forum; a journal of fact and opinion. 1957. q. Columbia University, New York, N. Y. Indexed: P. A. I. S.

CONTEMPORARY Issues. 1948. q. Contemporary Press, London and New York. adv. index. Indexed: P.A. I. S.

CURRENT: Significant new material from all sources on the frontier problems of today. 1960. m. Current, Inc., New York, N. Y. abstr. illus. index.

CURRENT History; the monthly magazine of world affairs. 1914. m. Events Publishing Co., Philadelphia, Pa. Bk. rev. index. Indexed: Abr. R. G. P. A. I.S. R. G.

EAST Europe; a review of East European affairs. 1950. m. Free Europe Committee, Inc., New York, N.Y. bk. rev. illus. index. Indexed: P. A. I. S.

FEDERALIST Newsletter. 1951. 11 times a year. United World Federalists, Inc., Washington, D. C. bk. rev. illus.

FOREIGN Affairs; an American quarterly review. 1922. q. Council on Foreign Relations, New York, N.Y. adv. bibl. bk. rev. cum. index: v. 1-25 (Sept. 1922-July 1947) Indexed: P.A. I. S. R. G.

FOREIGN Policy Bulletin. 1961. m. Foreign Policy Research Institute of South Carolina, Charleston, S. C.

FOREIGN Service Journal. 1924. m. American Foreign Service Association, Washington, D. C. adv. bk. rev. illus. index. Indexed: P. A. I. S.

HEADLINE Series. No. 148, July 20, 1961. bi-m. Foreign Policy Association, New York, N.Y. bibl. illus. maps.

HISPANIC American Report; an analysis of developments in

Spain, Portugal and Latin-America. 1948. m. Institute of Hispanic, American and Luso-Brazilian Studies, Stanford University, Stanford, Calif. bk. rev. index. cum. index. v. 1-7 (v. 8-12 in prep.)

INTERCOM: an information resource on world affairs, including monthly roundup of current materials and a special focus on a subject or area of current national interest. 1959. 7 times a year. Foreign Policy Association, World Affairs Center, New York, N.Y. bibl. bk.rev. Indexed: P.A.I.S.

INTERNATIONAL Conciliation. 1907. 5 times a year. Carnegie Endowment for International Peace, New York, N.Y. charts. index. Indexed: P.A.I.S. R.G.

JOURNAL of Conflict Resolution; for research related to war and peace. 1957. q. Center for Research on Conflict Resolution, University of Michigan, Ann Arbor, Mich. abstr. adv. bk. rev. charts. Indexed: P.A.I.S. Psych. Abstr.

JOURNAL of International Affairs. 1947. s-a. Graduate School of International Affairs, Columbia University, New York, N.Y. adv. bk. rev. index. cum. index every 3 years (v. 1-8 Spring, 1947-Spring, 1954) Indexed: Int. Ind. Soc. Abstr.

JOURNAL of Politics. 1939. q. Southern Political Science Association, University of Florida, Gainesville, Fla. adv. bibl. bk. rev. index. Indexed: Int. Ind. P.A.I.S.

MIDDLE East Journal. 1946. q. Middle East Institute, Washington, D.C. adv. bibl. bk. rev. index. Indexed: Int. Ind. P.A.I.S.

MIDWEST Journal of Political Science. (Midwest Conference of Political Scientists) 1957. q. Wayne State University Press, Detroit, Mich. adv. bk. rev. charts. index. Indexed: P.A.I.S.

ORBIS: a journal of world affairs. 1957. 4 times a year. Foreign Policy Research Institute, University of Pennsylvania, Philadelphia. adv. bk. rev. index. Indexed: P.A.I.S.

PACIFIC Affairs; an international review of the Far East and

Pacific area. 1928. q. University of British Columbia,
Vancouver, B. C. , Canada. adv. bibl. bk. rev. index.
Indexed: Int. Ind. P. A. I. S.

POLITICAL Quarterly. 1930. q. Stevens & Sons, London,
England. adv. bk. rev. index. Indexed: Br. Hum. Ind.
Int. Ind. P. A. I. S.

POLITICAL Science. 1948. s-a. School of Political Science and Public Administration, Victoria University of
Wellington, Wellington, New Zealand. adv. bk. rev. Indexed: P. A. I. S.

POLITICAL Science Quarterly. 1886. 4 times a year.
Academy of Political Science, Columbia University, New
York, N. Y. adv. bk. rev. index. cum. index published
irregularly; v. 1-45 (1886-1930); v. 46-65 (1931-1950) Indexed: Int. Ind. P. A. I. S.

POLITIQUE: revue internationale des doctrines et des institutions. N. S. 1951. q. C. E. L. S. E. , Paris, France.
bk. rev.

POLITISCHE Studien. 1950. m. Thierschstr, Munich,
Germany. adv. bk. rev. charts. index.

POLITISCHE Vierteljahresschrift (Deutsche Vereinigung für
Politische Wissenschaft) 1960. 4 times a year. West-
deutscher Verlag, Opladen, Germany. adv. bk. rev.

POPULAR Government. 1931. 9 times a year. Institute of
Government, University of North Carolina, Chapel Hill,
N. C. , bk. rev. cum. index every 5 years. Indexed:
P. A. I. S.

PUBLIC Administration News. (American Society for Public
Administration) 1951. q. Chicago, Ill.

PUBLIC Administration Review. (American Society for Public Administration) 1940. q. Chicago, Ill. adv. bk. rev.
index. cum. index published irreg. Indexed: Int. Ind.
Leg. Per. P. A. I. S.

PUBLIC Affairs Comment. 1955. bi-m. Institute of Public
Affairs, University of Texas, Austin, Texas. Indexed:
P. A. I. S.

PUBLIC Opinion Quarterly. 1937. q. Princeton University
Press, Princeton, N. J. adv. bk. rev. charts. index.
Indexed: Int. Ind. P. A. I. S. Psych. Abstr.

REVIEW of Politics. 1939. q. University of Notre Dame,
Notre Dame, Indiana. bk. rev. index. Indexed: Cath.
Ind. Int. Ind. P. A. I. S.

REVUE Politique. 1951. bi-m. Centre d'Etudes Politiques, Economiques et Sociales (C. E. P. E. S. S.) Brussels,
Belgium. index.

SAIS Review. q. School of Advanced International Studies,
Johns Hopkins University, Washington, D. C. Indexed:
P. A. I. S.

STATE Government; the magazine of State affairs. 1930.
q. Council of State Governments, Chicago, Ill. index.
Indexed: Int. Ind. P. A. I. S.

U. S. News and World Report. 1933. w. United States
Publishing Corp. , Washington, D. C. adv. charts. illus.
index semi-annually. Indexed: Abr. R. G. Fin. Ind.
P. A. I. S. R. G.

WESTERN Political Quarterly. (Western Political Science
Association; Pacific Northwest Political Science Association) 1948. q. Institute of Government, University of
Utah, Salt Lake City, Utah. adv. bk. rev. index. Indexed: Int. Ind. P. A. I. S.

YALE Political; a journal of divergent views on national issues. 1962. q. Yale Political Publishing Corp. , New
Haven, Conn. Indexed: P. A.I. S.

Appendix B

Government Documents

It would be superfluous to include a wide variety of information on government documents since there are a number of works available that treat the subject well and in great detail. What follows, therefore, is a select, annotated bibliography of general works and guides to both United States and United Nations documents.

American Library Association. Committee on Public Documents. Public documents...papers presented at the conference of the A. L. A., 1933-1942. Chicago, American Library Association, 1934-1942. 7v. (Not published, 1939-1941) (J1)

Ames, John Griffith. Comprehensive index to the publications of the United States government, 1881-1893. Washington, U.S. Govt. Print. Off., 1905. 2v. (Reprinted by Johnson Reprint Corp., 1962.)

A good index, although less detailed than the Documents catalog. Bridges the gap between Poore's Descriptive catalogue and the first volume of the Documents catalog. (J2)

Boyd, Anne Morris. United States government publications. 3d ed. Rev. by Rae Elizabeth Rips. New York, H.W. Wilson, 1949. 627p.

A useful, extensive guide listing the publications of each branch of government. (J3)

Brimmer, Brenda. A guide to the use of United Nations documents, including reference to the specialized agencies and special U.N. bodies. Dobbs Ferry, N.Y., Oceana Publications, 1962. 272p. (Bibliography: p.268-269)

The most current guide to the publications of the United Nations and their use. Also includes publications of many of the specialized agencies not handled in other works. (J4)

Brown, Everett Sommerville. Manual of government publications: United States and foreign. New York, Appleton-
Century-Crofts, 1950. 121p. (Bibliography: p. 116-121)

Although brief in nature, this manual covers the most useful government documents of foreign nations as well as the
United States.   (J5)

Childs, James Bennett. Government document bibliography in
the United States and elsewhere. 3d ed. Washington,
U.S. Govt. Print. Off., 1942. 78p.

A good coverage of foreign nations and the United States.
The catalogs, indexes and guides to documents are given
for each country with occasional brief annotations. (J6)

Greely, Adolphus Washington. Public documents of the first
fourteen congresses, 1789-1817. Papers relating to early
congressional documents. Washington, U.S. Govt. Print.
Off., 1900. 903p. (Supplement, 1904)   (J7)

Hirshberg, Herbert Simon. Subject guide to United States
government publications. With Carl H. Melinat. Chicago,
American Library Association, 1947. 228p.

"...a selection of those books and pamphlets, most of them
published during the past twenty years, believed to be the
most generally useful in libraries." - Pref.   (J8)

Leidy, William Philip. A popular guide to government publications. 2d ed. New York, Columbia University Press,
1963. 291p.

A useful guide for seeking authoritative information on a
wide variety of subjects. Gives complete information with
some annotations.   (J9)

Moor, Carol Carter. How to use United Nations documents.
With Waldo Chamberlain. New York, New York University Press, 1952. 26p. (Bibliography: p. 22)

A general manual of value to the researcher. Includes all
unrestricted, mimeographed, processed, and printed material.   (J10)

National Association of State Libraries. Collected public
documents of the States; a checklist. Comp. by William

S. Jenkins.   Boston, 1947.   87p.   (J11)

National Association of State Libraries.   Public Documents
Clearing House Committee.   Checklist of legislative jour-
nals of the states of the United States of America. Comp.
by Grace E. Macdonald.   Providence, R.I., The Oxford
Press, 1938.   274p. (Supplement, comp. by William S.
Jenkins, 1943.   107p.)   (J12)

Patch, William H.   The use of United Nations documents.
Urbana, University of Illinois Library School, 1962. 29p.

A brief guide to the current problems of using United Nations documents.   (J13)

Poore, Benjamin Perley.   A descriptive catalogue of the government publications of the United States, Sept. 5, 1774-
Mar. 4, 1881.   Washington, U.S. Govt. Print. Off., 1885.
1392p.

Arranges material chronologically and has a general index.
Weak index is not complete or detailed enough for quick
reference use.   (J14)

Pullen, William Russell.   A checklist of legislative journals
issued since 1937 by the states of the United States of
America.   Chicago, American Library Association, 1955.
59p.

Continues the listing of journals as those in the National
Association of State Libraries' Checklist of legislative journals...   (J15)

Schmeckebier, Laurence Frederick.   Government publications
and their use.   With Roy B. Eastin.   Rev. ed.   Washington, Brookings Institution, 1961.   476p.

Now brought up to date by Mr. Eastin, this work is a very
useful guide to government publications of all types. (J16)

U.S. Congress.   Senate.   Presidential vetoes.   List of bills
vetoed and action taken thereon by the Senate and House of
Representatives, First Congress through the 86th Congress,
1789-1961.   Comp. by the Senate Library under the direction of F.M. Johnson and R.D. Hupman.   Washington,
U.S. Govt. Print. Off., 1961.   244p.   (J17)

U.S. Congress. Senate. Library. Cumulative index of congressional committee hearings (not confidential in character) from the 74th Cong. (Jan. 3, 1935) through the 85th Cong. (Jan. 3, 1959) in the United States Senate Library. Indexed and comp. under the direction of F.M. Johnson and R.D. Hupman. Washington, U.S. Govt. Print. Off., 1959. 823p.   (J18)

U.S. Library of Congress. Division of Documents. Monthly checklist of state publications. Washington, U.S. Govt. Print. Off., 1910+

Basically a current bibliography that is arranged alphabetically by state.   (J19)

U.S. Superintendent of Documents. Catalog of the public documents of Congress and all departments of the government of the United States for the period of Mar. 4, 1893-Dec. 31, 1940. Washington, U.S. Govt. Print. Off., 1896-1945. 25v.

Most popularly known as the Documents catalog, this set of volumes is a dictionary catalog in form for congressional and departmental publications for the period covered.
                                                        (J20)
---- ----. Checklist of United States public documents, 1789-1909. 3d ed. Washington, U.S. Govt. Print. Off., 1911. 1707p.

This is a list of congressional and departmental publications. Volume 2 was to have been an index, but it was never issued.   (J21)

---- ----. Monthly catalog of United States government publications. Washington, U.S. Govt. Print. Off., 1895+

Currently this is the primary bibliography of all publications issued by branches of the government including those of Congress, departments and bureaus.   (J22)

---- ----. Tables of and annotated index to the congressional series of United States public documents. Washington, U.S. Govt. Print. Off., 1902. 769p.

Superseded by the third edition of the Checklist of U.S. public documents; however, the subject index is very useful as a key to the congressional set before 1893. (J23)

Wilcox, Jerome Kear. Bibliography of new guides and aides
to public documents use, 1953-1956. New York, Special
Libraries Association, 1957. 16p.

Contains some 70 items that include general, federal,
state, municipal, foreign and international guides. (J24)

---- ----. Manual on the use of state publications. Chicago, American Library Association, 1940. 342p.

Each section being written by a specialist, this work includes general descriptions as well as bibliographies of
basic state publications.   (J25)

---- ----. Official defense publications; guide to state, federal, and Canadian publications. Berkeley, Bureau of Public Administration, University of California, 1941-45. 9v.
in 3

Volumes 1-2 include official defense publications and a
guide to state and federal publications. Each volume contains a subject index.   (J26)

Appendix C

Agencies and Institutions Engaged

in Political Research

The number of agencies and institutions that are carrying on research projects in political science is at an all time high. Below is a list of several reference works with information concerning these agencies and institutions followed by a few examples in alphabetical order.

The Foundation directory. New York, Russell Sage Foundation, 1960+ (1964 is the 2d ed.)

Supersedes American foundations and their fields, VII (1955). It is arranged alphabetically by state with a special section for New York City. Data is provided on many non-governmental and non-profit foundations. Gives name, address, date of founding, donor, purposes and activities, financial data and officers. (K1)

Gale Research Company. Encyclopedia of associations. 4th ed. Detroit, 1964+

Consists of 2 volumes. v.1 is a listing of over 12,000 U.S. national organizations, associations, societies, federations, chambers of commerce, unions and other non-profit groups. These are grouped by field and indexed by name, key word and subject. For each one is given the name, address, membership, acronym, activities, purpose, etc. v.2 is an index of executives, listed geographically. (K2)

Governmental Research Association. A directory of organizations engaged in governmental research. Chicago, Governmental Research Association, 1935+

Includes a geographical arrangement, with alphabetical indexes by organization and individual. (K3)

Academie International de Science Politique et d'Histoire Constitutionelle. Paris. Founded 1936.

310

Academy of Political Science.   New York, Columbia University.   Founded 1880.

American Academy of Political and Social Science.   Philadelphia.   Founded 1889.

American Political Science Association.   Washington.   Founded 1903.

American Society for Public Administration.   Chicago.   Founded 1939.

Carnegie Endowment for International Peace.   New York.   Founded 1910.

Citizens' Research Foundation (CRF).   Princeton, New Jersey.   Founded 1958.

Council of State Governments.   Chicago.   Founded 1935.

Council on Foreign Relations.   New York.   Founded 1921.

Deutsche Vereinigungen für Politische Wissenschaft.   Berlin.

Foundation Nationale des Sciences Politiques.   Paris.   Founded 1945.

Foreign Policy Association.   New York.   Founded 1921.

International City Managers Association.   Chicago.   Founded 1914.

International Institute of Administrative Sciences.   Brussels.   Founded 1930.

International Political Science Association.   Geneva.   Founded 1949.

Istituto per gli Studi di Politica Internazionale.   Milan.   Founded 1934.

National Academy of Economics and Political Science.   Washington, American University.   Founded 1932.

National Center for Education in Politics (NCEP).   New York.   Founded 1947.

Public Administration Service.   Chicago.   Founded 1933.

Royal Institute of International Affairs.   London.   Founded
    1920.

Author Index

The designation following the author entry refers to the chapter and numerical position of the item.

Abbo, John A. , Political thought, F10.
Abbott, Leonard Dalton, ed. , Masterworks of government, F3.
Abbott, Lyman, Rights of man, F142.
Abraham, Henry Julian, The judicial process, C242.
Abraham, Louis Arnold, A parliamentary dictionary, C187.
Acheson, Dean Gooderham, A Democrat looks at his party, E59.
Acheson, Patricia C. , The Supreme Court, C249.
Adam, Melchior, Vitae Germanorum, B47.
Adam, Thomas Ritchie, Elements of government, B113.
Adams, John Clarke, The government of republican Italy, C155, E113.
Adams, Michael, Suez and after, I360.
Adrian, Charles R. , State and local governments, D1.
Advisory Commission on Graduate Education and Research in Government in the South, Graduate education and research in government in the South, B29.
Agar, Herbert, Price of union, E23.
Agard, Walter Raymond, What democracy meant to the Greeks, F223.
Ahmad, Mushtaq, The United Nations and Pakistan, I361.
Aids to the study of European governments, C134.
Akzin, Benjamin, New states and international organization, H251.
Alabama. University. Bureau of Public Administration, Alabama government manual, D183.
Alaska. Legislative Council, Legislative handbook on Alaska state government, D185.
Albig, William, Modern public opinion, E125.
Alden, Edmund K. , The world's representative assemblies of today, C171.
Alderfer, Harold Freed, American local government and administration, D2; Local government in developing countries, D246; Pennsylvania government, D229.
Alexander, Henry M. , Government in Arkansas, D188.

Appleby, Paul Henson, Big democracy, H1; Morality and
   administration in democratic government, H320; Policy and
   administration, H2; Public administration for a welfare
   state, H3; Re-examination of India's administrative system, H238; Report on India's administrative system, H116.
Apter, David Ernest, The Gold Coast in transition, H117.
Ardant, Gabriel, Technique de l'État, H239.
Arendt, Hannah, The origins of totalitarianism, F188.
Aris, Reingold, History of political thought in Germany, F72.
Armstrong, John Alexander, Ideology, politics, and govern-
   ment in the Soviet Union, C157; Politics of totalitarian-
   ism, E116; The Soviet bureaucratic elite, I289.
Arnold, Harry John Philip, Aid for developing countries,
   I378.
Arnold, Thurman Wesley, The folklore of capitalism, B115;
   The symbols of government, C3.
Aruego, Jose Maminta, Principles of political science, B116.
Ashford, Douglas E., Political change in Morocco, E7.
Ashton, E.B., The fascist, F145.
Ashton-Gwatkin, Frank Trelaway Arthur, The British For-
   eign Service, I239.
Asia Society, American institutions and organizations in-
   terested in Asia, I103.
Asian annual, C101.
Association for Education in Citizenship, Bibliography of so-
   cial studies, B48.
Association of American Law Schools, Directory of teachers
   in member schools, G62; Select essays on Anglo-Ameri-
   can legal history, G167.
Atlantic reporter, G94.
Aubrey, Henry G., Coexistence, I290.
Auerbach, M. Morton, Conservative illusion, F131.
Aufricht, Hans, Guide to League of Nations publications,
   I412; World organization, I395.
Aumann, Francis Robert, Government and administration of
   Ohio, D224; Instrumentalities of justice, D86.
Australian National University, Canberre, Federalism, H228.
Authoritarian personality, B268.
Avasthi, Amreshwar, Public administration, H4.
Avery, Mary Wilhamson, History and government of the
   State of Washington, D240.
Avery, Robert Sterling, Experiment in management, H261.
Ayer, Firm, Newspaper Advertising Agents, N.W. Ayer &
   son's directory of newspapers and periodicals, A71.

Babbitt, Irving, Democracy and leadership, F133.
Babcock, Robert S., State and local government, D5.

Benson, George Charles Sumner, The new centralization, D43.

Benson, Lee, Concept of Jacksonian democracy, E78.

Bentham, Jeremy, Bentham's handbook of political fallacies, C172.

Bentley, Arthur Fisher, Process of government, C5.

Berelson, Bernard, The behavioral sciences today, A4; Reader in public opinion and communication, E123; Voting, E171.

Berger, Adolf, Encyclopedic dictionary of Roman law, G45.

Berger, Morroe, Bureaucracy and society in modern Egypt, H185.

Berggrav, Eivind Josef, Man and the state, F79.

Berkes, Ross N., The diplomacy of India, I363.

Berle, Adolf Augustus, Natural selection of political forces, B121; Tides of crisis, I248.

Berliner, Joseph S., Soviet economic aid, I292.

Berman, Harold Joseph, Justice in the U.S.S.R., C246.

Bernard, Luther Lee, Sociology and the study of international relations, I49.

Bernstein, Eduard, Evolutionary socialism, F165.

Bernstein, Marver H., The job of the Federal executive, H146; The politics of Israel, H186; Regulating business by independent commission, H229.

Berolzheimer, Fritz, World's legal philosophies, G201.

Bertier de Sauvigny, Guillaume de, Some historical clues to French politics, C136.

Bertrand, André, The techniques of governmental work in the modern state, H37.

Best, Harry, The Soviet State, H154.

Besterman, Theodore, A world bibliography of bibliographies, A52.

Bhandari, Sukhsampattirai, A twentieth century political dictionary, B79.

Biblio, A67.

Bibliographic index, A53.

Bibliographical guide to the law of the United Kingdom, G28.

Bibliographical services throughout the world, I399.

Bibliographie de la France, A68.

Bibliographie der Sozialwissenschaften, B49.

Bibliography in politics, B50.

Bibliography of the studies on law and politics, B51.

Bickel, Alexander M., The least dangerous branch, C250.

Bingham, Alfred Mitchell, The techniques of democracy, F134.

Binkley, Wilford Ellsworth, American political parties, E24.

Biography index, A86.

Bosanquet, Bernard, The philosophical theory of the state, F105.

Botero, Giovanni, The reason of state, F106.

Boulding, Kenneth Ewart, Conflict and defense, I51.

Bouvier, John, Bouvier's law dictionary, G47.

Bowie, Robert Richardson, ed., Studies in federalism, F195.

Bowker, Richard Rogers, The reader's guide in economic, social and political science, B52.

Bowle, John, Western political thought, F11.

Bowles, Chester, Ambassador's report, I364; Coming political breakthrough, E60.

Bowman, Eric Fisher, An introduction to political science, B122.

Boyd, Andrew Kirk Henry, An atlas of African affairs, I107; An atlas of world affairs, I108; United Nations, I416.

Boyd, Anne Morris, United States government publications, J3.

Bozza, Tommaso, Scrittori politici italiani, B53.

Bradley, Phillips, A bibliography of the Monroe doctrine, I82.

Brady, Alexander. Democracy in the Dominions, C60.

Bramson, Leon, The political context of sociology, B284.

Branch, Melville Campbell, Aerial photography in urban planning and research, D172.

Brandt, Conrad, Stalin's failure in China, I327.

Brane, Dennis DeWitt, A sequential science of government, B5.

Branning, Rosalind Lorraine, Annotated bibliography on Pennsylvania State Government, D230.

Brecht, Arnold, The art and technique of administration in German ministries, H137; Federalism and regionalism in Germany, H230; Political theory, F12.

Breckenridge, Adam Carlyle, One house for two, D68.

Brewster, Robert Wallace, Government in modern society, C7.

Breycha-Vanthier, Arthur Carl von, Sources of information, I413.

Bridge, Lawrence Wilford, The Funk & Wagnalls book of parliamentary procedure, C219.

Bridges, Edward Ettingdene, Portrait of a profession, H100.

Brierly, James Leslie, The law of nations, I465.

Brimmer, Brenda, A guide to the use of United Nations documents, J4.

Brinton, Clarence Crane, English political thought in the 19th century, F61; From many, one, I130; Political ideas of the English romanticists, F62.

Brissaud, Jean Baptiste, A history of French private law, G186; A history of French public law, G187.
Britannica Library Research Service, Britannica home study guide. Political science, B90.
British national bibliography, A65.
British year book of international law, I510.
Broekmeijer, M.W.J.M., Developing countries and N.A.T.O., I379.
Brogan, Denis William, Political patterns in today's world, C8; The study of politics, B32.
Bromage, Arthur Watson, Councilmen at work, D104.
Brookes, Edgar Harry, The city of God and the politics of crisis, F236; The relationship between history and political science, B123.
Brookings Institution, Washington, D.C., The administration of foreign affairs and overseas operation, I240; Development of the emerging countries, I380; Institute for government research, B6; Major problems of United States foreign policy, I250; United States foreign policy, I226.
Brookings Institution, Washington, D.C. Committee on Training, Essays on research in the social sciences, A5.
Brookings Institution, Washington, D.C. International Studies Group, The administration of foreign affairs and overseas operation, H208.
Brooks, Alexander D., Civil rights and liberties in the United States, H44.
Brooks, Glenn E., When governors convene, D79.
Brooks, Robert Clarkson, Political parties and electoral problems, E27.
Brown, Bernard Edward, New directions in comparative politics, C9.
Brown, Delbert Franklin, The growth of democratic government, C10.
Brown, Donald Mackenzie, The white umbrella, F76.
Brown, Edwin Tylor, The sovereign people, H8.
Brown, Everett Sommerville, Manual of government publications, J5.
Brown, George Williams, Canadians and their government, C61.
Bruce, Harold Rozelle, American parties and politics, E28.
Bryce, James Bryce, Modern democracies, C11; Studies in history and jurisprudence, G204.
Brzezinski, Zbigniew K., The Soviet bloc, I293.
Buber, Martin, Paths in Utopia, F166.
Buchanan, Norman Sharpe, Approaches to economic development, H285.
Buchanan, William, How nations see each other, E129, I145.

Carroll, Wallace, Persuade or perish, I172.
Carswell's directory of Canadian lawyers, G63.
Carter, Byrum E., The office of Prime Minister, C224.
Carter, Gwendolen Margaret, Government and politics in the
   twentieth century, C13; The politics of inequality, C53.
Cartwright, Dorwin, ed., Group dynamics, I146.
Carver, Thomas Nixon, Principles of political economy,
   B239.
Case, Harry Lawrence, Personnel policy in a public agency,
   H262.
Cassinelli, C.W., The politics of freedom, C14.
Cassirer, Ernst, The myth of the state, F107.
Catlin, George Edward Gordon, The Atlantic community,
   I273; Political theory, B126; Preface to action, B127; The
   science and method of politics, B225; The story of the po-
   litical philosophers, F13; A study of the principles of poli-
   tics, B128; Systematic politics, B129.
Center for the Study of Democratic Institutions, The power
   of reason, F156; Tragedy and the new politics, B130.
Chadwick, Hecter Munro, The nationalities of Europe and the
   growth of national ideologies, I136.
Chamberlain, Joseph Perkins, Legislative processes, D70.
Chamberlin, Jo Hubbard, Careers for social scientists, A45.
Chamberlin, Waldo, A chronology and fact book of the United
   Nations, I431.
Chanda, Asok Kumar, Indian administration, H209.
Changing environment of international relations, I3.
Chapin, Francis Stuart, Urban land use planning, D173.
Chapman, Brian, Devolution of powers to autonomous insti-
   tutions, H231; Introduction to French local government,
   D247; The prefects and provincial France, H232; The pro-
   fession of government, H9.
Chapman, Sydney John, Political economy, B240.
Charles, Joseph, Origins of the American party system, E30.
Charlesworth, James Clyde, Governmental administration,
   H10; Mathematics and the social sciences, A6.
Chase, Allan, Falange, I173.
Chatters, Carl Hallack, An inventory of governmental activi-
   ties in the United States, H290.
Cheever, Daniel S., American foreign policy and the separa-
   tion of powers, I227; Organizing for peace, I385.
Chester, Daniel Norman, The nationalized industries, H240.
Childs, Harwood Lawrence, A reference guide to the study
   of public opinion, E148.
Childs, James Bennett, Government document bibliography in
   the United States, J6.
Childs, James Rives, American foreign service, I241.

Childs, Richard Spencer, Civic victories, D105, H11.
Chitty, Joseph, Chitty's Statutes of practical utility, G87.
Christensen, Asher Norman, ed. , The evolution of Latin
    American government, C64, H194.
Christenson, Rea Millard, comp. , Voice of the people,
    E124.
Christiansen, Bjørn, Attitudes towards foreign affairs as a
    function of personality, I53.
Ch'u, Tung-tsu, Law and society in traditional China, G175;
    Local government in China under the Chin, D248.
Chute, Charles Lionel, Crime, courts, and probation, D142.
Clagett, Helen (Lord), The administration of justice in Latin
    America, C245.
Clancy, Herbert John, The Democratic party, E62.
Clark, Frederick LeGros, ed. , Four thousand million
    mouths, I202.
Clark, Jane Perry, The rise of a new federalism, D45.
Clark, Joseph S. , The Senate establishment, C190.
Clarke, Jack Alden, Research materials in the social sci-
    ences, A32.
Claude, Inis L. , Swords into plowshares, I386.
Claunch, John Miller, ed. , Political and social problems of
    public administration in underdeveloped areas, H12.
Cobban, Alfred, The crisis of civilization, B131; Dictator-
    ship, F200.
Cochran, William Cox, Cochran's law lexicon, G48.
Codding, George Arthur, The federal government of Switzer-
    land, C164.
Code of federal regulations, G78.
Cohen, Bernard Cecil, Citizen education in world affairs,
    I34.
Cohen, Carl, ed. , Communism, fascism, and democracy,
    F167.
Cohen, Emmeline W. , The growth of the British civil serv-
    ice, H72.
Cohen, Morris Raphael, Law and social order, G207.
Cohen, Saul Bernard, Geography and politics in a world di-
    vided, B251.
Cohn, David Lewis, The fabulous Democrats, E63.
Coke, Edward, A catalogue of the library of Sir Edward
    Coke, G29.
Coker, Francis William, Organismic theories of the State,
    F108; Readings in political philosophy, F5.
Cole, Fred, International relations in institutions of higher
    education in the South, I35.
Cole, George Douglas Howard, A guide to modern politics,
    B132; Some relations between political and economic

Corry, James Alexander, Elements of democratic government, C15.

Corson, John Jay, Economic needs of older people, D143; Executives for the Federal service, H148.

Corwin, Edward Samuel, The President, office and powers, C228; The President's control of foreign relations, I228.

Council of Europe Directorate of Information, Handbook of the European organization, I446.

Council of State Governments, The American governors, D80; American legislatures, D71; State government, D26.

Council on Foreign Relations, Social change in Latin America today, I320.

Cowan, Laing Gray, Local government in West Africa, D249.

Cowley, John Duncan, A bibliography of abridgments, digests, dictionaries and indexes of English law to the year 1800, G30, G132.

Cowling, Maurice, The nature and limits of political science, B133.

Cox, Richard Howard, Locke on war and peace, F252.

Coyle, David Cushman, The United Nations and how it works, C77.

Cracknell, Douglas George, Constituional law and the English legal system, G240.

Craig, Gordon Alexander, ed. , The diplomats, I209.

Craig, John Herbert McCutcheon, A history of red tape, H73.

Crandall, Andrew Wallace, The early history of the Republican party, E64.

Cresap, Dean Russell, Party politics in the Golden State, E80.

Crick, Bernard R., In defense of politics, B134.

Critchley, Thomas Alan, The civil service today, H101.

Cross, Charles Albert, Principles of local government, D250.

Crouch, Winston Winford, California government and politics, D189; The initiative and referendum in California, D61.

Crump, Irving, Our State police, D144.

Cumulative book index, A58.

Cundliffe, John Bell, International trade and economic nationalism, I186.

Cunningham, Noble E. , Jeffersonian Republicans, E65.

Current law consolidation, G133.

Current thought on peace and war, I119.

Curtis, M.R. , Central government, C146.

Curtis, Michael, ed. , The great political theories, F6; The nature of politics, B99.

Cushing, Luther Stearns, Cushing's manual of parliamentary

practice, C220.

Cushman, Robert Eugene, The independent regulatory commissions, H210.

Cyclopedia of American government, C88.

Cyclopedia of law and procedure, G51.

Dahl, Robert Alan, Congress and foreign policy, I229; Modern political analysis, B7; Politics, economics, and welfare, H89; A preface to democratic theory, F136.

Dale, Harold Edward, The higher civil service of Great Britain, H102.

Dallin, Alexander, Soviet conduct in world affairs, I296; The Soviet Union at the United Nations, I297.

Dallin, David J., Soviet foreign policy after Stalin, I298.

Daly, Lowrie John, The political theory of John Wycliff, F253.

Dangerfield, Royden James, In defense of the Senate, I230.

Datta, Ansu Kamar, Tanganyika, C55.

Dauer, Manning Julian, Political science scope and method, B8.

David, Paul Theodore, Executives for government, H269; Presidential nominating politics in 1952, E173.

David, René, The French legal system, G190.

Davidson, William Leslie, Political thought in England, F63.

Davies, James C., Human nature in politics, B270.

Davis, Claude J., West Virginia State and local government, D242.

Davis, Deborah, Idaho civics, D198.

Davis, Harold Eugene, ed., Government and politics in Latin America, C65.

Davis, Harold Thayer, Political statistics, B290.

Davis, Harriet Ide (Egger) ed., Pioneers in world order, I408.

Davis, Henry William Charles, Political thought of Heinrich von Treitschke, F280.

Davis, Jerome, Contemporary social movements, F209.

Davis, Kingsley, The population of India and Pakistan, I203.

Davitt, Thomas E., The nature of law, G208.

Dawson, Robert MacGregor, The Government of Canada, C62.

Day, John Percival, Public administration in the highlands and islands of Scotland, H121.

Deadline data on foreign affairs, I120.

Dealey, James Quayle, Development of the state, F109; Growth of American State constitutions, D55.

Deane, Herbert Andrew, The political and social ideas of St. Augustine, F238.

politics, C89.
Ewing, Russell Howard, Political science seminar manual,
  B11.
Exline, Frank, Politics, B138.
Eysenck, Hans Jurgen, The psychology of politics, B273.

Fabre d'Olivet, Antoine, Hermeneutic interpretation of the
  origin of the social state of man and the destiny of the
  Adamic race, F110.
Facts on file yearbook, A89.
Fahs, Charles B., Government in Japan, H164.
Fainsod, Merle, How Russia is ruled, C158.
Fairbank, John King, The United States and China, I330.
Falk, Richard A., Law, morality, and war in the contempo-
  rary world, I468.
Fall, Bernard B., The Viet-Minh regime, H155.
Farber, William Ogden, Government of South Dakota, D233.
Farley, Miriam Southwell, United States relations with South-
  east Asia, I344.
Farrell, Henry Percy, Introduction to political philosophy,
  F21.
Fearey, Robert A., The U.S. versus the U.S.S.R., I148.
Federal reporter, G95.
Federal supplement, G96.
Feis, Herbert, Foreign aid and foreign policy, I222.
Ferguson, John Henry, The American federal government,
  C78.
Fesler, James William, Area and administration, H233.
Field, George Lowell, Governments in modern society, C18.
Field, Guy Cromwell, Political theory, F22.
Field, Oliver Peter, Political science at Indiana University,
  B33.
Fifield, Russell Hunt, The diplomacy of Southeast Asia,
  I345; Southeast Asia in United States policy, I346.
Figgis, John Neville, The political aspects of St. Augustine's
  'City of God,' F239; Studies of political thought from Ger-
  son to Grotius, F256.
Fine, Nathan, Labor and farmer parties in the United States,
  E91.
Finer, Herman, The British civil service, H104; English
  local government, D251; Governments of greater European
  powers, C124; Theory and practice of modern government,
  C19.
Finer, Samuel Edward, A primer of public administration,
  H14.
Finletter, Thomas Knight, Foreign policy, I253.

tional government and politics, F193; Foreign policy in
the making, I232; Man and his government, B12; The
philosophy of law in historical perspective, G211; Die
politische Wissenschaft, B139; Responsible bureaucracy,
H138.

Friedwald, Eugene Marie, Man's last choice, B140.

Fritz, Kurt von, Pythagorean politics in southern Italy,
    F226; The theory of mixed constitution in antiquity, F227.

Froman, Lewis Acrelius, People and politics, C79.

Frost, Richard Theodore, ed., Cases in State and local gov-
    ernment, D6.

Fuchs, Lawrence H., The political behavior of American
    Jews, B201.

Fuller, C. Dale, Training of specialists in international re-
    lations, I36.

Fuller, Lon L., The problems of jurisprudence, G212.

Furniss, Edgar Stephenson, American military policy, I217;
    France, troubled ally, I277; An introduction to American
    foreign policy, I254.

Furnivall, John Sydenham, Colonial policy and practice,
    H176; Educational progress in southeast Asia, H316.

Gale Research Company, Acronyms dictionary, A46; Encyclo-
    pedia of associations, K2.

Gallion, Arthur B., The urban pattern, D174.

Galloway, George Barnes, American pamphlet literature of
    public affairs, H46; Congress and Parliament, C173; His-
    tory of the House of Representatives, C193; The legisla-
    tive process in Congress, C194; Next steps in congres-
    sional reform, C195.

Gallup political almanac, E149.

Gammon, Samuel Rhea, Presidential campaign of 1837, E174.

Gange, John, American foreign relations, I255; University
    research on international affairs, I78.

Garceau, Oliver, The public library in the political process,
    D159.

Gareis, Karl von, Introduction to the science of law, G213.

Garner, James Wilford, Introduction to political science,
    B141; Political science and government, B142.

Garvey, Neil Ford, The government and administration of
    Illinois, D199.

Gaus, John Merriman, The frontiers of public administration,
    H15; Reflections on public administration, H16.

Gay, Peter, The dilemma of democratic socialism, F170.

Gee, Wilson, Research in the social sciences, A7; Social
    science research methods, A8; Social science research
    organization in American universities and colleges, A9.

tions, H19; American state government and administration, D28.

Gray, Albert Woodruff, Family legal adviser, G74.

Gray, John Chipman, The nature and sources of the law, G148.

Gt. Brit. Court of Criminal Appeal, The Criminal appeal reports, G118.

Gt. Brit. Courts, Reports of tax cases, G119.

Gt. Brit. Laws, Statutes, etc., Acts and ordinances of the interregnum, G89; The statutes, G90.

Gt. Brit. Patent Office, Patents, designs, and trade marks, G120.

Greaves, Harold Goring, The civil service in a changing state, H106.

Greaves, Harold Richard Goring, The foundations of political theory, F24.

Greely, Adolphus Washington, Public documents of the first fourteen congresses, J7.

Green, Bert F., Digital computers in research, A10.

Green, L. P., History of local government in South Africa, D252.

Green, Thomas Hill, Lectures on the principles of political obligation, F86; The political theory of T.H. Green, F281.

Greene, Alexander, Ohio government, D226.

Greene, Fred, Dynamics of international relations, I8.

Greene, Lee Siefert, Government in Tennessee, D234.

Greenfield, Margaret, Legislative reapportionment, D73.

Greenstein, Fred I., The American party system, E35.

Greer, Sarah, A bibliography of civil service and personnel administration, H47.

Greer, Scott A., Metropolitics, D129.

Grégoire, Roger, National administration and international organizations, H213.

Griffith, Ernest Stacey, Congress, C196.

Griffith, Llewelyn Wyn, The British Civil Service, H107.

Grimes, Alan Pendleton, American political thought, F51; Modern political ideologies, F25.

Grindrod, Muriel, The rebuilding of Italy, I279.

Grinnell College, Grinnell, Iowa, Internationalism and democracy, F150.

Gripp, Richard C., Patterns of Soviet politics, C159.

Gross, Bertram Myron, The legislative struggle, C197.

Gross, Feliks, Foreign policy analysis, I9.

Grotius; annuaire international, I512.

Grotius Society, London. Library, Catalog of books, I485.

Groves, Harold Martin, Decentralization in decision-making and finance, H293; Financing government, H294.

Groves, Harry E. , Comparative constitutional law, G243.
Grunder, Gorel A., The Philippines and the United States,
I339.
Grundstein, Nathan D. , Presidential delegation of authority
in wartime, C230.
Guins, George Constantine, Soviet law and Soviet society,
H308.
Gulick, Luther Halsey, American forest policy, D175.
Gurland, Arcadius Rudolph Lang, Political science in West-
ern Germany, B34.
Gutteridge, Harold Cooke, Comparative law, G137.
Gwyn, William B. , Democracy and the cost of politics in
Britain, E194.

Haas, Ernst B. , Dynamics of international relations, I10;
The uniting of Europe, I447.
Hacker, Andrew, Political theory, F26; The study of poli-
tics, B13.
Hackworth, Green Haywood, Digest of international law,
I506.
Haddow, Anna, Political science in American colleges and
universities, B35.
Haessly, Mathias John, Political and governmental terms,
B81.
Hagman, Harlan L. , The administration of American public
schools, D160.
Hague.   International Court of Justice, Reports of Judgments,
I498.
Hague. International Court of Justice.   Registry, Reports of
international arbitral awards, I499.
Hague. Palace of Peace. Library, Catalog par P. C. Mal-
huysen et E. R. Oppenheim, I486.
Hague. Permanent Court of International Justice, The case
law of the International Court, I500.
Hailey, William Malcolm Hailey, Native administration in the
British African territories, H124.
Halasz, D. , Metropolis, D29.
Hall, Mary Penelope, The social services of modern Eng-
land, H317.
Halle, Louis Joseph, Men and nations, B146.
Hallowell, John Hamilton, Main currents in modern political
thought, F27; Religious perspectives of college teaching
in political science, B36.
Halsbury's Statutes of England, G91.
Hamburger, Max, The awakening of western legal thought,
G215.
Hamilton, Howard Devon, ed. , Political institutions, B103.

Hamilton, Joseph Greyore de Roulhec, Party politics in
   North Carolina, E83.
Hammer, Ellen Joy, The struggle for Indochina, I348.
Hammond, Mason, City-state and world state in Greek and
   Roman political theory, F229.
Hamson, Charles John, Executive discretion and judicial
   control, H310.
Hankey, Maurice Pascal Alers Hankey, The science and art
   of government, C22.
Hanson, Albert Henry, Public enterprise, H243; Public en-
   terprise and economic development, H244.
Harari, Maurice, Government and politics of the Middle
   East, C165.
Harley, John Eugene, Documentary textbook on international
   relations, I127.
Harmon, Mont Judd, Political thought, F28.
Harmon, Robert Bartlett, A bibliography of bibliographies in
   political science, B57.
Harper, Samuel Northrup, The government of the Soviet
   Union, H156.
Harrington, James, Political writings, F257.
Harris, George Montagu, Comparative local government,
   D253.
Harris, Joseph Pratt, Registration of voters in the United
   States, E180.
Harris, Seymour Edwin, The economics of the political
   parties, E76.
Harrison, Horace V., ed., The role of theory in internation-
   al relations, I56.
Hart, Herbert Lionell Adolphus, The concept of law, G216.
Hart, Jeffrey, ed., Political writers of eighteenth-century
   England, F258.
Hartman, Frederick H., The relations of nations, I11;
   World in crisis, I12.
Hartz, Louis, The liberal tradition in America, F52.
Harvard Law Review, An introduction to law, G149.
Harvard University. Law School, Library, Annual legal
   bibliography, G4; Catalogue of the library, G17.
Harvey, Heather J., Consultation and co-operation in the
   Commonwealth, H214.
Haskell, Henry Joseph, This was Cicero, F230.
Hauptman, Jerzy, The dilemmas of politics, B147.
Havard, William C., The Government of Louisiana, D204;
   Henry Sidgwick & later utilitarian political philosophy,
   F282.
Hawaii University, Honolulu. Legislative Reference Bureau,
   The structure of the Hawaii State government, D196.

Hawley, Amos Henry, Papers in demography and public administration, H177.

Hayes, Carlton Joseph Huntley, The historical evolution of modern nationalism, I138; Nationalism, a religion, I139.

Haynes, Edmund Didney Pollock, Religious persecution, B274.

Haynes, Evan, The selection and tenure of judges, D88.

Hazard, John Newbold, Law and social change in the U.S.S.R., G194; Settling disputes in Soviet society, C247; The Soviet system of government, C160.

Heady, Farrel, ed., Papers in comparative public administration, H20.

Heard, Alexander, Money and politics, E77; A two-party South?, E84.

Hearle, Edward F.R., A data processing system for State and local governments, D35.

Hearn, William Edward, Aryan household, G217.

Hearnshaw, Fossey John Cobb, The development of political ideas, F29; Social and political ideas of some English thinkers, F64; Social and political ideas of some great French thinkers, F67; Social and political ideas of some great mediaeval thinkers, F242; Social and political ideas of some great thinkers of the Renaissance and the Reformation, F259; Social and political ideas of some great thinkers of the sixteenth and seventeenth centuries, F260; Social and political ideas of some representative thinkers of the age of reaction and reconstruction, F283; Social and political ideas of some thinkers of the Revolutionary Era, F261; Social and political ideas of some representative thinkers of the Victorian Age, F262.

Heater, Derek Benjamin, Political ideas in the modern world, F30.

Heatley, David Playfair, Diplomacy and the study of international relations, I210.

Hebden, Norman, State-city relationships in highway affairs, D168.

Heckscher, August, Pattern of politics, B148.

Heckscher, Gunnar, The study of comparative government and politics, C23.

Heidenheimer, Arnold J., The governments of Germany, C143.

Hemphill, William Edwin, Cavalier Commonwealth, D239.

Hendel, Samuel, ed., The Soviet crucible, C161.

Hensel, Herman Struve, Department management in Federal administration, H215.

Herlitz, Mils, Sweden, H139.

Hermens, Ferdinand Aloys, Introduction to modern politics,

Jenks, Jeremiah Whipple, Principles of politics from the viewpoint of the American citizen, F54.

Jennings, William Ivor, Cabinet government, C225; Commonwealth in Asia, H126; Party politics, E110.

Jensen, Christen, The pardoning power in the American states, D81.

Jensen, De Lamar, Machiavelli, F263.

Jessup, Frank, Problems of local government in England and Wales, D256.

Jessup, Philip Caryl, A modern law of nations, I473.

Jevons, William Stanley, Theory of political economy, B244.

Jewell, Malcolm Edwin, State legislature, D74.

Jewish yearbook of international law, I513.

Jhering, Rudolf von, Law as a means to an end, G218.

Joad, Cyrin Edwin Mitchinson, Introduction to modern political theory, F33.

Joeckel, Carleton Burns, Government of the American public library, D161.

Johnson, Claudius Osborne, American state and local government, D12.

Johnson, John J., Role of the military in underdeveloped countries. I381.

Jonas, Frank H., Bibliography on Western politics, D30; Western politics and the 1956 elections, E176.

Jones, Stanley Wilson, Public administration in Malaya, H179.

Jones, Stephen Barr, Geography and world affairs, B255.

Jones, Victor, Metropolitan government, D131.

Jorrin, Miguel, Government of Latin America, C67.

Joseph, Franz M., ed., As others see us, I151.

Journal of Political Economy, Landmarks in political economy, B245.

Jouvenel, Bertrand de, On power, F97; The pure theory of politics, B151; Sovereignty, F179.

Jowitt, William Allen Jowitt, Dictionary of English law, G52.

Judah, Charles Burned, 47th state, D219.

Kaeley, S.L., Simple study of political science, B152.

Kahin, George McTurnan, Governments and politics of Southeast Asia, C118; Major governments of Asia, C99; Nationalism and revolution in Indonesia, I349.

Kallen, Horace Meyer, Study of liberty, F157.

Kantor, Harry, Governing our metropolitan communities, D132.

Kaplan, Morton A., Political foundations of international law, I474; Some problems in the strategic analysis of interna-

Kingsley, John Donald, Representative bureaucracy, H109.
Kinnane, Charles Herman, First book on Anglo-American
law, G168.
Kirchheimer, Otto, Political justice, G220.
Kirk, George Eden, Contemporary Arab politics, C166.
Kirk, Grayson Louis, Study of international relations in
American colleges and universities, I39.
Kise, Joseph, Minnesota's government, D211.
Kisker, George W., ed., World tension, I62.
Klineberg, Otto, Tensions affecting international understand-
ing, I152.
Kling, Samuel G., Popular legal encyclopedia for home and
business, G75.
Knoll, Joachim H., Jugend, Politik und politische Bildung,
B38.
Knorr, Klaus Eugen, The international system, I63; NATO
and American security, I453.
Knowles, Stanley, The new party, E12.
Koenig, Louis William, the invisible presidency, C231.
Kogan, Norman, The government of Italy, C156.
Kogekar, Sadanand Vasudeo, Political science in India, B39.
Kohler, Josef, Philosophy of law, G221.
Kohn, Hans, Nationalism, I140.
Korbel, Josef, Danger in Kashmir, I370.
Korkunov, Nikolai Mikhailovich, General theory of law, G222.
Kornhauser, Arthur William, When labor votes, E177.
Kovner, Milton, The challenge of coexistence, I305.
Kracke, Edward A., Civil service in early Sung China, H80.
Kraines, Oscar, Government and politics in Israel, C167.
Kris, Ernst, German radio propaganda, I176.
Krislov, Samuel, ed., The politics of regulation, H235.
Kronenberg, Henry Harold, Pamphlets on public affairs, H50.
Krüger, D.W., ed., South African parties and policies, E9.
Kulaski, Wladyslaw Wszbór, Peaceful coexistence, I306.
Kunz, Josef Lauienz, Latin American philosophy of law,
G164.

Lacordaire, Jean Baptiste Henri Dominique de, Political and
social philosophy, F218.
Laing, Lionel Hassell, ed., Source book in European govern-
ment, C126.
Lalor, John Joseph, ed., Cyclopedia of political science,
B82.
Lamprecht, Sterling Power, The moral and political philoso-
phy of John Locke, F265.
Lancaster, Lane W., Government in rural America, D97.
Landau, Jacob M., Parliaments and parties in Egypt, E10.

Lane, Robert Edwards, Political ideology, F34; Political
life, B276.
LaPalombra, Joseph G., The initiative and referendum in
Oregon, D62.
Laponce, J.A., The government of the Fifth Republic, E104.
Larsen, Jakob Aall Ottesen, Representative government in
Greek and Roman history, C25.
Laski, Harold Joseph, American presidency, C232; Founda-
tions of sovereignty, F180; A grammar of politics, B154;
Introduction to politics, B155; Political thought in Eng-
land, F65; Studies in law and politics, G150.
Laslett, Peter, ed., Philosophy, politics and society, B104.
Lasswell, Harold Dwight, Analysis of political behavior,
B205; Comparative study of elites, C233; Comparative
study of symbols, H201; Decision process, B218; Democ-
racy through public opinion, E136; Future of political sci-
ence, B15; Language of politics, B95; Political writings,
F285; Politics, B156; Power and society, F98; Psycho-
pathology and politics, B277; World politics and personal
insecurity, I64.
Lauterpacht, Hersh, Development of international law, I476.
Laves, Walter Herman Carl, Unesco, H255.
Law in Eastern Europe, G196.
Law journal reports, G121, G122.
Law reports, G123.
Law times reports, G124.
Laws of England, G53.
Lawson, Ruth Catherine, International regional organizations,
I422.
Lawyers directory, G66.
Lawyers reports annotated, G108.
Lazarsfeld, Paul Felix, Academic mind, A15; Language of
social research, A16; People's choice, E178.
Leacock, Stephen Butler, Elements of political science,
B157.
League of Nations, Handbook of international organizations,
I400.
League of Women Voters of Massachusetts, Massachusetts
State government, D207.
League of Women Voters of New York, New York State,
D221.
Learned, Edmund Philip, Executive action, H202.
Lecky, William Edward Hortpole, Democracy and liberty,
F139.
Legal bibliography of the British Commonwealth of Nations,
G32.
Legal periodical digest, G41.

Lyber, Albert Howe, Government of the Ottoman empire, H81.

Maass, Arthur, ed., Area and power, D15.

Mabbott, John David, State and the citizen, F114.

McCamy, James Lucian, Administration of American foreign affairs, H150, I243.

McCandless, Carl Albert, Government, Politics and administration in Missouri, D213.

McCarthy, Eugene J., Crescent dictionary of American politics, C91.

McCleskey, Clifton, Government and politics of Texas, D235.

McCloskey, Robert Green, American Supreme Court, C252; Essays in constitutional law, G244.

McClosky, Herbert, Soviet dictatorship, I307.

MacCorkle, Stuart Alexander, City manager's job, D109; Texas government, D236.

McCormick, Thomas Carson, Methods of research in the behavioral sciences, A19.

McCoy, Charles Nicholas Reiten, Structure of political thought, F35.

McCulloch, Albert Johnston, Suffrage and its problems, E186.

McCulloch, John Ramsay, Literature of political economy, B232.

MacCunn, John, Political philosophy of Burke, F266.

Macdonald, Austin Faulks, American state government and administration, D16; Elements of political science research, B18; State and local government in the United States, D17.

MacDonald, H. Malcolm, ed., Readings in American government, C81.

McDonald, Lee Cameron, Western political theory, F36.

McDonald, Neil A., Study of political parties, E1.

Macdonell, John, ed., Great jurists of the world, G197.

McGeary, Martin Nelson, Development of congressional investigative power, C200.

McGovern, William Montgomery, From Luther to Hitler, F147; Strategic intelligence and the shape of tomorrow, B256.

McGovney, Dudley Odell, American suffrage medley, E187.

McHargue, Daniel S., Michigan government in brief, D210.

McIlwain, Charles Howard, Growth of political thought in the West, F37.

MacIver, Robert Morrison, The modern state, F115; Web of government, C27.

Mack Effie Mona, Nevada government, D216.

Mackaye, James, Politics of utility, F190.

Mangone, Gerard J., Elements of international law, I503;
   Guide to United States foreign policy, I235; Short history
   of international organization, I393.
Mannheim, Karl, Ideology and utopia, F220, I156.
Manning, Charles Anthony Woodward, Nature of international
   society, I68; University teaching of the social sciences,
   I40.
Manning, Clarence Augustus, Forgotten republics, H158.
Mansoor, Menahem, English-Arabic dictionary of political,
   diplomatic, and conference terms, B84.
March, James G., Organizations, H204.
Marcuse, Herbert, Soviet Marxism, F176, I308.
Mariner, Elwyn E., This is your Massachusetts government,
   D208.
Maritain, Jacques, Man and the state, F84.
Marke, Julius J., ed., Deans' list of recommended reading,
   G9.
Markel, Lester, Public opinion and foreign policy, E140,
   I179.
Marquard, Leopold, Peoples and policies of South Africa,
   H128.
Mars, David, comp., Suggested library in public adminis-
   tration, H51.
Marshall, Geoffrey, Parliamentary sovereignty and the Com-
   monwealth, C147.
Martin, Curtis, Colorado politics, D191.
Martin, Everett Dean, Some principles of political behavior,
   B207.
Martin, Kingsley, French liberal thought, F68.
Martin, Ronald Russell, Teach yourself public administra-
   tion, H24.
Martindale-Hubbell law directory, G68.
Marvick, Dwaine, ed., Political decision-makers, B219.
Maryland. University. Bureau of Governmental Research,
   Political science, B60.
Mason, Edward Sagendorph, Promoting economic develop-
   ment, H299.
Massachusetts Institute of Technology. Dept. of Economics
   and Social Science, International relations, I19.
Masters of political thought, F8.
Mathiot, Andre, British political system, C148.
Mathisen, Trygve, Methodology in the study of international
   relations, I79.
Mattei, Rodolfo de, La storia dottrine politiche, B61.
Mattern, Johannes, Concepts of state, sovereignty and inter-
   national law, F116; Geopolitik, B257.
Matthews, A. T. J., Emergent Turkish administration, H190.

Moore, John Bassett, Digest of international law, I507.

Moos, Malcolm Charles, Republicans, E70.

Morgan, Glenn Guy, Soviet administrative legality, C248.

Morgenthau, Hans Joachim, Dilemmas of politics, B105; Politics among nations, I21; Principles and problems of international politics, I22; Scientific man vs. power politics, B167.

Morlan, Robert Loren, Capitol, courthouse, and city hall, D19; Intergovernmental relations in education, D163.

Morrah, Dermot, Work of the Queen, C226.

Morral, John B., Political thought in medieval times, F244.

Morris, Allen Covington, Our Florida government, D194.

Morris, Charles Richard, History of political ideas, F40.

Morris, George Sylvester, Hegel's philosophy of the state and of history, F286.

Morris-Jones, Wyndraeth Humphreys, Parliament in India, C218.

Morrison, Herbert Stanley, Government and Parliament, H112.

Morrison, Leonard Samuel, Government of New Hampshire, D217.

Morse, Alan Leslie, Internal control in the administration of local government, H129.

Morstein Marx, Fritz, Administrative state, H95; Elements of public administration, H26.

Mosca, Gaetano, Ruling class, H96.

Mosher, Frederick C., Program budgeting, H301.

Mott, Rodney Loomer, Home rule for America's cities, D123.

Muller, Steven, Documents on European government, C127.

Mund, Vernon Arthur, Government and business, H302.

Municipal index, D36.

Municipal yearbook, D37.

Munro, William Bennett, Bibliography of municipal government, D31; Governments of Europe, C128; Invisible government, C32.

Muret, Charlotte (Tonzalia), French royalist doctrines since the revolution, F70.

Murphy, Walter F., Congress and the court, C201.

Murray, Alexander Rainy Maclean, Introduction to political philosophy, F41.

Murray, Robert Henry, Political consequences of the reformation, F267.

Musolf, Lloyd D., Public ownership and accountability, H248.

Mustard, Harry Stoll, Introduction to public health, D152.

Myers, William Starr, Republican party, a history, E71.

Myers, John Linton, Political ideas of the Greeks, **F233.**

Nandi, A., Introduction to political science, **B168.**
Nash, Howard Pervear, Third parties in American politics, **E93.**
National Association of Legal Aid Organizations, 1949 legal aid directory, **G69.**
National Association of State Libraries, Collected public documents of the states, **J11.**
National Association of State Libraries, Public Documents Clearing House Committee, Checklist of legislative journals of the states of the United States of America, **J12.**
National Civil Service League, Law of civil service, **H265.**
Naude, Gabriel, Bibliographia politica, **B63.**
Needler, Martin C., Latin American politics in perspective, **C68.**
Neibuhr, Reinhold, Reinhold Niebuhr on politics, **F287.**
Nelson, George R., Freedom and welfare, **H319.**
Nelson, William H., Theory and practice in American politics, **C83.**
Neuberger, Richard Lewis, Adventures in politics, **D75.**
Neue politische Literatur, **B64.**
Neumann, Franz Leopold, Democratic and the authoritarian state, **F117.**
Neumann, Robert G., European and comparative government, **C129.**
Neumann, Sigmund, Modern political parties, **E5.**
Neustadt, Richard E., Presidential power, **C237.**
New York Public Library, Political parties in the United States, **E16.**
New York, State Library, Albany, Checklist of books and pamphlets in the social sciences, **A39.**
New York. State Library, Albany, Legislature Reference Library. Source material for the study of public administration, **H66.**
New York supplement, **G97.**
New York times index, **A81.**
New York Tribune, New York daily tribune index, **A82.**
New York University. School of Law. Library, Catalogue of the law collection, **G18.**
New Zealand. Dept. of External Affairs, United Nations and specialized agencies handbook, **I433.**
Nicolson, Sir Harold George, Diplomacy, **I212;** Evolution of diplomatic method, **I213.**
Nigro, Felix A., Public administration readings and documents, **H27;** Public personnel administration, **H266.**
Niles, Mary Cushing (Howard), Essence of management, **H28**

Nineteenth century readers' guide to periodical literature, A73.

Nock Albert Jay, Our enemy the state, F118.

Nomand, Max, Skeptic's political dictionary, B112.

Norman, E. Herbert, Japan's emergence as a modern state, H167.

North, Robert Carver, Content analysis, B208; Moscow and Chinese Communists, I334.

North Atlantic Treaty Organization, The North Atlantic Treaty Organization, I454; NATO bibliography, I455.

North Atlantic Treaty Organization. Information Service, Facts about NATO, I456.

North Dakota. Legislative Reference Service, Legislative handbook of state governmental agencies, D223.

North eastern reporter, G98.

North western reporter, G99.

Northrop, Filmer Stuart Cuckow, European union and United States foreign policy, I259; Ideological differences and world order, I159.

Northwestern University, Evanston, Ill., World population and future resources, I204.

Notz, Rebecca Laurens (Love), Legal bibliography and legal research, G22.

Nova, Fritz, Contemporary European governments, C130.

Nurkse, Ragnar, Problems of capital formation in under-developed countries, I383.

Nussbaum, Arthur, Concise history of the law of nations, I477.

Odegard, Peter H., Pressure politics, E94.

Odum, Howard Washington, Introduction to social research, A21.

Ogburn, William Fielding, Social sciences and their interrelations, A22; Technology and international relations, I23, I164.

Ogg, Frederick Austin, Modern foreign governments, C33.

Ogle, Marbury Bladen, Public opinion and political dynamics, E141.

Oppenheim, Lassa Francis Lawrence, International law, I478.

Oppenheim, Leonard, Materials on legal bibliography, G11.

Oppenheimer, Franz, The state, F119.

Orbis; encyclopaedia of extra-European countries, C135.

Oregon. University. School of Business Administration, The study of administration, H40.

Organization for European Economic Cooperation, General catalogue of books, I458; History and structure, I459.

Organization of American States, Annals, I461.
Organski, A.F.K. , World politics, I24.
Osgood, Robert Endicott, NATO, the entangling alliance,
    I457.
Ostrogorskii, Moisei Iakovlevich, Democracy and the organ-
    ization of political parties, E6.
Overacker, Louise, Australian party system, E101; Money
    in elections, E184; Presidential primary, E179.
Owen, Wilfred, Cities in the motor age, D111; Metropolitan
    transportation problem, D134.

Pacific reporter, G100.
Padelford, Norman Judson, Dynamics of international poli-
    tics, I25.
Palande, Manohr Ramchandra, Textbook of Indian adminis-
    tration, H130.
Palgrave, Sir Robert Harry Inglis, Palgrave's dictionary of
    political economy, B233.
Palmer, Norman Dunbar, Indian political system, C105;
    International relations, I26.
Pan American Union, Status of Inter-American treaties and
    conventions, I464.
Pan American Union.   Columbus Memorial Library, Biblio-
    grafia de las conferencias interamericanas, I462; Bibli-
    ography on public administration in Latin America, H54.
Pan American Union.   Dept. of Legal Affairs, Organization
    of American States and the United Nations, I463.
Panikkar, Kavalan Madhava, Principles and practice of di-
    plomacy, I214.
Parkinson, Cyril Northcote, Evolution of political thought,
    F42.
Parks, Wallace Judson, United States administration of its
    international economic affairs, H221.
Parson, Ruben L. , Conserving American resources, D178.
Partridge, Percy Herbert, Thinking about politics, B169.
Pascjal, Crisolito, Nature and elements of the law, G151.
Passerin d'Entrèves, Alessandro, Dante as a political
    thinker, F245; Medieval contribution to political thought,
    F246.
Passfield, Sidney James Webb, Methods of social study,
    A23.
Patch, William H. , Use of United Nations documents, J13.
Pate, James Ernest, Local government and administration,
    D20.
Patterson, Caleb Perry, Presidential government, C238.
Pearcy, George Etzel, World political geography, B259.
Peaslee, Amos Jenkins, International governmental organiza-

tions, I404.

Peel, Roy Victor, ed., Introduction to politics, B170.

Pekelis, Alexander Haim, Law and social action, G152.

Peltason, Jack Walter, Federal courts in the political process, C253.

Perkins, Dexter, United States and Latin America, I322.

Perleberg, Max, Who's who in modern China, C104.

Perticone, Giacomo, Filosofia del dritto e dello stato, a curad, B65.

Petersen, Svend, Statistical history of the American Presidential elections, E162.

Pettersch, Carl Alfred, Teaching of government in the United States, B40.

Pfiffner, John McDonald, Public administration, H29; Research methods in public administration, H62; Supervision of personnel, H277.

Phillips, Jewell Cass, Municipal government and administration in America, D112; State and local government in America, D21.

Phillipson, Sydney, Nigerianization of the Civil Service, H131.

Pickles, Dorothy Maud, Fifth French Republic, C140; Introduction to politics, B171.

Pierson, William Whatley, Governments of Latin America, C69.

Pimsleur, Meira G., Check lists of basic American legal publications, G12.

Pinner, Frank A., Old age and political behavior, B209.

Pinson, Koppel Shub, Bibliographical introduction to nationalism, I88.

Pistrak, Lazar, Grand tactician; Khrushchev's rise to power, I309.

Pitamic, Leonid, Treatise on the state, F120.

Pittenger, Benjamin Floyd, Local public school administration, D164.

Plamenatz, John Petrov, Mill's utilitarianism, F191.

Plano, Jack C., American political dictionary, C93.

Plischke, Elmer, American diplomacy, I89; American foreign relations, I90; Contemporary government of Germany, C145; International relations, I129.

Plucknett, Theodore Frank Thomas, Bibliography and legal history, G13; Early English legal literature, G33.

Polaschek, R. J., Government administration in New Zealand, H132.

Political dictionary, B86.

Political handbook and atlas of the world, C50.

Political party platforms, E163.

Political register and impartial review of new books, B66.
Politische literature, B67.
Pollock, Sir Frederick, bart., Introduction to the history of
the science of politics, B227; Jurisprudence and legal es-
says, G227.
Pollock, James Kerr, Direct primary in Michigan, D63;
German democracy at work, E107; Initiative and referen-
dum in Michigan, D64.
Polsby, Nelson W., Community power and political theory,
D113; Politics and social life, B210.
Pontius, Dale, State supervision of local government, D124.
Poole's index to periodical literature, A74.
Poore, Benjamin Perley, Descriptive catalogue of the gov-
ernment publications of the United States, J14.
Porter, Charles Orlando, Struggle for democracy in Latin
America, C70.
Porter, Kirk Harold, comp., National party platforms, E164.
Possony, Stefan Thomas, Century of conflict, I181.
Pott, William Sumner Appleton, Chinese political philosophy,
F59.
Potter, David Morris, ed., Party politics and public action,
E45.
Pound, Roscoe, Criminal justice in America, D90; Forma-
tive era of American law, G165; Introduction to the phi-
losophy of law, G228; Spirit of the common law, G169.
Pounds, Norman John Grenville, Atlas of European affairs,
I110; Atlas of Middle Eastern affairs, I111; Political ge-
ography, B260.
Powell, Norman John, Major aspects of American govern-
ment, C84.
Pratt, Julius William, History of United States foreign policy,
I260.
Prelot, Marcel, Science politique, B172.
Press, Charles, State manuals, blue books, and election re-
sults, D38.
Presthus, Robert Vance, Statistical analysis in comparative
administration, H311.
Preston, Ralph Clausius, Teaching world understanding, I41.
Price, Miles Oscar, Effective legal research, G23.
Pritchett, Charles Herman, Congress versus the Supreme
Court, C202.
Problems of communism, Russia under Khrushchev, I310.
Progress of continental law in the nineteenth century, G198.
Proudfoot, Mary (Macdonald), Britain and the United States
in the Caribbean, H195.
Public Administration Clearing House, Chicago, Public ad-
ministration in Latin America, H196.

Public affairs information service, bulletin, A42.
Public policy, H67.
Puget, Henry, Essai de bibliographie des principaux ouvrages de droit public, B68.
Puleston, William Dilworth, Influence of Power on International Relations, I165.
Pullen, Wm. Russell, Checklist of legislative journals, G77, J15.
Putnam, Carlton B., How to find the law, G24.
Pye, Lucian W., Guerrilla communism in Malaya, I352; Politics, personality, and nation building, I353.

Quarterly check-list of economics and political science, B69.
Quigley, Harold Scott, New Japan, C112.

Radin, Max, Handbook of Anglo-American legal history, G170; Law dictionary, G54.
Raghu, Vira, Comprehensive english Hindi dictionary of governmental and educational words and phrases, B87.
Raj, M. Joseph, Dynamics of politics, B173.
Raleigh, Thomas, Elementary politics, B174.
Ramachandra Rao, P.R., India and Ceylon, I372.
Rankin, Robert Stanley, Government and administration of North Carolina, D222; Political science in the South, B41; State constitutions, D57.
Ranney, Austin, Democracy and the American party system, E46; Doctrine of responsible party government, E58; Essays on the behavioral study of politics, B211; Governing of men, B175.
Ranney, John Calyer, Major foreign power, C131.
Ransone, Coleman Bernard, Governments under which we live, D184; Office of governor in the United States, D83.
Rappoport, Angelo Solomon, Dictionary of socialism, I97.
Rauch, Geary von, History of Soviet Russia, I311.
Ray, Donald P., ed., Trends in social science, A24.
Ray, Perley Orman, Introduction to political parties and practical politics, E47.
Read, Herbert Edward, Politics of the unpolitical, B176.
Readers' guide to periodical literature, A75.
Recent developments in the social sciences, A25.
Recent publications in governmental problems, H55.
Reed, Edward, ed., Readings for Democrats, E72.
Reed, Thomas Harrison, Preparing college men and women for politics, B42.
Reeve, W.D., Public administration in Siam, H181.
Reeves, Charles Everand, School boards, D165.
Reeves, John Estill, Kentucky government, D203.
Reichardt, Martin, Psychologie und Politik, B280.

Reischauer, Edwin Oldfather, Japan, Past and present, H168,
I335; United States and Japan, I336; Wanted: an Asian
policy, I338.
Reischauer, Robert Karl, Japan, government-politics, C113.
Reiss, Hans Siegbert, ed., Political thought of the German
romantics, F75.
Remmlein, Madaline (Kinter), Law of local public school ad-
ministration, D166.
Renne, Roland Roger, Government and administration of
Montana, D214.
Research frontiers in politics and government, B23.
Reshetar, John Stephen, Concise history of the Communist
Party of the Soviet Union, E119; Problems of analyzing
and predicting Soviet behavior, I312.
Retzlaff, Ralph Herbert, Village government in India, D257.
Review of Politics, Image of man, B106.
Revised reports, G126.
Reynolds, Philip Alan, War in the twentieth century, I166.
Rice, Stuart Arthur, Quantitative methods in politics, B228.
Rich, Bennett Milton, Government and administration of New
Jersey, D218; State constitutions: the governor, D84.
Rich, Clifford A. L., ed., European politics and government,
C132.
Riddell, Walter Alexander, Documents on Canadian foreign
policy, I261.
Rienow, Robert, Contemporary international politics, I27.
Riesenberg, Peter N., Inalienability of sovereignty in med-
ieval political thought, F182.
Riesman, David, Faces in the crowd, B177.
Riggs, Fred Warren, Comparative bureaucracy, H97; Con-
vergences in the study of comparative public administra-
tion and local government, H30; Models in the compara-
tive study of public administration, H31; Some problems
of public administration in Southeast Asia, H182.
Riggs, Robert Edwon, Politics in the United Nations, I423.
Riker, William H., Study of local politics, D22.
Rippy, James Fred, Globe and hemisphere, I323.
Ritchie, David George, Natural rights, F144; Principles of
state interference, F268; Studies in political and social
ethics, F207.
Rivers, William Halse Rivers, Psychology and politics, B281.
Roback, Abraham Aaron, Dictionary of international slurs,
I98.
Robb, Louis Adams, Dictionary of Legal terms; Spanish-
English and English-Spanish, G55.
Robbins, Lionel Charles Robbins, Politics and economics,
B248.

Robert, Henry Martyn, Rules of order, C221.
Roberts, Henry L., Russia and America, dangers and prospects, I313.
Robertson, Arthur Henry, Council of Europe, I449; European institutions, I450.
Robinson, Claude Everett, Straw votes, E156.
Robinson, Daniel Sommer, Political ethics, F208.
Robinson, Dorothy Fulwiler, Making of Arizona, D186.
Robinson, Edgar Eugene, Presidential vote, E166, E165.
Robinson, James Arthur, Congress and foreign policy-making, I236.
Robson, William Alexander, Civil service in Britain and France, H113; Great cities of the world, D114; Justice and administrative law, H312; Problems of nationalized industry, H249; University teaching of social sciences, B43.
Roche, John Pearson, Dynamics of democratic government, C34.
Rockefeller Brothers Fund, Mid-century challenge to U. S. foreign policy, I262.
Rocker, Rudolf, Anarcho-Syndicalism, F185.
Rockow, Lewis, Contemporary political thought in England, F66.
Rodee, Carlton Clymer, Introduction to political science, B178.
Rodgers, Cleveland, American planning, D179.
Rodney, Thomas, Anglo-American law of the frontier, G171.
Rogers, William Cecil, International administration, I397.
Rogow, Arnold A., Power, corruption, and rectitude, B179.
Roman, John Henry, Office of the Philippine president, H222.
Ronning, C. Neale, Law and politics in inter-American diplomacy, I479.
Rood, John Romain, Political science primer, B180.
Rosenau, James N., Calculated control as a unifying concept in the study of international politics and foreign policy, I80; International politics and foreign policy, I70; National leadership and foreign policy, I182; Public opinion and foreign policy, E142, I183.
Rosenberg, Hans, Bureaucracy, aristocracy, and autocracy, H84.
Rosenblum, Victor G., Law as a political instrument, G153; Public administration and public law, H313.
Rose's notes on the United States Supreme Court reports, G114.
Ross, Russell Marion, Government and administration of Iowa, D201.
Rossiter, Clinton Lawrence, American presidency, C239;

United States in world affairs, I269.
U. S. Air Force Reserve Officers' Training Corps, Military aspects of world political geography, B263.
U. S. Bureau of the Census, County and city data book, D40.
U. S. Congress, Biographical directory of the American Congress, C208; Congressional index, C209.
U. S. Congress. House, Constitution, Jefferson's manual and rules of the House of Representatives, C210.
U. S. Congress. Senate, Presidential vetoes, J17; Senate manual, C211; Senate procedure, C212.
U. S. Congress. Senate. Library, Cumulative index of congressional hearings, J18.
United States Dept. of Justice, Digest of the Official opinions of the attorneys-general, G109; Official opinions of the attorneys-general, G110.
U. S Dept. of State. Bureau of Intelligence and Research. External Research Staff, Political behavior, B215.
U. S. Dept. of State. Office of the Legal Advisor, Treaties in force, I492.
United States, Federal register, G79.
U. S. Laws, Statutes, etc., Federal code annotated, G80; Index to the federal statutes, G81; Revised statutes of the United States, G82; Statutes at large, G83; United States code, G84; United States code annotated, G85; United States Code Congressional Service, G86.
U. S. Library of Congress, Catalog of books, A60, A61; Library of Congress author catalog, A62; National union catalog, A63.
U. S. Library of Congress. Catalog Division, List of American doctoral dissertations, A77.
U. S. Library of Congress. Division of Bibliography, Brief list of books on political parties, E17; List of references on party government, E18; List of references on the national committees of political parties, E19; List of works relating to political parties, E20; Selected list of recent books on modern political systems, B72; Selected list of references on the convention system, E21; Short list of references to recent writings on American politics and political parties, E222.
U. S. Library of Congress. Division of Documents, Monthly checklist of state publications, J19.
U. S. Library of Congress. General Reference and Bibliography Division, Current national bibliographies, A56; Guide to bibliographic tools for research in foreign affairs, I116.
U. S. Library of Congress. Law Library, Anglo-American legal bibliographies, G19; Bibliography of international law

Vaughn, Charles Edwyn, Studies in the history of political philosophy before and after Rousseau, F47.

Vecchio, Giorgio del, Formal basis of law, G234.

Vella, Walter Francis, Impact of the West on government in Thailand, H184.

Verba, Sidney, Small groups and political behavior, B216.

Vermont. Commission to Study State Government, Operation of Vermont State government, D238.

Verney, Douglas V., Analysis of political systems, B27.

Vertical file index, A64.

Viereck, Peter Robert Edwin, Conservatism, F132.

Villari, Luigi, Development of political ideas in Italy, F78.

Vinogradoff, Paul, Outlines of historical jurisprudence, G235.

Virginia. State Library, Richmond, Finding list of the social sciences, B73.

Vlekke, Bernard H.M., On the study of international political science, I44.

Voegelin, Eric, New science of politics, B231.

Vogt, William, Road to survival, I207.

Von Goeckingk, Johanna, United Nations Technical Assistance Board, H260.

Von Mehren, Arthur Taylor, Civil law system, G141.

Von Mises, Ludwig, Omnipotent government, C44.

Von Rosenstiel, Werner H., Comparative law, G142.

Vorees, Edith, Political parties in the United States, E54.

Wade, Emlyn C.S., Constitutional law, G246.

Wager, Paul Woodford, County government across the nation, D99.

Wagstaff, Henry McGilbert, State rights and parties in North Carolina, E90.

Wahlke, John C., ed., Legislative behavior, C176.

Waldo, Dwight, Administrative state, H36; Political science in the United States of America, B45; Study of public administration, H41.

Walker, Harvey, Legislative process, C203.

Walker, Robert Averill, Planning function in urban government, D181.

Wallace, William Kay, Passing of politics, B192.

Wallas, Graham, Human nature in politics, B283.

Walsh, William Francis, History of Anglo-American law, G172.

Walters, Francis Paul, History of the League of Nations, I410.

Waltz, Kenneth Neal, Man, the state, and war, I168.

Wang, Kan-yü, Local government of China, D258.

Ward, Norman, Government in Canada, C63.
Ward, Paul William, Sovereignty, F183.
Ward, Robert Edward, Guide to Japanese reference and re-
search materials in the field of political science, B92;
Studying politics abroad, B28.
Ware, Edith Ellen, Study of international relations in the
United States, I45.
Waring, Luther Hess, Political theories of Martin Luther,
F275.
Warner, William Lloyd, American federal executive, C241.
Warth, Robert D., Soviet Russia in world politics, I318.
Washington University, St. Louis. Libraries, Guide to re-
search material in political science, B93.
Wasserman, Louis, Handbook of political "isms," F48.
Wasserman, Paul, Decision-making, B221.
Watkins, Frederick Mundell, Political tradition of the west,
F160; State as a concept of political science, F121.
Watkins, James Thomas, General international organization,
I406.
Webster, Donald Hopkins, Urban planning and municipal pub-
lic policy, D182; Washington state government, D241.
Weekly law reports, G129.
Weekly notes, G130.
Weeks, Oliver Douglas, Research in the American state leg-
islative process, D78.
Weidner, Edward W., American county-patchwork of boards,
D100.
Weigert, Hans Werner, Principles of political geography,
B265.
Weiner, Myron, Party politics in India, E97.
Weisiger, George Bates, Manual for the use of law books,
G25.
Weldon, Thomas Dwar, States and morals, B193, F122;
Vocabulary of politics, B97.
Welles, Sumner, Seven decisions that shaped history, I134.
Wendell, Mitchell, Relations between the Federal and State
courts, D94.
Westerfield, Bradford, Foreign policy and party politics:
Pearl Harbor to Korea, E55.
Wharton, John Jane Smith, Wharton's Law-lexicon, G58.
Wheare, Kenneth Clinton, Civil service in the constitution,
H115; Federal government, C45; Government by commit-
tee, H227; Legislatures, C177.
Whitaker's cumulative book list, A66.
White, Carl Milton, Sources of information in the social sci-
ences, A35.
White, Leonard Dupee, Civil Service in the modern state,

Subject Index

The designation following the subject entry refers to the page on which the item is found.

F